A Job with a Difference

A Job with a Difference

Robin Blue

Published in 2006 by Stamford House Publishing

© Copyright 2006
Robin Blue

The right of Robin Blue to be identified as the author of this work has been asserted by him in accordance with the Copyright, Designs and Patents Act 1988.

All Rights Reserved

No reproduction, copy or transmission of this publication may be made without written permission. No paragraph of this publication may be reproduced, copied or transmitted save with the written permission or in accordance with the provisions of the Copyright Act 1956 (as amended).

ISBN: 1-904985-41-6

Printed and bound in Great Britain by:

Stamford House Publishing

7 The Metro Centre, Woodston,
Peterborough PE2 7UH

CONTENTS

Chapter One	*Fifteenth Birthday*	1
Chapter Two	*Training*	4
Chapter Three	*Aden*	19
Chapter Four	*UK and Tranquillity*	47
Chapter Five	*Malta*	49
Chapter Six	*42 Commando Royal Marines*	83
Chapter Seven	*Spearhead*	95
Chapter Eight	*Civilian Employment*	222

PREFACE

This account which you are about to read, is written by a nobody for anybody to enjoy. It is about events and incidents I have experienced in my life. Some good, others not so. There is no hero, just an ordinary man experiencing events. There is nothing exceptional about events in this short novel.

The main story is about life in the Royal Marines. Most of the boys I served with joined up for travel, adventure and a little excitement. So please read on and enjoy this short memoir.

Chapter One
Fifteenth Birthday

February, 1959, was my 15th birthday. The routine in those days was that you left school once you were 15. I was 15 years old on a Tuesday, so I had to leave on Friday of that week. At the beginning of Autumn term, our school class had started with 40 boys. Each week one or two left, which was the requirement at Harper Secondary School, Bedford, in 1959. For my last Friday at school I received a letter from the Youth Employment Bureau. I was to report to their offices on Monday, at ten in the morning. Nobody at the Harper Secondary School left with any qualifications in those days. You were expected to go out and work. It was drummed into all the children there that nobody owed you a living. The general attitude then was – "no work no food". We were also told that jobs suitable for us were: farm hands, factory workers, labourers on building sites and the armed forces.

On the Monday morning when I reported to the Youth Employment Bureau, the woman in charge told me that a large garage in town required a Stores Boy. I was to report to the Stores Manager at three in the afternoon. I was not asked what I would *like* to do. To tell you the truth, I did not have a clue. At five to three I arrived at the Stores Department and asked to see the gentleman in charge of Stores. The man at the front counter said, 'You must be the new Stores boy.' It sounded as though I had this job before the interview was carried out. I was shown into the Stores Manager's office. He told me what my duties were. I would be required to start work Tuesday morning at eight, till six in the evening, with one hour for lunch. As I only lived a mile away it was possible for me to cycle home for a snack lunch. I was not asked if I wanted this job, it was assumed that it would be accepted. The wages structure was not explained, or what holidays I would be entitled to. I told the manager that I would start at eight the following morning; then I was given a piece of blank paper and told to write down my name, address and date of birth. I was now employed as a Stores Boy, my first job.

On Tuesday morning I arrived and the senior storeman showed me around. He also told me what my duties were. Basically, I was the *Go-For-Boy*. Go, make the tea, clean the offices, run errands to Red Star Parcels and collect stores. I was in the most menial position there. I did not mind, however, as some money would be coming in. The staff were kind and friendly, I was shown how to read stores catalogues and parts lists. The time passed slowly, routine and more routine . . .

I had been there now for two years, and looking ahead I could see that the future held nothing for me. One of the stores assistants had served with the Royal Marines during the last war. He would tell me stories concerning his time then and how good it had been. He also told me about the great battleships he served on. Then he had moved over to the Commando Units. He always emphasised the comradeship, excitement, interest, opportunities, adventure and travel. The more I thought about it the more I wanted to join up and have some of this life which had been described to me; it sounded good. I decided that it was time for me to take up a different type of employment.

The Naval Recruiting Office for the Bedford area was in Cambridge. I had a week's holiday to come, so it was booked and taken. One day during the holiday I caught a bus to Cambridge. The Naval Recruiting Office was above a butcher's shop, stairs leading to it clearly marked. I proceeded up the stairs, knocked and entered.

A large Royal Marine Colour Sergeant was seated there, and he immediately asked what I wanted.

I replied, 'To join the Royal Marines.'

Then he told me medical and written tests had to be passed before I could be accepted. I had to sit two written tests, which I passed. Then I was given a form to pass on to my Doctor, which he would complete and forward to the Ministry of Defence, London.

Once all the forms were completed I was asked how I had travelled to Cambridge.

I said, 'I purchased a return bus ticket this morning.'

Then the Colour Sergeant gave me the price of a return bus ticket, also 3/6d for a meal. I thought to myself that things were going well. Three weeks later I received a letter telling me that I was required to report to HMS Discovery on the Thames Embankment, London, at eight in the morning. Also, I would be required to have a final medical. A railway warrant was in the envelope.

A week before I was due to report for my final acceptance into the Royal Marines notice was given concerning my departure. I knew that this was a risk, as events could go wrong, I may not be up to the required standard. I thanked all the staff for their friendship and help.

*

At HMS Discovery that Monday morning, there was a large group of young men wanting to join the Royal Navy and Royal Marines. Only eight boys were for the Royal Marines, the remainder were for the Royal Navy. Boys who wanted to join up in the Royal Marines were taken to one side. The Royal Naval Chief Petty Officer told us all to strip to our underwear. Once we were all down to our underwear we were told to move on deck and onto the Thames Embankment. A Royal Navy Doctor was waiting on the Embankment.

The doctor told us, when he called us forward, that we had to run between two lampposts a 100 yards apart. Once this was completed, ten press-ups had to be done. Once completed he listened to our hearts, one of the boys asked, 'Why aren't the naval personnel required to do this?'

The doctor replied, 'Training that lies ahead of you is the most physically demanding of all three services.

Anyway, I did what was required, and was accepted as physically fit to join the Royal Marines. Three of the boys were turned away as they were not fit enough. They were told that their hearts could not take what would lie ahead.

In the afternoon five future Royal Marines took an oath and signed on to serve for nine years. I was now on my way to the Depot, at Deal in Kent, to commence my training.

Chapter Two
Training

A Royal Marine was waiting at Deal Railway Station to meet us, and we were told to follow him. He told us that we would spend the next four months training here, then move on to Portsmouth and HMS SHEFFIELD. On arrival at the Depot, we were taken to the marines' dining hall, as it was afternoon teatime. The marine told us to go and have a mug of tea, also a large rock cake each. As we entered this dining hall, all young marines under training banged their hands on the dining tables. This was an accepted custom each Monday afternoon. The new arrivals had been welcomed in the age old way. Once tea had been finished, the marine led all of us to a stores complex. We were issued with bedding, bucket, towel and soap. Then we were taken to a New Intake Block, and told that this was to be our accommodation for the next two weeks. We grabbed an empty bunk each and laid out our bedding. One of the young boys who had been there a week told us to make up our beds, then we would be shown where everything was. Also, he told us that once the numbers in this block reached 40 then a recruit squad would be formed.

After supper all of us returned to our accommodation block, everyone at the moment feeling like a fish out of water. This was a totally different way of life to what everyone had experienced before joining up. For most of the boys this was their first time away from home. That evening the boys in New Intake Block went round and introduced themselves to each other. Everybody was curious, wanting to know where everyone came from and what they did before. There were boys from all over Britain, Scotland to Lands End. The average age of these boys was 17 or 18 years old, all very young.

On Tuesday morning a Corporal arrived at the New Intake Block and told all of us that we had to draw some of our kit, as a training squad would be formed. We were issued with very basic kit. The remainder would be issued as training progressed. In the afternoon we were all taken to a Barber's Shop in barracks and told that this first haircut was free, on the Royal Marines. One of the young boys had thick black hair styled in the way of Teddy Boys. He told the barber, 'Only a light trim is required,' as his hairstyle was his pride and joy. The barber, a miserable old bloke, did not take any notice of this request, and all his hair was cut off. We all had short hair on leaving the Barber's Shop, our escort Corporal told us that was how long our hair had to be all through training. Most of the boys expected a short haircut, but not a shaved head, with no hair whatsoever. The next two days passed slowly, more bits and pieces of kit were issued. The squad now numbered 42.

On Friday morning all of us had to form up outside the New Intake Block. The Corporal who had shepherded us around for the previous three days was now replaced by a Sergeant Drill Instructor. He introduced himself as Sergeant Jones, from now on it was his responsibility to train, teach and escort the squad, at Deal. The first thing he did was to inspect all of us. All the boys were different in their appearance, we had the same style of clothing on, but none of us were uniform as a squad. Bootlaces were done up differently, berets were on wrong and clothing was worn incorrectly. All of us were taken back into the New Intake Block and shown how to dress correctly. We were also told that detailed instructions would be given on all matters of dress and behaviour. Detailed instructions would be from all training personnel and none of us would be in any doubt as to what was expected. Sergeant Jones said, 'For the next 19 weeks you will all see a lot of me, and any problems you may have must be brought to me.'

In the afternoon all of us had to be in one large lecture room. The Adjutant, Regimental Sergeant Major and Company Sergeant Major introduced themselves and explained their duties. Also, we were instructed on what standards would be expected, - "Very High". After 15 minutes the Commanding Officer arrived. He was a full Colonel. He welcomed us and explained some of the training which lay ahead, and also told us all about traditions in the Royal Marines. It was explained that all training was thorough, detailed, and some would be individual. We were all informed of our proud traditions and reminded that a third of the Corps had served in Nelson's fleet at Trafalgar. Just before the colonel left he reminded all present of Nelson's famous signal at Trafalgar, "England expects that every man will do his duty".

On Saturday morning our squad was marched to the Sick Bay, where injections and inoculations were administered. On completion of pin-cushion treatment, our Drill Instructor told us that some of the injections would make us feel bad. Training would commence on Monday, and the remainder of Saturday was free. We were also excused church parade on Sunday so that side effects from the inoculations and injections could wear off. On Saturday evening most of the boys in our squad felt bad, Sunday was spent on our bunk beds recovering. On Sunday evening our Drill Instructor came around to see what state of health we were in and most of the boys now felt better. I can't remember what the injections and inoculations were for, but it was explained that they would combat diseases prevalent in Eastern countries.

Monday morning came and training started in earnest, drill, schooling and physical fitness training. For the first three weeks we did not have a personal weapon. Every Friday morning all recruits under training marched through Deal, this was the only time we were allowed out. Schooling was one whole day each week, and this was good. Royal Naval Officers who took us for schooling were interesting, caring and very helpful, better than the teachers I'd had at Harper Secondary School, Bedford. Lectures were given by the Padre, Adjutant and Sergeant Major. All physical training instructions were in the gymnasium. Physical Training Instructors told us that we would be physically fit by the time we left Depot Deal for Lympstone, to carry out infantry training. Sport was played once a week. Also three hours swimming instructions were undertaken each week, it was pointed out, "If you go to sea you should be able to swim". After three weeks our rifles were issued, and the Weapon Training Instructors started teaching. We were instructed in groups of four, either by a Corporal or Sergeant. All infantry weapons were taught, and emphasis was always put on safety, cleanliness and care. It was explained that your weapon is your best friend, it could save your life one day. Whole days were spent on the rifle ranges at Dover.

During our time at Depot Deal, three of the boys in our squad were discharged. One had flat feet, another was muscle bound, which meant he could not move fast, and the third had a defect in one eye.

Our squad had two special entry cooks, they had been allowed to join up, but only as cooks, the reason being that they had achieved a low mark on their entry test. Both of them had to do the full training, but were not expected to reach a high standard. One was from Liverpool, and was always telling jokes, and full of laughs. The other boy was from an island in the Outer Hebrides. He was likeable, but a disaster waiting to happen. Our Sergeant Jones told us we had to inspect and ensure that young Hebrides Jock's dress was correct before he went on parade. We did inspect him, but between the barracks room and parade ground all his dress would go out of line. Belt buckle out of line with buttons, cap over one side of his head, tie loose, and a general mess. His whole body was wrong, but he was immensely strong and well-liked by us all.

One day on parade, all of us were told to strip our weapons for inspection by the Adjutant. The Adjutant came to young Hebrides Jock, he showed him the main body of his weapon, but no moving parts (breech block, slide and cocking piston). The Adjutant asked him, 'Where are the moving parts for your weapon?'

Young Hebrides Jock replied, 'In my locker, as the removal of moving parts reduces its weight and makes it easier to carry all day long.'

This did not go down very well with the Adjutant and young Hebrides Jock was awarded eight hours extra drill, to be carried out on Saturday afternoons. After the Adjutant left, Sergeant Jones gave all of us a verbal lashing.

Each Sunday at ten in the morning, all personnel under training had to attend Church Parade. Young Hebrides Jock approached Sergeant Jones and told him that he believed in atheism. He was told that this was alright, and he was excused Church Parades. Young Hebrides Jock rubbed it into the rest of us, concerning his good luck. Sunday morning at seven, a Corporal came over from the Guardroom with special instructions for him and told him, 'As you are an atheist and not attending Church parade, and have spare time on your hands, then the day can be spent in the Dining Hall wash-up.'

On Monday morning, young Hebrides Jock found religion, he joined the rest of us for Sunday Church parades. As they always say, "Go with the flow".

Our squad completed the 16 weeks at Depot Deal, all of us were fitter, better and now prepared for infantry training at Lympstone. Before Lympstone we had two weeks on board HMS Sheffield, sea training, followed by a week at Royal Marines Poole.

Once we boarded HMS Sheffield, the first item all of us were issued with was a hammock. The Chief Petty Officer showed all of us how to make it up and sling a hammock. This was a new experience for all of us, and for a few, not a pleasant one. Hammocks look nice in films, but take some getting used to. After a few nights everybody mastered their hammock and slept soundly in it. Most of the training on HMS Sheffield involved seamanship, rowing, and duties to be carried out on board a ship. One morning we were all taken to HMS Victory and shown around, this was very interesting and enjoyable. HMS Sheffield was a new experience and an eye opener.

Royal Marines Poole was excellent, no training staff to bother us, only our Sergeant Jones; he left us alone most of the time. Most days were spent on landing craft, going out to Studland Bay. Also, Special Boat Sections showed us what work they carried out, which was interesting and informative. I decided that this type of work was too dangerous for me. It takes a special kind of person to pass the Special Boat Section selection course. They are some of the bravest and most intelligent men in the Royal Marines.

*

Our squad left RM Poole Sunday morning, arriving at Lympstone Infantry Training Centre, Royal Marines, in the afternoon. Sergeant Jones led us to our accommodation. The hut which we were to occupy housed 40 men. These huts had been built during the war and each one had two coke burning stoves for main heating. The accommodation at Deal was new and purpose built, with all modern comforts, including central heating. The washing facilities here were shared by four squads. If you wanted hot water, you had to be first there. Normally the first 20 had hot water, then warm, and finally cold.

On Monday morning we had to parade outside our hut, Sergeant Jones passed us over to a Platoon Weapon Instructor's team for infantry training. He gave us some sound advice before departing, telling the squad to stick together and help each other. Sergeant Jones had been caring, helpful and considerate at all times. When he said his final farewell there was a tear in the corner of one eye. Sergeant Jones finished his time in the service as a RSM, I served with him twice on completion of training.

The training team consisted of a Lieutenant, two Sergeants and five Corporals. The Lieutenant addressed his new squad, telling all of us that we would see him and his team every day during our Infantry training. Training would be tough and very physical, and if you were not up to the required standard at the end of ten weeks, then you would have to do it all over again. His statement sent a cold shiver down everybody's spine. The first two weeks would be spent in camp, then out in the field, Woodbury Common and Dartmoor.

The remainder of this first morning was spent drawing kit and rifles. That afternoon we were all introduced to the assault course, from now on it would be Battle Physical Training, always in an open field and on a large assault course. Eight Physical Training Instructors plus our training team were present, the ratio of recruits to instructors was nearly two to one. Somebody was watching and observing every move you made. First of all we were taken around and shown how to negotiate each obstacle on this assault course, and this took about 40 minutes. All instructions were detailed, also our training team would scale and negotiate each obstacle, demonstrating the correct method of assault. Once it had been explained, our squad was put into small teams of three. Each team set off at one minute intervals and timed. Also, each team had an instructor accompanying them, who would run to one side, encouraging and ensuring that everything was done correctly. One obstacle I found hard was to scale a six-foot wall at the very beginning, this being due to my height. The remainder of the course was OK. The really large boys in our squad tired early, one PTI said, 'Large men have no stamina or endurance.' Sadly he was proved right; in the final weeks of our training one of our boys broke his leg on the assault course. He made a full recovery and completed recruit training eight months after we all left Lympstone. Our squad now numbered 38. The first week passed quickly, lectures and plenty of Battle Physical Training; the strange thing was that I found it most enjoyable.

Saturday was a half-day, recruits were allowed out of camp from two in the afternoon till midnight. A few of us went to Exeter, others Exmouth. The train carriages were old types with no connecting corridors. Some boys used to go from one compartment to another by climbing along the outside of carriages. One night the boys who went to Exmouth, were returning to camp late and were moving from one compartment to another, and as their train approached a tunnel a young recruit was knocked off. Sadly this boy died, falling under the wheels of the moving train. Our squad now numbered 37.

Second week in camp was very physical, a four mile run each day. Battle physical training was three times that week. On Saturday a four-mile run was completed, followed by Battle Physical Training. Everybody in our squad was tired and feeling the full effects of fatigue. The Colour Sergeant Physical Training Instructor accused our squad of being lazy. He decided that before we were dismissed our squad would climb up the 30-foot ropes and over the supporting bar. A bar 30 feet up from the ground supported four ropes, and we formed lines behind these ropes. The first four boys climbed up and successfully went over this bar and descended. The next four went up, and as one of our boys was going over the bar he knocked a boy next to him. The boy who had been knocked lost his grip and fell 30 ft, landing on his side. He broke a leg badly. The next boy waiting to climb up was told to pull him out of his way. The boy lay there for half an hour with a compound fracture. The last four to finish were told to go into the Gymnasium and bring out a stretcher to take our injured mate down to Sickbay. The Colour Sergeant filled in an Accident Report and all was forgotten. Our squad now numbered 36. Saturday afternoon all of us spent time in bed to catch up on some sleep. That evening all of us went in to Exmouth and had a good time.

On Monday morning stores were drawn, as our squad was going to spend this week on Woodbury Common. Stores were loaded on to a truck, and we all marched to the common. The first week in the field was most enjoyable. We were shown how to make small bivouacs, using blocks of turf and ground sheets. Field craft was taught and practised, we were also show how to care for ourselves in the field. Small patrols were carried out each night, our Sergeants and Corporals led each time.

During the day cooked meals were brought out from camp and dished out. After our meal the Instructors would talk and explain past experiences. The two Sergeants had served in Yugoslavia during World War II with Tito's Partisans. The Royal Marines had three Commando Units fighting alongside Tito's forces. Two stories I will never forget were told to us by one of our Sergeants:

A group of them were moving with Tito's Partisans, and had to cross a large area sown with anti-personnel mines. To go around this area would have put at least two hours on their journey. The Partisan Leader told his men to go to a nearby village and round up all the children, then to bring them back. The children were brought to him, accompanied by crying mothers. They were then placed in a tight bunch and three of the Partisans were behind them with sub machine guns. They were forced to walk across this minefield . . . but at a high price, eight children died. They had cleared a path across the mined area. Their Royal Marine Officer approached the Partisan leader and stated that their action was barbaric. The Partisan leader said, 'A path has been cleared. People from this village can make more children. Children only eat, and contribute nothing.'

A few weeks later in one of their camps a young man and woman were taken before their leader. They had been caught fraternizing together, and this was a cardinal sin. After a trial that lasted two minutes both of them were taken out and shot. None of the marines ever went near the women because Tito's Partisans would not hesitate to shoot anyone if their women were threatened or approached for sex. It was also emphasised that other peoples do not have the same outlook to life as we do. Every country is different, they are not like the British.

On Friday afternoon we returned to camp, Saturday morning there was a four-mile run and Battle Physical Training. We managed to reach the end of the week with no further losses.

Week four of our infantry training commenced. Monday was spent in camp. The morning was spent doing Battle Physical Training, and there were two lectures concerning fire and movement. During the afternoon stores were drawn, also blank ammunition and 24 hour ration packs. The blank ammunition was for .303 weapons, and one of our marines pointed this out to his Corporal. Our Lieutenant said that old .303 rifles would be drawn from stores, and used only for firing these blanks. We would still have to bring our self-loading rifles along, they would be slung across our backs and carried all the time. Tuesday morning we marched to Woodbury Common, the first two days we were shown how to carry out fire and movement. The remainder of this week was spent practising what we had been taught. From eight in the morning till five it was continuous movement. Small night patrols were carried out, also guard duties throughout the night. We left Woodbury Common on Saturday morning, running the six miles back to camp. We were all looking forward to fresh food, as the past four days all of our squad had lived on 24-hour ration packs. All the squad were practically dead on their feet.

In the dining hall our friend from Liverpool sat with us, his nickname now was "Scouse the Cook". He was complaining that our Lieutenant was picking on him. We explained that our training Lieutenant was everywhere, everybody had received some criticism from him during the past week. It was part of his duties to chase us up, also, in six weeks time we would have another training team. We told him to just go along with what he wanted, that way he would stay off his back. But Scouse the Cook said it was personal, and if he got a chance then the odds would be evened up. We told him not to do anything foolish.

The next five weeks were spent on Dartmoor, live firing. All exercises involved live ammunition and constant movement. Marches, map reading and more physical exercises. We always returned on a Friday night, Saturday was spent doing Battle Physical Training and a four-mile run. Saturday afternoons were spent in bed. Scouse the Cook was still complaining about our Lieutenant. Week ten was test time. If you passed all the tests then you moved on to "X "Troop (Commando course). None of us had any desire to do the Infantry training again, it was intense and extremely physical.

Week ten commenced with weapon tests, nobody had any problems as we had received intense, detailed instructions. Tuesday was spent on Woodbury Common doing field craft and camouflage. On the return to camp one of the boys collapsed and died. We were running back when he swayed and fell to the ground. Our Sergeant Instructor checked him and no pulse was found. This boy had suffered a heart attack, one of the valves in his heart closed up and did not reopen. He was the largest member of our squad, and had been liked by everybody. The medical staff did some checking into his family, it was found that they had a history of sudden deaths, all due to heart failure. This brought home to everyone how fragile life is, here one second, gone the next. We were now down to 35.

Wednesday morning first period was the Battle Physical Training test. This was timed, and nobody failed. The remainder of this day was spent attending lectures, which everyone enjoyed, as it was relaxing and restful.

Thursday was live grenade throwing on Woodbury Common. We were taken up in trucks, which was a nice change from marching. The area for grenade practice/throwing was on the side of a hill, and well away from all other training. There were two shelters, one either side of the throwing bay. The squad sat in one shelter, moved forward one at a time and threw two live grenades. Our Lieutenant was in charge of the throwing bay, trenches behind were shaped like a "W". If a grenade was dropped, then each person could run away to safety. The "W" shape ensured that a blast and grenade fragments were dissipated into the trench. Once we had thrown the two grenades we just sat in the rest/waiting shelter. Scouse the Cook said that this would be his "get even" day, and also that he would go last. Everybody told him not to be stupid, he only had one day to go then Infantry training would be finished.

Thirty four of our squad were sitting and waiting. The two grenades belonging to "Scouse the Cook" were heard to explode. The Lieutenant came into our waiting shelter and detailed four marines off to guard and escort "Scouse the Cook". What he had done was this: he had thrown the first grenade correctly, and with the second grenade he had withdrawn the pin and released the trigger mechanism, setting off the .22 firing cap which ignited a four second internal fuse. After two seconds he threw his grenade into the air, telling our Lieutenant to catch it and see how far he could throw a primed grenade. The Lieutenant caught this grenade and threw it. The grenade exploded about two feet in front of the throwing trench. A fool had spoilt a good day. "Scouse the Cook" received 48 days in cells, and he had to do all his Infantry training again. I met him three years later and he said, 'It was worth it!'

On Friday morning we were told that two of the boys in our squad had not come up to standard, they would be back-squadded and do all the Infantry training course again. Thirty-two would move forward to the next stage, which commenced on Monday.

*

On Monday morning 23 young Royal Marine Officers, in training, and 51 Army personnel joined the squad. The Army personnel came from the Royal Artillery and the Royal Engineers, making a total of 106. A Royal Marine Lieutenant, two Sergeants and nine Corporals would take all of us through "X" Troop training. The attitude and manner of this Lieutenant-in-charge was very relaxed, telling all present that his team did not teach, they only took us through tried and tested procedures. All Royal Marines had completed their Infantry training, and Army ranks pasted on, as they were considered suitable to undergo Commando training. If anybody failed a test then the Royal Marines would be back-squadded and Army ranks returned to their Unit. Over the next five weeks the Commando course would be carried out. All ranks were issued with a special woollen headdress, this signified to other people in camp that they were undergoing Commando training. This headdress was introduced during the war, and Royal Marines maintain this tradition. We were then told what the tests would be, and that three live firing exercises on Dartmoor would be carried out. The following tests would be carried out during the final week: a 30-mile march, a nine-mile speed march, an endurance course and a Tarzan course. Each test had to be completed in a specified time. The course was split into two teams, large and small. All personnel under 5'8" were in the small half, and those taller were in a large group. I was in the small group.

During the first week six Army ranks were returned to their Unit, they were well below the required fitness standard. The Infantry training had been hard, intense and very physical, and now we all realised why, it stood all Royal Marines in a good position concerning fitness.

The team of instructors were excellent, they talked to us, never pushing or dominating as previous people had. Each week the number dropped. The three exercises on Dartmoor were hard, but enjoyable.

The final week came. The prediction that large men have less stamina was proved correct. Eight large men failed the 30-mile march, and another six the nine-mile speed march. A speed march is one mile covered in ten minutes. The marines did as much as possible to help their squad mates, but the pressure was too great. The advice Sergeant Jones had given just before he left was practised, and this helped most of us through this training.

Friday morning of week five, all ranks on this course had to parade outside the main dining hall to hear who had passed and failed. Our squad had already lost three members. First of all names were read out of men that had failed, and reasons given. Three more boys from our squad failed, the reason given was that they had not tried hard enough. Two Royal Marine Young Officers were failed for the same reason and 12 Army ranks were not up to the required standard. Twenty-six members of our squad would go forward to Kings Squad; this involved two weeks of parade ground work and a pass out before some dignitary. On Saturday morning the Commanding Officer presented all personnel that passed "X" Troop training with their Green Berets. We had nearly completed training.

On Monday morning our squad returned to the parade ground, we were now in our final two weeks of training. Another tradition in the Royal Marines is that Kings Squad wears a white lanyard. This is to distinguish it as the senior recruit squad in our Corps. Our instructor was a Sergeant Drill Instructor, taking us through the next two weeks. We were told that the first week would be spent refreshing everybody about parade ground work, bringing us all back up to standard. Week two we commenced our set piece drill display; it was practised over and over again. Thursday morning we would have a full dress rehearsal in front of key training personnel within the camp. The Sergeant Drill Instructor was a little nervous, as we were. If a poor show was given his head would be on the chopping block. However, our senior training staff within camp were happy and content with the display.

Thursday afternoon we had to have a lecture from one of the Royal Naval Doctors, all it said on our training programme was "Briefing on General Health". Our squad assembled in one lecture room at two in the afternoon. A Royal Naval Surgeon Lieutenant Commander and Chief Petty Officer were waiting to give this lecture. None of us had any idea what it was going to be about. The doctor opened the lecture by telling us that we were going to learn about Sexually Transmitted Diseases, commonly called venereal disease (VD). Firstly, we were told that VD is normally caught by having sexual relations outside of marriage, and by being promiscuous. Then we were told what types of venereal diseases there were, including gonorrhoea, which is the most common. We were told what symptoms to look for and what treatment would be administered. Then we were told about syphilis, which is more serious, and what symptoms to look out for. Both types of VD are preventable and treatable. The first method of prevention was not to go riding local "bicycles", and the second was to wear a condom. Then the Chief Petty Officer walked around and showed us photographs of both diseases, which were not pretty. After the photographs we were all given a condom each. The doctor said, 'Condoms are available and free from all sickbays within the Royal Navy, and they can be purchased from barbers' shops.'

I now realised what occurred in barbers' shops. Quite often whilst waiting for a haircut a man would come in, approach the barber, and whisper something in his ear. The barber would stop cutting hair, go to a cupboard and remove something small. He would return to the waiting man and place something in his hand. All the time during this exercise nothing was shown to other men in his shop. The whole procedure was carried out quietly and with great secrecy.

The doctor said, 'No disciplinary action will be taken against any person who catches a venereal disease.' He again emphasised the importance of reporting sick if any symptoms occurred concerning what we had just been told. The doctors parting words were 'Always wear your cycle clips if you want to ride the neighbourhood bicycle.'

Once we left the lecture room most of the boys were in shock. In the 1950's and early 60's sex was not taught in schools. Sex was a taboo, we were all very naïve. Young Hebrides Jock said that he had not ridden the island bicycle yet, but he would ensure that he had cycle clips on when he did. One of the other boys said, 'Don't wear them around your ankles.' Everyone thought it was a good joke.

On Friday afternoon our squad assembled on the parade ground. Young Hebrides Jock had to have all his dress adjusted, as normal. We were dressed in Number Ones, best blues and very smart; this was a proud occasion for all of us. A Royal Naval Vice Admiral was the passing out and reviewing officer. The drill display was performed, then our passing out officer said a few words. Nowadays a recruit squad passing out at Lympstone is a major event, with families and friends attending. Once the Admiral left the dais and was out of sight, we were marched into the parade ground drill shed. Our Sergeant Drill Instructor wished us all good luck for our future life, and handed us over to the Movements Sergeant. We were now going to find out where each one of us would be posted to. First, Young Hebrides Jock was going to Chatham to train as a cook. Then three boys were to join a Royal Navy ship, and the remaining 22 to Aden, joining 45 Commando Royal Marines. The Movements Sergeant told all of us to pack our kit and attach labels, which he gave us. All kit was already packed. Before departing for Aden all of us would have two weeks' leave, flight details and instructions would be posted to our home addresses.

I had now completed training in the Royal Marines. I felt very proud, this was my first accomplishment in life.

Chapter Three
Aden

Boys for Aden arrived at RAF Brize Norton late in the evening, ready to fly out the following morning. The aircraft that transported us out was a VC 10 belonging to the Royal Air Force. Service on board was very good. The whole flight was excellent, a very good aircraft. We were met at the airport and transported to Little Aden in three trucks, with an armed escort.

The camp at Little Aden was old accommodation originally used by Italian oil workers. It was adequate and reasonably comfortable. The really good thing about it was that we were close to a good beach. On arrival we drew our bedding and were told which hut to occupy. The first weekend we were all free. On Monday, all of us would commence acclimatisation training. The training was for two weeks.

On Monday morning we were joined by three young Officers, who had done the same Commando course as ourselves. In addition, five Corporals and six Sergeants would do this course. The idea of this acclimatisation course was to prepare individuals for conditions they would encounter over the period in the Unit. The first morning we all went for a four-mile run, which made everybody sweat a great deal. Our run finished on the beach, so all of us walked into the lovely cool seawater, which was very pleasant and refreshing. Later in the morning everybody drew their personal weapon and kit. Two water bottles were issued. Each morning began with a four-mile run, as this helped us to acclimatise to physical exercise in a hot climate. By the end of this first week our four-mile run was becoming easier. The second weekend was spent relaxing, swimming, drinking a few cold beers and watching a picture show on the Saturday night.

Monday commenced as normal with a run and a swim. Also, this week we would spend three days on the rifle ranges. Running down from 600 yards to 100 was hot, sticky, and not very nice the first few times. Sweat and bright sunlight in your eyes made shooting straight a lot harder. Friday morning was our last day, no physical exercise. We were to have a morning of lectures. The

Unit Intelligence Officer, a Royal Navy Lieutenant, was the first person to give his lecture. He told us about the dissident tribesmen up country, and that the Armed Services were the people who brought Law and Order to the region. He told us that Communists were always stirring up trouble, and that the British Armed Services operated under the Geneva Convention. Dissident tribesmen did not. Also, we were told, 'You always keep the last bullet for yourself.' This shocked most of the boys in our squad, and the three Young Officers. Then the Intelligence Officer told all present what had happened two years previously:

A small patrol of one Corporal and seven marines, straight out of basic training, were carrying out an information-gathering patrol, near the border with North Yemen. The area they were walking through was very rugged, with many small rocky peaks. This area could hide a thousand men behind these rocky peaks. The patrol was advancing along a narrow path between the peaks, when suddenly they were addressed by somebody on a Tannoy Loudspeaker in clear perfect English. They immediately took cover behind rocks. The person on the Tannoy told them that it was useless taking cover as they were totally surrounded. Then he told the men to stand up, which they did. The patrol was told to look up and around them, and they did. There were about 200 tribesmen up on the high ground looking directly down on the patrol. The Corporal knew that he could not fight his way out, or go back. His patrol was in a no-win situation, with no means of escape. The man on the Tannoy told them to surrender, nothing would happen to any of them, he guaranteed their safety.

The Corporal told his men to lay down their arms and move away from their weapons, and they did so. Once they had complied with the surrender request tribesmen moved down, picking up their weapons and removing all personal kit from the patrol. The patrol was then marched across the border into North Yemen and placed in one large cell, in an old Turkish fort. The cell was about 30ft by 20ft, it was cool and well ventilated, with a hole in one corner for a toilet. The first ten days no food was given to any of them, only water. On the 11th day, early in the morning, the Section Corporal was escorted away by Tribesmen Guards. Nothing was heard from him for the rest of the day.

Everything passed on as normal. That evening the young marines were told that a special meal had been prepared for them. They were led into a large room. In the centre was a large dining table with a white tablecloth, silver cutlery and cut glass. There were large jugs of water and salt and pepper containers. Then they were led to a large bathroom and told to wash, fresh clean clothing was provided. After half an hour they sat down and enjoyed an excellent meal of pork stew with fresh vegetables. After the stew they were given apple pie and custard. The man, who spoke perfect English with no accent, was present all the time. One of the marines asked him where he had been educated. He replied, 'At an English Public School, and then at Oxford University.'

Once the sweet dish was finished coffee and cigars were brought in, which were offered around. The English speaker said that he knew how Western people liked their food and pleasure. After half an hour all captive marines were relaxed and feeling comfortable, also very laid back. Then the English speaker said that he had a very good surprise for them, they would be reunited with their Corporal. He clapped his hands, the door opened and a servant walked in with a large silver tray. In the middle of this tray was the head of their Section Corporal, he was the meat in their pork stew!!! Also, a large number of tribesmen came in to laugh at and belittle the marines. All the marines vomited up their food.

It was another six weeks before they were released and returned back to Aden. The American Consulate in North Yemen negotiated their release. All of them were returned to the UK, and they subsequently suffered some mental problems. I met a Corporal Driver some years later, he confirmed the story, as he was one of the marines captured. Sometimes he used to go away for long periods of rest. On leaving the Royal Marines he committed suicide.

The Intelligence Officer finished his lecture by stressing how important it was never to be taken prisoner. This confirmed what one of our Infantry Training Instructor Sergeants had said: "Not everyone is the same as us".

The Unit Movements Officer came into the lecture room, and told us which rifle troop each one of us would be in. The squad was split up, only three of us went to one rifle troop, but each individual in a separate section. Some of the boys in these sections had been in Aden nearly nine months, so they were old hands. The Troop Lieutenant was one of our Young Officers, who had done Commando training with us at Lympstone.

Our Troop Sergeant was in his late thirties, he immediately took all four of us aside and laid down the law. He said there was to be no heroics, no gung-ho-get-up-and-go, and all training was to be authorised by him. The Troop Officer was not to do anything without his say-so, and he reminded us that all of us knew only the very basics. We had two enemies, heat and dissident tribesmen. Whenever we put our equipment on both water bottles had to be full. Then he finished by saying, 'No marines or Young Officers have ever been lost in my Troop.'

On the Monday, I carried out my first guard duty and fell in with the camp routine. Normal training each day and fatigue parties. Volleyball is played on the beach, always followed by a swim.

All three Section Corporals were in their late twenties, and had served in Cyprus during the emergencies. The Troop Sergeant was very caring and kind, he had served with our Commanding Officer during the war. In his room there was a photograph of himself and our CO on the Normandy beach during "D Day Landings". The CO then was a Lieutenant, and our Sergeant a young marine. Over the next week not much happened. On Saturday I made a visit to Aden town with some of the boys. There were many shops on the main road that sold duty free goods. Also, we visited the Mermaid NAAFI Club, which was fully air-conditioned. The big attraction about this club was that draught Red Barrel and Flowers Keg beer was available. I had a couple of beers and caught the six o'clock transport back to camp. That evening a good John Wayne movie was being shown, I did not want to miss it.

On Monday morning the Rifle Troop had to be at the Guardroom at three thirty, three trucks were waiting to transport us out 20 miles. Our Troop Sergeant had organised a 20-mile march. The trucks would drop us 20 miles out from camp, then we would march back. The day starts to heat up after eight thirty, so we would miss most of it. Before we were loaded on to the trucks everybody went into the Guardroom. All of us put our water bottle pint mugs into a large bowl of limes with blocks of ice floating in it. Lime helped to eliminate the awful taste of the water in Aden. We only had our small packs, rifles and 20 rounds of live ammunition. The drive out took just over half an hour to our drop off point. The march back was steady, averaging about four miles per hour. When we were about a mile from camp our Young Lieutenant suggested that the remaining distance should be covered running. Our Troop Sergeant told him that the distance had to be covered at a steady pace, also everybody should still have one full water bottle left. We finished our march on the beach, everybody was saturated in sweat. The CO came down to the beach and our Troop Sergeant told him that he had a very keen young Subaltern to break in. The CO said, 'Young officers out of training have a lot of theory but are short of experience, but he will learn.'

*

Patrols were sent out daily. Now it was our Section's turn to carry out a patrol. This would be my first, all the other boys in our Section had done numerous patrols out here. They told me there was nothing to worry about, I was to stay in the middle at all times, as this was still part of training for me. Our Section Corporal made a scale model of the area to be patrolled, also a North direction indicator was placed in one corner. It was always important to know where North is as this helps with your bearings. The Company Commander, Troop Officer and our Sergeant were present during this briefing. Our Section Corporal followed the standard procedure and format, which is laid down by NATO. Our mission was to patrol around the outskirts of three villages, checking on them. We were not to enter any village, but to ensure that they were aware of our presence. The patrol would last no more than two days. Ammunition and one 24 hour ration pack was issued, all equipment was checked. The drop off point would also be our rendezvous collection pick up. The first day we would visit two villages, covering a good distance during nighttime.

The transport dropped us off at the beginning of the foothills. All villages to be visited in this area were located around here. The first one was about six miles away, and the second eight miles. Everything was OK at both villages. At the second village all water bottles were filled. I was given the job of collecting water bottles, going to the village well and filling them up. Everybody had to put a water sterilisation tablet and neutralising pill in their water bottles; the water tasted foul at the best of times. I collected all the water bottles and went to the well head. Women from the village were collecting water so I waited for them to go. One woman was hanging back, all I could see were her toes protruding out from under a black dress, which covered the head and whole of her body. All of them were dressed in black and their faces were covered. As this woman came close to me she spoke in clear English saying, 'Please ask your Corporal to take me back with you.'

I filled up the water bottles and told my Section Corporal of this event. He replied that she had married the Headman's son and was wife number four, water carrier. The Headman's son had been to England on a university course and had met her there. Life out here was not a picnic and was very hard for her. Also, I was told, 'If she did come back with us, none of the Section would reach our rendezvous point alive. She has made her choice, now she has to live with it.'

We left the village and travelled for two hours, our Corporal said that we would stop for four hours and rest. We would be outside the third village by eight the following morning. We were detailed off to carry out an hour's guard watch, in pairs. At midnight our Section Corporal had to make a very brief radio call to headquarters, informing them, in code, of our location and well-being. The radio and battery which were carried by our section had a combined weight of 60 pounds, its battery was 40 pounds. The radio message had to be brief, as the dissident tribesmen had good locating equipment. Our radio had valves and was a product of the last war. Each one of us carried this radio for an hour at a time, it was passed over to the next man without fail. Nobody liked carrying it, but it was necessary.

Just before four in the morning we set off for our last village. We arrived outside the village, or to within about half a mile of it, just before eight. We ensured that they saw us, then we commenced our return journey. Our truck was waiting for us, in the rear were four five-gallon containers of fresh water as our water bottles were nearly empty. Everybody had a good pint of fresh water, then we filled our bottles up. It is always better to have two full water bottles, as you didn't know what would be around the next corner. We arrived back at camp just before six that evening. Our Section Corporal made his report to the Company Commander. My first patrol had been a minor success, and an experience.

The patrols continued on a steady basis, as a routine, without any major problems. I only intend to write about what were unusual events.

About two months after my first patrol our section had to carry out a "Hearts and Minds", taking two Medical Assistants out around five villages. The normal routine was followed, model and mission clearly laid out. We were to escort the two Medical Assistants from our Unit, they would give inoculations and sweets with Polio vaccine in them to village children, as well as limited advice on health. We never went into any villages, always staying just outside. Buildings are very good places for ambushes and snipers. The women brought their children out and the Medical Assistants always ensured that the children put the sweets in their mouths, after they were given to them. Vaccines and inoculations were administered. Also we were told that there were a lot of sexually transmitted diseases amongst the village inhabitants. Men and women were pointed out to us, their walking was uncoordinated as they were in the final stages of syphilis. Our Medical Assistants said that they would be dead within six months. This "Hearts and Minds" patrol was judged to be a success by the powers that be. Over the next six months they were sent out on a regular routine, in fact every section in our Unit carried out Hearts and Minds patrols.

Our troop was detailed off to guard some Royal Engineers working up country repairing a road. The road ran through some mountain passes and they were making it safe from rock falls. We would sit high up and ensure that no Dissident Tribesman took pot shots at these Royal Engineers. They started work early each day and finished at sunset. It was hot, dusty and hard work for them. They had bulldozers, tractors, lorries and determination to complete their task. We all got on very well with them. They envied us a little as they said, 'You just watch us work all day!' All the water for washing, cooking and drinking came from a well. Large quantities of purification tablets had to be added, also the water was boiled; but it still tasted terrible. It was discovered that the water purification tablets were running low, and life was not possible without them. It was decided that three Land Rovers would leave early the following morning and collect five boxes of them from an Army base 30 miles away. We set off just before sunrise, travelling on a road high up in the mountains. We could look down and see everything below us, for about four miles. Our Troop Sergeant was in the lead vehicle, it would take two hours to cover 30 miles. The road which we travelled on was full of potholes and ditches. We had to stop and fill in numerous ditches for the vehicles to pass over them, it was hot work.

After we had been travelling for about an hour shots and small explosions were heard below in the valley. The vehicles travelled on for about a mile. One mile to our left there were about 200 dissident tribesmen, behind good cover, pinning down an Army Troop of Infantry. Our Sergeant had a very good pair of high-powered binoculars, which gave him a clear view of this situation. The tribesmen were about 100 feet above the Army Infantry men, shooting down. It was hopeless for the soldiers to move in either direction or return any rifle fire. The tribesmen were not aware of our presence, and our Sergeant said that the Bren guns and rifles we had were no good, as the distance was too great. Then he handed me the map saying, 'Give me a six figure grid reference of this enemy position.' I did this, it was like sitting high up on a table and looking down. The map reference was checked by him, and as we were on very high ground the radio reception was excellent. Headquarters was contacted, and a map reference and clear description of the enemy layout were given. Ten minutes later four RAF Hawker Hunter jets appeared as from nowhere, they made one pass firing their two-inch rockets. The tribesmen were forced out of their cover and left the area. The aircraft had appeared suddenly, and then vanished to the wild blue horizon. The Army boys then had a clear route out, our collection party had saved their skins. I asked our Sergeant why he had asked me to give the map reference. He replied, 'It was good to see if you were capable of clear thinking under pressure.' We collected the water tablets and returned safely back to our camp up country. Our CO received a letter of thanks from the Army Infantry Battalion, he passed it on to our Troop Sergeant.

*

In the Unit there was a marine who always managed to worm his way out of patrols. Every time his Section or Troop was detailed off for a patrol he went sick, complaining of some imaginary illness. The boys in his Section resented him, it made their patrols harder as there were fewer of them to share carrying loads. He was over six feet tall, but very thin. He had been in this Unit about two months longer than myself. It was better to go out on patrol, in camp there were guards, fatigues and senior staff to stay clear of. Each time we had to do a guard there was a parade in khaki drill, which had to be starched and pressed with sharp creases, our white belts had to be Blancoed and our boots highly polished. The Regimental Sergeant Major always inspected guards, but none of us liked him. He hated his Aden posting, so he made life uncomfortable for all the Corporals and marines.

One Sunday, in the dining hall, everybody was sitting enjoying their roast beef and Yorkshire puddings when the main entrance doors were opened. Three Corporals in khaki drill, white belt, best boots and white peak caps were stood in the doorway. Nobody knew what they wanted at first. One Corporal was carrying a white pillow with a large white feather in the centre. Then one of these Corporals asked for total silence, "as a very important presentation was to be made". Then all three marched to where the Patrol Dodger was sitting. One of them took a sheet of paper out of his pocket, it was handed to the first Corporal, who had called for quiet. The Patrol Dodger was then addressed correctly by his full name, a list of patrols that he had missed was read out. Then they said that he was being presented with the order of "White Feather". The feather was placed in front of his dinner plate, he did not say a thing. The three Corporals turned around and marched out of the dining hall. There were four other marines sat at the same table as the Patrol Dodger. These four marines picked up their plate and moved to other tables. The Patrol Dodger had now been accused and branded a coward, for letting his mates down. From that Sunday on he was sent to Coventry and treated like a social leper. To be accused of cowardice by your mates is a very serious offence.

Two weeks later I was on guard. Opposite the Guardroom were the ammunition magazines. Before a patrol left camp they always drew their hand grenades and bullets. A patrol was drawing ammunition and preparing to leave. The Patrol Dodger was filling his rifle magazines up. Once he had completed arming and packing his grenades away he sat down. The remainder of his section ignored him. I watched him for a few minutes, then he took a full rifle magazine out of his ammunition pouch. The magazine was put on his rifle, then he went to one side. Then he cocked his rifle, feeding a live round into the breech. The Rifle barrel was placed in his mouth, then he pulled the trigger. The bullet and gases from the cartridge took the back of his head off. Rather than go on patrol and take his chances with the rest of the marines in our Unit, he took the coward's way out. It is not another experience I would wish to witness, suicide for him was final. The saying, "If you can't stand the heat get out of the kitchen", was taken to extremes.

*

Not all patrols go as planned. During my next patrol all planning fell apart, but in the final details it saved our lives. Also, the exacting training all marines go through stood us in very good stead.

This patrol was to be five days/four nights, going deep up country. The intelligent reports stated that there were no dissident tribesmen in this area, or surrounding villages. We were to leave early morning in the rear of trucks, for a five hour journey. Once we disembarked from the trucks we would be given a lift on three tanks, over soft ground. This area which would be covered by tanks was nearly 30 miles, walking/marching across soft ground is hard and tiring. The tanks dropped us off at the edge of the desert, and all of us had a good drink of water. One thing about vehicles is that there is no problem carrying containers of water. That day we covered nine miles on foot and found a favourable location to spend the night. One hour before dawn we proceeded to our first village. The inhabitants were glad to see us, and very friendly. All our water bottles were filled and we stopped and made some tea. The children were given sweets, as we were issued with two large bags to distribute to village inhabitants. We visited two other villages that day as routine, and all was well. That evening we found a nice spot to camp, and a fire was lit. Everything was going well, there were two nights to go. That morning another village was visited, our second one was about 14 miles away, so we set off at a steady march.

We were proceeding along the side of some foothills when there was a shot. The marine bringing up our rear was carrying a radio, and a bullet from a rifle hit it. It lodged in the radio rendering it useless, but at the same time it saved the life of the marine carrying it. We all took cover amongst some rocks and our Corporal checked the ground behind using his binoculars. Nothing was seen, but it was decided that we would stay amongst the rocks. After an hour a large group of tribesmen came down from the foothills. As the radio was damaged and useless we were instructed to dump our spare batteries. The radio could not be dumped as it had to be taken back with us to substantiate our story; also, we did not want this enemy to know of our shortcomings.

The tribesmen spread out, there were about 60 of them. We opened up with rifle fire and our Bren gun. I think about eight were hit, the remainder took cover. While this turmoil was taking place amongst them we commenced our withdrawal. We moved as fast as possible. When we arrived amongst some large rocky boulders it was decided to rest for a short period, to gain our bearings and check on the enemy. We were in this position for about 20 minutes and our Corporal observed about 20 Tribesmen pursuing us. We left the spot and found an area with better cover, but the tribesmen were still looking for us. One of the marines in our Section said, 'People out here like Heinz soup, we could leave a very unpleasant surprise for them.' Three cans were taken out of our packs, the bottoms were removed very carefully. The contents was shared out amongst us. Once we had three empty tins three hand grenades were taken out. The pins were removed and empty soup cans placed over them. These three cans were then placed on a rocky ledge, ensuring that they would not be missed. It was reasoned that the tribesmen would pick them up and our grenades would drop out. This little venture should cause more casualties amongst them. We proceeded away, trying to keep out of sight. Half an hour later three explosions were heard, but we did not know what damage was inflicted on the dissident tribesmen. We kept moving, and were pursued by about 15 tribesmen. Their numbers were dropping. We moved into what looked like a small valley, but it was a cul-de-sac, the only way out for us – was up. It was now getting dark, the light was fading. Our Corporal decided that we had to climb out during the night. We checked the area and found a low cliff about 30 feet high. It was decided that this would be our avenue of escape.

There were seven rifles and one Bren gun, the slings were removed from our weapons and they were joined together. Also, we carried nylon cord in our packs. This cord attached to rifle slings made it possible for the first person to go up and pull some of our equipment out. The Corporal was first to scale the cliff face and assess our escape route. He told us to be careful as some footings gave way under him. As each member of our Section reached the top, the makeshift rope was dropped down to pull up his weapon.

Marine David Fulsome was the last member to come out. As he reached up to go over the lip at the very top his footing gave way. He fell the full 30 feet, lying at the bottom, conscious, but in great pain. Our Section was very lucky as one of our members had trained as a male nurse before joining the Royal Marines. Marine Michael Caruthers, our male nurse, and I descended down again. Marine Caruthers checked David Fulsome for injuries, and it was found that he had a broken left arm and collarbone. Both these injuries were very painful and we now had the major problem of how to get him to the top. His arm was immobilised, by tying it tight to his body, but he was in great pain. Our made-up rope was put round his body and under his armpits. Our Corporal carried two small injections of morphine and one was administered to our injured colleague. I was amazed how quickly the morphine acted to relieve his pain. It took all of us nearly half an hour to get Marine David Fulsome to the top. Now we had to move away from the spot, our Corporal reasoned that the tribesmen pursuing us would enter the cul-de-sac and conduct a search. We left and found what was considered a safe spot to rest up. Two hours before dawn six members of our Section made their way round to the entrance of our cul-de-sac, one was left to look after and guard out injured mate. We took up an ambush position about half a mile from the entrance. Half an hour after sunrise we watched eight tribesmen enter the cul-de-sac. Our Corporal checked the surrounding area to see if there were any other tribesmen around. None were seen. We all went forward carefully, using rocks and low bushes for cover. About 100 yards in front of the entrance we took up a good ambush position, with plenty of cover from view and return fire.

After an hour all eight came out, they were walking and talking as though there was nothing whatsoever to worry about. Once they were well clear of the entrance our Corporal fired the first shot. The first shot was also our order to open fire. The Bren Gunner let off a full magazine with one burst. All eight were hit and eliminated. We advanced very carefully towards them, not one had returned fire. The first thing we checked for was water bottles. All of them had large canteens of water, holding about four pints each. Our water was running low, also the injured marine was dehydrating fast as broken bones lose moisture internally. All of the dead tribesmen were in their early twenties, about the same age as ourselves. Our Corporal had a small finger print set. All fingerprints were taken, also the bodies were checked for any identification. Nothing was found. They all had old .303 rifles.

Now we had to dig a grave to hide the bodies, this was for two reasons: first, if found by other dissident tribesmen they would disembowel them and blame the British Armed Forces, and secondly, to stop wild dogs eating their bodies. The sun was hot, it took nearly two hours to dig and bury the bodies. The bolts from their rifles were buried with them, and we covered the graves with stones and rocks so it did not look as though the ground had been disturbed. Eight old rifles were taken away and neatly stacked about 200 yards from the graves. They were placed together, but hiding four grenades with their pins removed from them, as a good booby trap. The weight of the rifles placed on top of grenades would keep the trigger mechanisms down. But this would make a nice surprise for those that might come along later, rifles to tribesmen were like candy to children.

We returned to our injured mate, and there was now sufficient water for the return journey. It was decided that all excess rations would be dumped, just keeping our hard tack biscuits, as they could be eaten on the hoof. Two men supported our injured mate back, and his kit was carried by others in the Section as they would only have their rifles and two magazines. Our Corporal checked his map, and it was discovered that we were 30 miles from our rendezvous pick up point. The three tanks would be waiting from five till eight the following morning. We had no radio to contact the outside world for any assistance and it was now midday, and the temperature was over $100^{O}F$. We would start our move back at three thirty, as the day cools a little then. Nobody rested, we were all on the lookout for more dissident tribesmen. At around two an Army Otter Spotter aircraft was seen, it was about three miles away. We could not light a fire or flash mirrors, if the pilot saw smoke, and other means to attract his attention, so would the dissident tribesmen. An hour later six RAF Hawker Hunters flew by, they were high and travelling fast. We all realised that we were on our own.

At three thirty we set off for our return journey, it was reasoned that two miles per hour could be covered. Our injured colleague was in great pain. Marine Caruthers said he would give him the final morphine injection around midnight. Every half an hour we would stop and give our injured mate a little water.

Just before dusk we heard four small explosions, they were about four miles to our rear. Somebody had disturbed the pile of rifles, but as it was now getting dark we all hoped that dissident tribesmen would not pursue us. There was no moon that night, just a clear sky and stars. We were all sweating, carrying extra kit and two of us were supporting our injured mate. The Section Corporal ensured that our water was meted out slowly. Marine Fulsome kept passing out and collapsing and it was getting harder all the time to keep him on his feet. At midnight we stopped and rested for half an hour, and the final dose of morphine was given to our injured mate. We knew that the morphine would only last four hours, but it made life easier for him, and for those supporting him. It was estimated that we had covered about 14 miles, still a long way to go. We set off again.

At around five in the morning our injured mate passed out completely, so now four of us had to carry him. One thing to be grateful for was that he was small and light. The dawn came, but we still had three miles to cover. Now we had very little water left, and it was getting hot. We all kept going, sweating hard now and losing body moisture fast. Most of us started to feel the early signs of dehydration, but we had to keep going. Just after seven thirty we reached the three tanks. The boys from 16/5th Lancers doubled forward and picked up our injured mate. He was laid out on a stretcher and mugs of water were poured into his mouth, it was important to get water into him fast. Seven five-gallon cans of fresh water, one for each one of us, were passed out. I put my mouth around the spout and just drank. After 15 minutes I was feeling refreshed. We all agreed that if the distance had been another two miles, none of us would have made it. The tank crews took our equipment off us and stowed it away. All of us sat inside the three tanks for our return journey, in air-conditioned comfort. They radioed ahead and asked for an Ambulance, and also informed our Unit that we were OK. When we met the trucks our injured mate was put into an Ambulance and taken to the RAF hospital for treatment.

Once we arrived back at camp, our Corporal gave a briefing to the CO and Unit Intelligence Officer. The radio was taken away, it was discovered that a musket ball one inch in diameter had lodged in the body of it. The musket ball had been fired from an old-fashioned black powder rifle, with an eight-foot barrel. This type of weapon was still used, they were accurate from a range of 800 yards. The Section was stood down for 48 hours. After a good night's sleep, all of us went to the RAF hospital to see our injured mate. He had his arm in plaster and shoulder immobilised. We told him how lucky he was to be surrounded by good-looking nurses. He thanked all of us for looking after him, we all knew that our care would have been reciprocated. He was flown home after seven days, six weeks ahead of his tour schedule ending.

The information passed on proved invaluable. All patrols in that area were now carried out by Army armoured cars, and closely monitored by reconnaissance aircraft.

*

Ten days after our near disastrous patrol, it stated on Company Daily orders that breakfast would be at four the following morning. Nobody had any idea what all this was for. At breakfast we were joined by a Mortar Troop. They told some of us that we would all be going on a two-day patrol, none of them knew where. Also, some of the vehicle drivers were present. I ensured that my plate was full up with food as 24-hour ration packs were not at all appetizing. When we went to draw ammunition, all of the Corporals and marines were given two four-inch mortar bombs each. Once everybody had been given their allocation of ammunition, we were told to form up outside the Guardroom. Our Company Commander, Company Officers, Sergeant Major, and all the troop Sergeants arrived.

The Company Commander addressed us, stating that we would provide an escort and protection patrol, and that we would also carry bombs for our Unit Mortar Troop. Six Mortar teams would accompany our Company. Intelligence had been received that a group of about 200 dissident tribesmen had gathered in a valley, preparing to raid villages for slaves. The area to be attacked was 120 miles up country, trucks would take us the first 80 miles. The next 30 miles would be covered in tanks, the reason being that the areas had been mined. Dissident tribesmen had laid anti-personnel Russian mines, and the small metal detection rings had been removed. Without the metal detection ring it was impossible for mine detection equipment to locate these devices, as they were made of plastic. Tanks could travel over them and set off the mines without any damage. We would travel on the back of tanks which had set off the morning before. We should rendezvous with the tanks at five that evening, and it was estimated that the next drop off point will be at around nine. From our drop off point we would have a ten-mile march, the patrol was to be on top of a plateau by one. Mortars would be set up, and bearings and settings would be given to each individual Mortar team. Our plateau was nearly 300 feet high. It was a gradual climb to the top, there was no need for ropes. Each Mortar team would fire 30 bombs after the order was given, following confirmation received from Army Spotter Aircraft.

Our Company and Mortar troop embarked onto the trucks. The side canopies had been removed and a nice breeze was flowing through. The first 20 miles was on a decent road, smooth and comfortable. The remainder of the journey was very uncomfortable, it was a track full of potholes and littered with small boulders. The trucks were going from side to side and the day was getting hot. The dry wind was drying us out, but thankfully there was plenty of water on each vehicle. The continuous movement of the vehicles was tiring and I was glad when we met up with 16/5th Lancers. 16/5th Lancers were at the rendezvous point and a meal had been prepared for us. Large mugs of tea helped wash down tinned corned beef stew, it was a good meal. After an hour we climbed onto the backs of tanks, about 15 individuals to each vehicle. The tanks travelled slowly, but still kicked up a lot of dust. After travelling for an hour we started to hear small "popping" noises; it was the anti-personnel mines going off. These mines could take off a foot. The ground for the first one and a half hours of travel was flat and level, then we entered small rolling hills. The continuous up and down motion made some of the boys a little sick. We were all glad to reach our final drop off point. The tanks would await our return.

The Company Commander led, and our Sergeant Major brought up the rear. Small sharp stones were on a hard surface, cutting into our boots as we marched over this ground. After nearly three hours we reached our plateau and the climb up was easy. Once at the top I gave my two mortar bombs over to a team. Mortars were set up in a short time, the bombs were fused and placed neatly, ready for firing. The Company took up a defensive position around the edge of this plateau and we waited for dawn to break.

Dawn came up just before six, the night had been cool and calm. At around ten past six I saw the Army Spotter aircraft to our west. The aircraft flew low and close to the mountains. As the aircraft flew over a valley we could hear rifle fire. The dissident tribesmen were trying to shoot down our Spotter plane. Five minutes later the order was given for Mortars to fire. The range from our plateau to the valley, where the dissident tribesmen were, was 3,000 yards. All the bombs were fired off at three second intervals, fitted with air burst fuses. They had been despatched in 90 seconds. Two minutes after the last bomb had been fired all Mortar teams were packed up and ready to move.

Our journey back was slow and without any incidents. Once we entered camp the Commanding officer welcomed us. Also, he said that the expedition had been a great success.

*

The Unit was to spend nine weeks away from Aden, two on board HMS Bulwark and seven in Kenya. Also, every company was to have one week's Rest and Recuperation at Silver Sands rest centre. I was looking forward to this trip, as it would be a nice break. Also, I would be seeing another country and way of life, this is what had attracted me to the services. HMS Bulwark was an aircraft carrier, converted to carry troops; it was known in the Royal Navy as a Commando Carrier. All the navy had done was to put some extra bunks into the stores that had been used for aircraft spares. The only aircraft onboard were helicopters, which were used to carry troops ashore. The marines called them Flying Taxis.

Once onboard, our Rifle Company was allocated bunks on the large S2 mess deck, and the accommodation was shared with members from Headquarters. This large mess deck accommodation held 200 men. The bunks were stacked three high, I was grateful that we did not have to sling hammocks. Comfort was limited, but you don't worry about that at the age of 19 years. One thing about this ship was that it was awkward, if you had to move around below decks it involved going up, across, and down again. The ship sailed from Aden at four that afternoon, we all lined the flight deck. The evening meal was excellent; also fresh water on board was sweet and free from all additives. HMS Bulwark had two large evaporators for making fresh water.

The following morning the CO addressed his Unit and informed everybody that an operation would take place early next day. We were to place a cordon around a village 500 miles North of Aden. Raiders had been going into Oman, and had been attacking the Sultan of Muscat. The raiders had taken slaves, food and high value goods. That morning our Company Commander informed us that we would conduct a search of the village.

Also, rum was issued just before lunch. All the boys under 20 years old were not entitled to a ration of rum. But we were entitled to two cans of beer. Jolly Jack lived very well.

Early next morning long before dawn, helicopters and landing craft left the ship. Our Company went ashore on landing craft. The first thing we did was to round up all the men in the village. They were taken onto the beach, also three informers accompanied our Unit. Their head covered with hoods, all the men from the village were lined up. Our informers picked out 22 rebels who were handcuffed and taken out to HMS Bulwark on landing craft. A search was conducted of the village, large quantities of arms and also five bars of gold were found. Also, 14 young children were found in a deep cellar; they had been captured in Oman, and were to be sold as slaves. The two principal families lived in splendour, but the remainder of the village occupants were in squalor and filth. Three doctors, plus ship's medical staff also came ashore, and administered inoculations. The general health of people living there was poor. The ship sailed at eleven that morning, heading north to Oman. We had 22 rebels and 14 young children to be handed over to the Sultan's forces and later in the afternoon the helicopters took off and did this. The children were returned to their parents, and the rebels tried according to their laws, and dealt with. That evening we turned south for Kenya.

There was a traditional ceremony conducted as we crossed the Equator, permission was asked and granted by King Neptune. The crossing ceremony was interesting, also enjoyable. Another experience not to be forgotten.

*

The following morning we arrived in Mombasa. Before our Unit was disembarked we were going to have a lecture from a Game Warden. The Game Warden addressed the whole Unit, telling us the following:

"All animals in the game parks are dangerous".

"Don't approach animals from up wind".

"Don't try and befriend rhinos, buffalos, elephants, lions or any animals".

"Don't pick up lion cubs or young leopards".

"Don't stand on snakes, as they are poisonous".

"Don't swim in any of the rivers, as there are crocodiles and hippos".

"Don't wander around the bush at night, as that's when most animals hunt".

Then, at the end he asked, 'Are there any questions?'

'What <u>can</u> we do?' asked one of the marines, which raised a good laugh from everybody.

Our Company was to live and operate from a tented camp, on the edge of the game park.

We arrived late afternoon and erected our ten man tents. As we had plenty of tents, six men shared each one, which was comfortable. A large ditch was dug for rubbish and food waste.

Three cooks also accompanied the Company and prepared meals each day, which were appreciated by all. Lanterns were hung around the camp to discourage wild animals entering during nighttime. Six marines would share the night patrolling, and as a fire watch, around the camp.

Early next morning just after dawn, one of the cooks woke everybody up with shouts of 'Snakes, snakes!' He had gone to the rubbish pit to dispose of some waste, and the pit and area around it was full of poisonous snakes. Rats had been attracted to the food waste and snakes, including cobras and vipers, had been attracted to the rats.

The Sergeant Major said, 'The best thing to do is to burn all waste each day.' A gallon of petrol was thrown over the rubbish and then set alight, this procedure was carried out each day. One marine on fatigues was told to go and burn the rubbish, he poured five gallons of petrol over it. Instead of standing back and throwing a match in he stood directly over the pit. The match dropped in and the flames shot upwards, he lost eyebrows, hair, and skin from his face, but his shirt saved his chest. A Land Rover had to take him to hospital in Nairobi.

The first week our Rifle Troop went for long walks, always finishing up at a Game Lodge for lunch and drinks. All of us carried a rifle, live ammunition and two water bottles. We saw various types of animals from a safe distance; this was a good week.

The next three weeks were spent practising contact procedures and drills, everything was quiet. During our fifth week we were doing Troop Advance to Contact, and my section was to the left. We were all advancing through elephant grass, which is about six feet high. There was a shout from one marine in the point Section, 'Run, run.' I heard them all going past our sections running shouting 'Run.' We all turned around and ran to our rear. After about a mile everybody stopped. Our Lieutenant was last to catch up with everybody, and he demanded to know what all the fuss was about. The Corporals and marines in Point Section told him that they had bumped into a sleeping pride of lions, right in front of them. The Troop Sergeant said that we would "call it a day". On the way back to camp one of the marines gave a shout saying that he had been bitten by a snake. He then sat down, saying that he was feeling faint and strange. We carried him to a track and radioed our Headquarters telling them what had happened. Now this was his "football pools win", the Unit Doctor replied. He asked for our map grid reference, which was given. The doctor replied that he would be with us soon. Two minutes later a helicopter torched down. The marine who had been bitten by a snake was by now unconscious, and the doctor gave him 20 injections of different types of anti-venom. Once he had completed giving him all these injections he was put on a stretcher and airlifted to a Nairobi hospital. The marine was in hospital for six weeks having been bitten on his leg by an Egyptian Cobra; which are very deadly. For once everything turned out alright, a real "football pools win" for this young man.

In week six our Company was joined by two Royal Navy Commanders from HMS Bulwark. Each of them were given a ten man tent to themselves, in the area known as the "Officers' Mess". This area was well away from the Corporals and marines. In addition they had one tent used only as a dining room. Most evenings they sat down to eat at eight, followed by numerous drinks. Our Company Commander always ensured that ice and beer was available for the other ranks, known as his boys, as he was a good caring man.

As this was our last week on the edge of this game reserve, it was decided that we would go for long walks observing animals each morning, finishing up for lunch at a game lodge. One of the Commanders was told to accompany us; as our Company Commander said, 'The exercise will do him good.' The Commander was overweight, as he led a very sedentary life on board ship. Two water bottles and a web belt were issued to this commander and our Troop Sergeant told him to stay between the marines on their sight-seeing trip through the game reserve.

The days were hot and humid, which caused everybody to sweat profusely. The first morning we walked slowly for about eight miles, gazing and observing animals. By now all of us could name and identify all the various species. Lunch at the Game Lodge was excellent, also the beer was nice and cold. Once we were ready to move, our Royal Navy Commander asked, 'Is transport going to pick us up now?'

Our Lieutenant told him, 'No, we are going to walk back, and be in camp by five.'

That afternoon we returned back to camp, walking alongside a river. We kept well back but observed crocodiles and hippocampus. Somebody suggested to the Commander that the water was cool and inviting, he should try it. The suggestion did not go down very well with him. By the time we returned back to camp the Commander was nearly dead on his feet. The following morning he was reluctant to accompany us, but the Company Commander insisted that he go out for a daily walk. By the end of the week both Commanders had lost some weight and said that they were fitter and healthier for the exercise.

On Sunday morning we were packing up camp and moving to Silver Sands Rest Centre. On the Saturday night the Officers had a special dinner and numerous drinks, retiring to their camp beds at around two that morning. A special area was cordoned off as a lavatory, well lit with lanterns to deter snakes and other nasties. Just before dawn one of the two Commanders had the call of nature, but being somewhat "under the influence" instead of going to the lavatory he wandered into a small copse of trees close to camp. He had his carpet slippers and pyjamas on, wandering around in the copse. The call of nature was completed, but by now he had lost his bearings. Staggering around, he tripped over a tree root. To steady himself he reached up, grabbing at a hanging branch. As he fell the so-called branch gave way and a large lump fell on him. He was now totally confused, the large lump was a small antelope which had been placed in the tree by a leopard, for safekeeping. He stood up, still with a hind leg in his hand. Then he received the biggest shock of his life as a large male leopard attacked him. This had a very sobering effect and brought him to his senses. He let go of the antelope and started to fight for his life.

In the morning his absence was noted. The Officers asked if anybody had seen him. The two Wandering Pickets said no-one had noticed the Commander wandering around, but they had heard a commotion in the nearby copse just before dawn. Both of them were sent over to check out the copse. One returned, telling the Company Commander that the Commander had been found, and that a stretcher party was required. Nearly everybody went over to the copse, where the Commander was found lying on a pile of leaves, covered in blood. His pyjamas were ripped and his face and body were covered in deep claw marks. He was conscious, but only just, and he was a very sorry sight. He was carried back to camp. Marine Caruthers washed him with an antiseptic solution and prepared the torn Commander for his helicopter return to HMS Bulwark. There were claw marks all over him, it looked like a map of Clapham railway junction. He made a full recovery, but had a permanent reminder, which would always be with him.

We packed up camp and arrived at Silver Sands Rest Centre in the evening. There we learned that a Corporal in our Unit had been trampled to death by a herd of elephants, whilst doing troop attacks in long grass. A marine had also been trampled to death by a herd of buffalos, but this was his own fault. Before joining up, he had worked on a farm as a herdsman. He told everybody that buffalo were only wild cattle and could be rounded up. He set off to show everybody that it could be done, telling them: "You have to show these buffalo who is master".

He approached the buffalo with a large stick, waving his arms and shouting. A mother with calf thought she was going to be attacked and charged. Her calls attracted other buffalo and about eight had charged him; he started to run, but not fast enough. By the time the buffalo had passed over him he was well and truly dead. He had forgotten the lecture from the Game Warden, a fatal mistake.

*

Silver Sands Rest Centre was on the coast of Kenya. The sands were silver, they stretched for miles North and South. The week spent there was restful and enjoyable.

*

Our return trip to Aden was relaxing. Once back in Aden four marines in our Section were returned back to the UK. The Royal Marines operate a trickle draft system in all their Units.

Five new members joined our Section, one of them a replacement for Marine David Fulsome. All five were straight from training, four teenagers and one man, 30 years old. The four teenagers were normal decent types, they had joined for adventure and travel. The 30 year old told our Section Corporal that he would have his position within a couple of weeks, and that by the end of the year he would be our Commanding Officer! Then he told all around him that he was "a hard man". Our Corporal looked at him and said, 'In your dreams!' One of the other new arrivals told us that the 30 year old had had to do his infantry and commando training twice before passing out.'

The 30 year old was getting on when he joined the Royal Marines, for which the maximum age for entry is 28. His name was Winslow Nation. He did not try to make friends or endear himself to anybody. When someone joins a new Unit it is best to stand back, watch and learn, and not to go around insulting other marines and telling stupid stories. Marine Caruthers told him that it would be better if he buttoned his lip and "engaged brain before starting mouth". Then I pointed out to Winslow that he had a bald patch on his head, a big red nose, a double chin, large stomach and skinny legs. Also, that he would be a liability on patrol as he did not look as though he had any strength or stamina in him.

Our Corporal asked him, 'What did you do before you joined the Royal Marines?'

Winslow replied, 'I was a telephone engineer for the Post Office Telephones.'

Marine Caruthers asked, 'Why did you join up if the job in civilian life was so good?'

He answered, 'Because I can gain fast promotion and be in charge of the Royal Marines within five years.'

I said to him, 'You are a fool, and dangerous to all around you.'

For the next two weeks we continued on normal training, but Winslow was always at the rear on a march. He struggled with any form of physical exercise. Marine Caruthers told him to "lay off the drink".

Winslow replied, 'Only a fool would stop drinking, the cost of spirits here is ridiculously cheap.'

Our Troop Sergeant also heard that Marine Winslow Nation was in the NAAFI every night getting drunk. He was given a warning and told to stop, but he did not heed the advice. One week later he collapsed on a march. On investigation it was discovered that large amounts of brandy had been consumed the night before. Winslow was charged, given seven Guard duties and also fined £20. On his first Guard, Winslow met the RSM, Winslow's dress turnout was below the required standard, so the RSM gave him another seven extra Guards.

One week later our Section was detailed off to carry out a reconnaissance patrol up country. I knew the area as we had been there before. The morning we had to leave Winslow had to be pulled out of his bed; he stank of brandy. We pushed him into the shower, trying to sober "this thing" up. He was late arriving at the Guardroom and our Section Corporal laid into him. Before we set off all of us had a drink of Limers from the Guardroom tub, except Winslow. We had a six-hour drive ahead of us and the day was hot. As you travel inland the atmosphere becomes drier.

We disembarked and proceeded on our way. Winslow was hanging back. After an hour he collapsed, we checked his water bottles, both were dry and empty. Marine Caruthers checked for a pulse, but none was found. It was now three in the afternoon, we radioed back and relayed our problem. We were told, 'Wait where you are as a RAF helicopter will collect the body.' Two hours later a RAF Whirlwind arrived and collected the body of Marine Winslow Nation. We continued on our patrol, nobody was sorry to see the last of him. The patrol was a success, but hard.

Once we returned back to camp the Unit Doctor sent for us. He asked us, 'Who certified Marine Winslow Nation dead?' The marine was alive now but sun-blind. When he was taken to the RAF hospital his body was taken down into their mortuary. When the staff changed shifts his body was looked at, someone noticed that one of his little fingers moved. The doctors put him on a drip, as he was severely dehydrated. He was alive but sun blind. He should not have been left lying on his back, looking up at the sky with his eyes open. His sight would return, but it would take a couple of weeks. Marine Caruthers said he assumed that the body would have been checked by a doctor on arrival at the hospital. The doctor said that the marine was so severely dehydrated that his heart would have dropped to something like one beat per minute.

Our Corporal said that he would have a word with the Troop Sergeant in order to be rid of Marine Winslow Nation. Subsequently the Troop Sergeant had a word with the Company Commander, explaining that Winslow Nation was a liability and incapable of fulfilling his duties. Also, we found out that he was only a linesman for Post Office Telephones, not an engineer. He was a "big Poser". In due course, Marine Winslow Nation was discharged, "services no longer required", never to be seen again. Also, the Section Corporal said that Winslow was too old when he joined up at the age of 28. At that age a person's character has formed and it is not easy to adjust to a different way of life. He had many bad habits and was unwilling to change.

The Troop Sergeant and Section Corporal were to be going home in a week's time and that weekend we had a small beach party, to say goodbye to both of them. The Troop Sergeant was going on to retirement, as he only had three months left to complete his 22 years for pension. Just to show that he had planned for the future he had booked a place on a Teacher Training course. During his time in the Corps, he had done numerous correspondence courses, preparing for civilian life. Our Section Corporal was to attend a Sergeant's course later in the year. He passed and was promoted, later completing his 22 years as a Sergeant Major. The Commanding Officer gave the Troop Sergeant a glowing reference; they had known each other for a long time. The Troop Lieutenant paid both of them compliments and thanked the Sergeant for his guidance.

A Corporal Roger Haphazard was our new Section Leader, he was a Platoon Weapons Instructor. His first tour abroad had been spent on board a ship, then the last six years at Lympstone training. This was his first time in a Commando Unit. He was like an old mother hen, constantly checking up on everybody. I only did one patrol with him. The model and orders were perfect, but on patrol he was very nervous. I think he was expecting us to confront numerous enemy personnel, and whenever we came near any close country he became edgy. Marine Michael Caruthers told him that the area we were in was safe, but it had no effect. We were all glad when this patrol was over.

Marine Michael Caruthers returned home a week after the patrol, he went on to become a Major. I served with him several times during future years.

Now it was time for me and the boys from my squad to return home, as we had completed our year's tour in Aden. Before we left, we were gathered together and addressed by our CO. He told all of us that our training was now complete, we had knowledge and experience which would help us in future years. We all flew home on the same flight.

45 Commando Royal Marines stayed in Aden till November 1967. Once they returned to the UK their operational role was altered to Arctic and Mountain Warfare. Dry desert to cold arctic and snow.

Chapter Four
UK and Tranquillity

After my foreign service leave I joined 43 Commando, based in Plymouth. I soon fell into barracks routine, compared to Aden it was very easy. Guards came round every six weeks. Whole weeks were spent on the ranges shooting, also the services took delivery of a new weapon. The General Purpose Machine Gun was brought in to replace the Bren Gun. This new weapon was belt fed, which meant that a great rate of fire could be put down. The Bren Gun was magazine fed, but very accurate. Also, lots of sport was played.

I had been in this Unit for 18 months when Company Orders asked for volunteers to serve with the Royal Navy for a short period. I volunteered and was accepted. Six weeks later I and 20 other marines travelled to Portsmouth, joining a squadron of Daring class destroyers. We were distributed amongst these six ships. Early the following morning all the destroyers put to sea. We spent six weeks at sea, the marines only did bridge watches. This period at sea was excellent. None of the ships went into any ports, all supplies were carried out at sea. Once I returned to Plymouth I put my name forward to serve on a Royal Marines Ships Detachment.

One year after volunteering I joined HMS Tartar. The Sergeant Major was Colour Sergeant Jones, my old squad instructor. He remembered me, and he was an excellent Sergeant Major. The frigate spent 18 months in the Caribbean, it was like an extended holiday. We visited numerous islands and ports.

One comment which always remains with me is from our visit to Corpus Christi, Texas, on the Gulf of Mexico. Whilst walking along by the docks I came across a small café, and displayed by the entrance was a menu board. What stood out was "Plate of gravy and two slices of bread, price 5 cents". I stopped and gazed at this menu, and then the owner came out. I started talking to him and commented on how cheap gravy and bread was. He replied that nobody starves in the USA, if you cannot afford the cheapest item on the menu, knock on the side door and it will be given to you for nothing. During our visit to this port all of us were treated well by the Americans.

After two and a half years on the frigate I returned to 43 Commando. Colour Sergeant Jones told me that once I had completed seven years service with a good record, it was possible to sign on for the pension, which was payable after completing 22 years. I signed on, also placing my name on the promotion list. One year later, I attended my Corporals course at Lympstone.

The course was eight weeks long, harder than Infantry training. As a Corporal you had to be able to teach and lead a Rifle Section. The average sleep we had each night was five hours. One of the main purposes was to see how a person reacted under pressure. Thirty marines commenced the course but only 20 passed. I am grateful to have passed, this was now behind me. One year later I was promoted to Corporal.

Two years later 41 Commando was posted to Malta, I volunteered to serve in this Unit. Malta is considered a good posting, also foreign drafts are few. I was accepted and given a joining date to fly out.

Chapter Five
Malta

My flight to Malta was courtesy of the RAF, they were at their normal standard – excellent. I was met at RAF LUQA by a marine driver and driven to St Andrew's Barracks. The driver dropped me off at Unit Movements office, which was housed in Headquarters Block. The Headquarters Block accommodated the following offices: - Commanding Officer, Second in Command, Adjutant, Regimental Sergeant Major, Movements officer. Orderly room and Guardroom. I reported to the Movements' staff, they welcomed me, also informed me that I would be in Headquarters Company. The Movements' Corporal told me to take a seat, he would telephone HQ Company and somebody would collect me from their staff. Being a nice Spring day I moved outside on to the veranda, which was at the rear of the building. The Movements' Corporal came outside, he explained that we were overlooking the parade ground, which was the equivalent size of four football pitches. On the far side of this ground there were three buildings – on the far left was the Sergeants' Mess and accommodation, in the centre the Marines' NAAFI, and the small one on the right was the Corporals' Club. (The Movements Corporal assured me that the Corporals' Club organised some excellent functions, also hired good local entertainers.) The long low building to our immediate right was the Medical Centre. There were 12 accommodation blocks to the rear of the Medical Centre, also company offices and stores at the far end of the camp.

It being nearly one o'clock all three messes had personnel coming and going from them. Three men emerged from the Marines' NAAFI, the one in the middle was being supported by the two either side of him. They went across the parade ground to the Medical Centre. The person in the middle had blood around his mouth and appeared to be in some distress. The Movements' Corporal stated that there must have been some trouble in the Marines' NAAFI. Five minutes after the three personnel had entered the Medical Centre the Corporal of the Guard came out of the Guardroom accompanied by four marines. He proceeded to Marines' NAAFI and entered by the main entrance. About four minutes later he re-emerged marching five marines across the parade ground. The marine in the middle did not have any head dress on as he was under close arrest. He was about five feet nine inches tall, broad build with jet black hair and a square face. As I was a good distance away I could only see his silhouette and outline of his build. Also, I could see that there was some discussion going on between the escort Corporal and the person under close arrest. The discussion looked heated, as the man under arrest appeared to be bad tempered and aggressive. I watched them enter the Guardroom.

A few minutes later a marine came over from Headquarters and showed me to my accommodation. I was to share a room with the Armourer Corporal. Also, the marine from HQ told me that lunch was nearly over, but I could have a late meal with today's Guard Commander. I went over to the dining hall, being easy to find, as there are normally some cooks at the rear of the building. I went over to the hotplate and helped myself, there was a table occupied by members from today's Guard. I recognised Corporal Roger Haphazard and asked if I could sit with them. It is nice to talk to other members in the Unit as you can start to feel its character. Corporal Haphazard made me feel welcome and told me that he had been in the Unit for 17 months. The two young marines had only been out here one month, both had come straight from training. The normal chat took place, what Company, where from and what job was I going to do?

I then mentioned to Corporal Haphazard that I had seen him escort a marine under close arrest from the NAAFI to the Guardroom. He replied that the so-called marine was Rupert Mansfield, not a very nice fellow. He continued that he knew Mansfield well as they were both in the same Rifle Company, as was his friend that he mixes with. Mansfield had been in Corps about five years, was in his early 30's and was a nasty type. He was not a career serviceman, all he ever wanted to do was drink, fornicate, fight and sleep. He had a general resentment to any form of authority. Also, he was ill-suited to the Royal Marines, joining at 28 years of age. His Sergeant and Section Corporal were always reprimanding him, he had numerous minor charges on his record, for failing to carry out his duties correctly. He was trying to convey the impression amongst marines that he was a hard man, but nobody was afraid of him. The Corporals and older marines were always telling him to behave himself. Mansfield was terrified of his Sergeant Major, and also of the RSM, both of whom had no times for him. Mansfield had struck a Corporal from the Army Pioneer Corps in the Marines' NAAFI simply because he had knocked the elbow of Rodney Blair, who was bringing beer over from the bar. The NAAFI was packed, and he'd had to force his way through the crowd. Only a little beer was spilt but Blair and Mansfield demanded that two fresh pints be brought for them. The Pioneer Corporal apologised, but refused to buy them fresh pints as only a little had been spilt. Mansfield then proceeded to hit the Army Pioneer Corporal several times, knocking him to the floor. The Pioneer Corporal was only five feet two inches tall. The other marines pulled Mansfield off his victim and two of his mates took him to the Medical Centre. It was from the Medical Centre that the Pioneer Corporal phoned and ordered Mansfield's arrest.

I said 'That beer Mansfield and Blair spilt is going to prove very expensive. Who is the RSM?'

Corporal Haphazard said, 'The Unit RSM is a Mr Jones, a Drill Instructor, he knows you.'

I replied, 'Yes, he was my instructor during recruit training.' Then I asked, 'What were you talking about to Mansfield on your the way over to the Guardroom?'

He answered, 'Mansfield said that his friends would ensure that no one would testify against him, and if they did then they would receive a good beating. I replied that I would pass that information on to the RSM, and at that point Mansfield realised that he had said too much. He didn't "engage brain before starting mouth".'

I reminded Corporal Haphazard of Marine Winslow Nation, he was in his late 20's when joining the Corps. Because he was set in his ways it was hard for him to conform and adjust to a different type of work. Also, he was kicked out of the Corps.

"Mansfield will go the same way. They are the types that think everything has to change for them".

One of the young marines related to us, 'Rodney Blair is Mansfield's best friend. Blair is nearly six feet tall, blond hair and a really nasty type, who thinks that he is the brains. Mansfield takes his orders from Blair, who starts the fights, then gets Mansfield to finish them off. Blair runs hot and cold, he can be very charming or extremely dangerous, he has a split personality, a real Jekyll and Hyde straight out of Robert Louis Stevenson's novel. Also, he is a coward, always ensuring that his opponents are small than himself, and he tells everybody that money can be made easily, with a little dishonesty, and that all Officers and non-commissioned ranks are fools.'

He went on, 'Mansfield thinks he can earn a lot of money being an enforcer for any East End London criminal gang, and he is known to fight bare-fisted in public houses. Overall, this shows how low his intelligence is. Blair worked in a warehouse in Southampton and Mansfield on the London Docks before joining up. The marines call both of them "the two buffoons", and the four marines they knock around with are idiots, too, two of them work in vegetable preparation, (spud peelers) and the other two work as camp pioneers (road sweepers and toilet cleaners). These four, who are known as "The Four Stooges" are nearing the end of their service contracts and have no ambition to stay in the Royal Marines. None of them want promotion as that would involve hard work, dedication and using their brains.'

Corporal Haphazard said, 'The four of them are overweight and generally lazy. They never take part in any sport, although the RSM ensures that they report to the Guardroom each morning for inspection before they start work. Most weekends they are drunk, but they stay clear of other marines.'

I said, 'The duties they carry out are normally done by fatigue parties.'

Corporal Haphazard replied, 'They are best left to carry out these duties, as they are no good in Rifle Companies.'

We all finished our meal and left the dining hall.

The following day I commenced my joining routine and met RSM Jones. He made me feel welcome telling me that most training is done in barracks as the Unit has to go away for exercises. He said, 'There is plenty of sport and shooting, to which I replied,

'Sun, sea and mild winters are one of the main attractions of Malta.'

Marine Mansfield was formally charged, his Company Commander said, 'As this is a very serious offence it will have to be dealt with by the Commanding Officer.' For the same reason Mansfield was kept under close arrest and escorted by Provost Staff.

That evening in the Corporals' Club, one of the Provost Corporals said, 'Blair had an interview with the Adjutant, RSM and Provost and he was told that if any intimidation takes place then a Court Martial will follow. The Adjutant informed him that he could be sentenced to six months in jail and given a dishonourable discharge.'

One of the Corporals said, 'Blair would welcome a discharge, but not jail. Both Blair and Mansfield do not have any honour, but they understand fear.

The Provost Corporal replied, 'The Adjutant and the RSM visited Mansfield in his cell, explaining the seriousness of his offence. Mansfield emphasised that he had been attacked and provoked by the Army Pioneer Corporal, but the RSM said that while he is at Colchester Detention Correction Centre there would be plenty of time to reflect on this incident over split beer. Also, he explained the options the CO had, and that it would be advisable to plead "guilty" as there were two independent witnesses. If he refused to accept the CO's punishment then he will be put forward for a Court Martial, which would have greater powers of punishment. And if he lost a Court Martial then he could go to jail for 18 months.'

Thursday morning Mansfield was escorted into the Commanding Officer's Office, by the Provost Sergeant and two Corporals from his staff. The Company Commander, Adjutant and RSM were also present. The charge was read out and Mansfield was asked if he understood the charge and seriousness of the offence.

He replied, 'Yes, but not guilty.'

Then the Adjutant read out the injuries: - "Loss of two teeth, broken nose and 14 stitches to the mouth". The Army Pioneer Corporal was marched in and the CO asked him to explain what had happened. Then the CO told him that he could speak without fear or retribution from anybody in the Unit. The Pioneer Corporal gave his evidence, emphasising that he recognised the accused.

Then the CO said to Mansfield, 'This Corporal was small and slightly built, but I don't think he attacked you. Also, your service record is not good.'

Then Mansfield was given 28 days Detention Quarters, to be served at Colchester Detention Correction Centre. Mansfield was marched out of the CO's office, back to his cell.

The RSM reprimanded him while he was there saying, 'You are a coward and a disgrace to the Corps.'

The Provost Sergeant told Mansfield, 'When you return to this Unit you will be kept under close observation.

Mansfield was escorted to RAF LUQA and put on the midday flight to the UK.

*

As I had just joined the Unit my name was top of the list for Guard Commander and I would be on duty that weekend, Friday and Sunday. Friday morning I reported to the RSM for any special instructions concerning my duty. He informed me that I would be the Guard Commander, as I was the senior Corporal. The relief Corporal had been promoted this week, it was his first duty as a Junior Non-Commissioned Officer. Also, I was informed that a marine called Rodney Blair would be on duty the same weekend. The RSM was not at all happy with Blair, he knew that he was the cause of the trouble in the Marines' NAAFI. It was pointed out that Blair would try and take first or last watch, which he was not to have. Blair would be the oldest marine on guard, the remainder were young boys just out of training. The RSM also explained to me that both Blair and Mansfield were troublemakers, who should not be in the Royal Marines, and that the four marines who went around with them were no good, but they would not cause any problems as they were just biding their time for discharge. Blair had some brains and ability, but he was lazy, manipulative and very cunning. If he'd had any sense he would have gone for promotion and a structured career, but he put more effort into dodging work than doing it. Mansfield was Blair's "go-for" boy, he obeyed Blair's orders without question, and that's why he had gone off to detention quarters rather than Blair.

The guard assembled just after lunch on Friday, and this was the first time I had met Blair. He was six foot, slender build, blond hair and round face with deep-set eyes. I took him to one side and told him, 'You will do the middle watch on both duties.'

He immediately protested and said, 'This is victimisation.'

I said, 'Yes, because you are camp low-life.'

Then a welcome face walked into the Guardroom, Sergeant David Fulsome. He looked fit, and came over and shook my hand. Then he confirmed to Blair, 'You are to have all middle watches.' Sergeant David Fulsome was the duty Senior Non-Commissioned Officer for the weekend guard. We had a chat and spoke of Aden.

'The relief Corporal drew up the duty roster,' Blair was sneering at the list telling everybody present, 'it's not fair. I am being victimised.'

I told Blair that he was right, and he would do as he was told.

Everyone settled down and started to carry out his duties. At tea time a young marine came to me, his face was red and swollen. He told me that he had agreed to swap watches with Blair, from last watch to middle. I told him to go and have his tea, and that he would still be doing the last watch. I continued, 'I will deal with the problem.'

I went to the rear of the Guardroom and found Blair, who was acting very cockily, telling me that he had swapped watches and there was nothing I could do about it.

I said to him, 'You are still doing the middle watch, and as an added bonus you can scrub the toilets out at the rear of this building.'

Sergeant Fulsome came in and asked what the problem was, and I explained the past events. He then said to Blair, 'If the young marine says that you have struck him then you will be placed in cells immediately. Also, when he returns from tea you will tell him that you have changed your mind and wish to do the middle watch. This will be done in the front office of the Guardroom in the presence of two Corporals and myself.'

Blair was glowing red with rage, he carried out his instructions, but grudgingly. I knew that I had an enemy now, but this did not worry me. I inspected Blair's toilet cleaning, ensuring he went over items he had missed. By the time guard finished on Saturday morning Blair was tired and fed up. Before the guard left I told him to look forward to Sunday. He gave me a black look.

Sunday's duty went off quietly and without any trouble.

Monday morning after guard, Sergeant David Fulsome and I had to report to the RSM. We outlined what events had occurred, but stressed that we had no firm evidence. The RSM said, 'Blair will overstep the boundary one day, then he will be thrown out of the Corps.' I returned back to my Company and continued with work.

In the Corporals' Club the talk always turned on Blair and Mansfield. As Blair was without his friend and sidekick everyone assumed that all was quiet. One of the NAAFI staff came over to the club and explained that there had been an incident in the Marines NAAFI that evening. The story was as follows:-

Blair and the Four Stooges were drinking in the Marines NAAFI when a marine came in and sat at the next table, close to them. The marine was drinking orange juice, eating a packet of crisps and reading a newspaper. Blair was drinking his beer fast and staring at the marine, whose orange juice was on the table. Then Blair started making remarks about his drink saying that he was not man enough to drink beer, and only weak men drank orange juice.

The Four Stooges were very quiet, they did not comment or pass any remarks. Blair became more aggressive as the drink started to have effect. The marine drinking orange finished his drink and started to walk towards the main entrance. Blair felt affronted as the marine had not answered him back, but ignored him. He then proceeded to call him names and put his drink down and left his seat. He walked to the main entrance and placed himself in front of the door. Blair, like a fool, told the marine that he was a coward and he tried to move him out of the way.

There was one blow to Blair's jaw and he went out like a light. He was out for nearly three minutes, the Four Stooges laid him out on a bench. When Blair came round it was explained to him that the marine who drank orange juice was also the Navy and marine light heavyweight boxing champion. This marine was the new driver for the Commanding Officer. Blair just said that he was feeling bad and wanted to go and lie down. The Four Stooges told him he could go once they had finished their beer, as it was his round and that he had to pay. Blair bought his round of beer, and left the NAAFI.

Another lesson had been learnt the hard way. Blair had learnt that quiet people are not cowards, he thought "gentlemen" were afraid and weak. Also, the Four Stooges were not the fools he took them for.

*

Two weeks after the event in the Marines' NAAFI, Rodney Blair reported sick, telling Medical Staff that he had a bad itch between his legs. The doctor examined him and told him that he had Gonorrhoea, caused by "riding bicycles without cycle clips on". He was put on two weeks' light duties. Blair reported to his Sergeant Major, telling him that the Unit doctor had placed him on light duties, also that he was excused all training over the next two weeks. Blair now had the idea that he could do nothing and nobody would bother with him.

The Sergeant Major asked him, 'Why are you excused?'

Blair replied, 'It is personal and confidential.'

The Company Clerk, a marine, said, 'He probably has the clap.'

Blair said nothing, but the Sergeant Major picked up the telephone and rang the Unit Medical Centre. They confirmed that Blair had Gonorrhoea. The Sergeant Major then said, 'Riding bicycles without cycle clips on. One night with Venus, the rest of your life with Mercury, but at the moment it's a week with penicillin injections.'

Then the Company Commander came into the office; the Company Clerk said, 'Blair has the Clap.' He laughed and said, 'Penicillin injections in the rump are painful.'

The Sergeant Major then told Blair, You can clean four Company bathrooms and toilets, a Sergeant will come and inspect them at 12, then you can go to lunch.' He was also told to report back at one, as there were other jobs which would be found for him. Blair was not at all pleased, no dodging work, and he was being made a joke of. He cleaned the toilets and went to lunch. Blair collected his food from the hotplate and sat down. The marines in the dining hall were pointing and laughing at him.

Then the Company Clerk came in and one of the Sergeant Cooks asked him what the big joke was. The Company Clerk, being very tactful, shouted out, 'Blair has Gonorrhoea, he's been riding bicycles without his cycle clips on.' This raised a big laugh. One of the Cook Sergeants went over to Blair and told him to sit at a table by the entrance, and to take his plates and cutlery with him, because "there was the risk that he could contaminate decent men". Blair moved to the table designated then somebody shouted, 'Blair is now in Rose Cottage.' Blair wanted to leave the dining hall quickly. Marines going out had to pass him, and they made funny remarks as they passed.

The CO's driver, and a bunch of marines from Motor Transport stopped by Blair and the CO's driver said, 'You are very jinxed and very unlucky. Blair did not reply or say a word in retaliation. He decided that he would go over for meals late, to miss the main body of diners.

At one o'clock Blair reported to his Sergeant Major and he was told to go over and see the Unit Armourer Colour Sergeant. He went over to the Armourers and reasoned that there was not much work for him. The previous week 200 new rifles and 30 General Purpose Machine Guns had been delivered, and as these were new they were all packed in thick grease. Blair reported as ordered and the Colour Sergeant took him to a large paraffin bath. He was issued with a leather apron and told to start cleaning the grease off the weapons, also that they had to be dry when completed. Blair spent the next two weeks cleaning the weapons and he stank of paraffin, and even after a shower he still smelled of this cleaning fluid. It took about two weeks for the smell to wear off. Another drawback for Blair came when the Unit doctor banned him from drinking and going into the NAAFI for two weeks. In the end he was glad to return to normal duties. The Armourers had worked him hard, and there was always a NCO present.

In the Corporals' Club somebody said, 'Rupert Mansfield should be back in the Unit now.'

The Orderly room Corporal then said, 'Mansfield will be away for another two weeks before he returns. He was rude an abusive to one of the instructors at Colchester, so was charged, and awarded 14 days extra detention.

Then one of the other Corporals said, 'Will the fool ever learn that it is better to go with the flow than against it?' The talk continued about Blair and Mansfield, somebody always mentioned their names.

Rupert Mansfield arrived back in the Unit after serving an extra 14 days in detention quarters. He had been insubordinate to an instructor and charged with this, being awarded 14 extra days. He thought he was safe in detention as he had been sentenced by his Commanding Officer so no extra punishment could be awarded. The staff at Colchester were from other branches of the Armed Forces and he reasoned that they would be a pushover. All he did was mark himself out by the insubordination incident, after which he received the undivided attention of all instructors. They ensured that his prolonged stay was beneficial to them and not Mansfield. He received extra training on the assault course. By the end of each day he was absolutely worn out, fit only to sleep. When I saw Mansfield in the dining hall he had lost nearly two stone. He looked lean and fit, and for the moment he had lost his cockiness, but it would return in time.

*

On returning to the Unit from Detention Quarters a marine has to see his Commanding Officer. Mansfield was marched into the

CO's office, this time minus an escort. The CO, his Company Commander, Adjutant, RSM and Provost Sergeant were present. The CO welcomed Mansfield back, but he explained that the performance at Colchester was a failure. It was pointed out to him that he was no longer in a position to misbehave and any future punishment would be more severe. Also, his Company Commander would submit a monthly report for three months, as he was still under close observation and rehabilitation.

At the end of three months a written report had to go off to Colchester Detention Quarters, Mansfield was then asked if he had learnt his lesson. He replied, 'Yes.' Also, he had to report to the Unit Guardroom each evening at nine and he was not to be involved in any heavy drinking. Over the next three months he would attend school and sport each afternoon, but Mansfield had big plans to go out drinking and return to his old ways. On leaving the CO's Orderly room, the RSM told Mansfield to wait outside his office.

The RSM saw Mansfield and told him that he believed that at the first opportunity he would return back to his old ways, and that all NCOs would be watching for any failure in his behaviour. Mansfield spent the next three months well behaved, showing that fear played a big part in his life.

During the Mansfield rehabilitation period, the Four Stooges returned to the UK and civilian life. They intended to apply for unemployment benefit. They were the types to apply for everything they were entitled to, plus whatever they could get away with. Maximum effort applying for benefit, minimum effort for gainful employment. All the Corporals reasoned that our Corps were better off without them. No loss.

Mansfield completed his rehabilitation without incident, but both he and Blair were becoming fed up with training and constant supervision, they reasoned that the two vacancies in vegetable preparation should be theirs. Both of them put their requests into the Company Office, but they were turned down.

The news of their requests filtered through to the RSM, who summoned them to report to him. The RSM made it clear to Blair that he knew he was the one with ideas to work in vegetable preparation room. As they were in the Royal Marines they would carry out the duties of a Rifleman. Also, it was pointed out that the vast majority enjoyed their work, as they had all volunteered to join.

*

The inter-Unit boxing championships were coming up and volunteers were requested to put their names forward to represent their Companies. I had no intention of volunteering, boxing did not appeal to me. As far as I was concerned it was a spectator sport, let other people be used as a punch bag. I was happy playing hockey and going swimming. The Physical Training Instructors were keen on any sport, there was a Sergeant and two Corporals. Whenever you saw them in camp they were running, never still for more than a minute. Six bouts would take place, so 30 volunteers were asked to step forward. Blair and Mansfield volunteered, they thought this was a golden opportunity to escape rifle troop training. The training for boxing championships started four weeks before the actual bouts would take place. One of the Sergeant Majors was a qualified referee and Marquis of Queensbury's rules would be adhered to very strictly.

The training programme was published, all volunteers were required to go on a five mile run every morning before breakfast. Training with one's rifle company each morning was followed by two hours boxing practice each afternoon. Blair and Mansfield did not take kindly to an early morning run as they were both at their worst first thing each day. Both Physical Training Instructor Corporals went around the accommodation and ensured that all members of the boxing team were up. Blair and Mansfield discovered that drinking too much the previous night made life hard each morning. The PTI Sergeant told them to stop drinking or risk being thrown off the boxing team. The RSM heard about their behaviour and stated that they had volunteered, so they would both complete boxing training. They continued with training but did not enjoy it at all. It was harder than they imagined. If they could miss an early morning run or afternoon training, they did. Physical Training Instructors were not happy with either of them, but reluctantly kept them on to represent their rifle company. Also the RSM had an influence in this decision.

As time passed by a number of volunteers dropped out, through injuries and not meeting standards set down. Only 12 contestants were required. The boxing tournament was to take place in the camp cinema. A boxing ring had been placed on the stage and was well lit. The RSM was master of ceremonies, a Sergeant Major the referee for all six bouts, and Officers on each side of the ring to count points. Unit doctor and Medical staff were present, with a portable stretcher. All Officers, Senior Non-Commissioned Officers, Corporals and marines would fill all the seats in camp cinema. On the evening of the Boxing Championships the camp cinema was full. The atmosphere was happy and jolly.

The National Anthem was played before commencement of a bout. The RSM announced the order of six bouts, stating that they consisted of three two-minute rounds. Mansfield was in the opening bout and Blair was in the final one. Mansfield arrived, accompanied by a second from his rifle company. His opponent was the same height as him, but a little thinner. The Referee called them both over to the centre of the boxing ring and emphasised the Rules of the Marquis of Queensbury to both opponents, ensuring that they understood. Both boxers returned to their corners and waited for the bell to go. The bell rang and both advanced to the centre, Mansfield was immediately hit with a flurry of punches. Mansfield was driven back, he came back but only managed to hit his opponent once in the first round. The bell rang at the end and Mansfield returned to his corner, his face was swollen and red. His opponent in the opposite corner had no marks on him. Mansfield rinsed his mouth out and waited for round two to commence.

The bell rang for the second round, it was a repeat performance of the first. Mansfield was totally outclassed, although he did managed to land two glancing punches. His opponent was quick with his punches, and very agile on his feet, he would not stand still long enough for Mansfield to strike him. The bell went at the end of round two. Mansfield returned to his corner and sank onto his stool, his face more swollen and one eye now closed. The referee went to him and asked if he wished to continue with the third round. Mansfield said that he was not finished yet, and that he could win.

He was standing before the bell rang for the third round, and on hearing the bell ring he ran over to his opponent, put his arms around him in a bear hug ensuring that he was held tight, then he gave him a head butt. Everyone heard the bones break in the opponent's nose, followed by blood gushing onto the canvas ring. His opponent was knocked out, also blood was everywhere in the ring. The referee had to pull Mansfield off and force him to release his hold. He was immediately disqualified. He was booed out of the camp cinema, his opponent was taken to the Unit Medical Centre and kept there for 48 hours under observation.

The following four contests were good clean bouts, one being a draw. There were no head butts, below the belt punches or any dirty tricks from any contestants.

The final bout was now ready to take place, this involved Blair and a Corporal from Support Company. Blair came in, accompanied by a second, he had a very expensive robe on and all silk boxing shorts and a correct pair of boxing boots. His opponent wore white baggy shorts and plimsolls. As Blair came down the isle towards the boxing ring he was dancing up and down throwing punches at an imaginary opponent. One of the marines shouted out, 'Give him an upper cut.' There was a roar of laughter, as everyone knew what had happened to Blair in the NAAFI, concerning the CO's Driver. Blair looked around him, he knew that he was the butt of a joke, and he did not like it.

Both boxers took their corners, the referee called them into the centre to explain the rules. Both boxers returned to their corners and the bell rang. Blair advanced to the centre and lunged at his opponent, but missed. Blair was telegraphing his punches, not one of them connected. In turn he received about 20 punches to his body. The bell rang for the end of the first round. Blair went straight over to his corner and sat down. There was an atmosphere building up against Blair. The marines were saying that he was not up to it and totally out of his class.

The bell rang for the second round. Blair did not leave his corner, The referee went to him and asked if anything was wrong.

Blair said that he had not heard the bell ring. The referee turned his back to return to the centre and Blair ran behind him and tried to hit his opponent in the body, with both fists held together. The Corporal stepped aside and Blair ran into the opposite corner, colliding with the corner post. A great cheer went up from the audience. Blair was now glowing with rage, his plan had failed. The Corporal advanced towards Blair. Blair saw him coming and started to run around the edge of the ring. The referee told both boxers to advance to the centre and box. Blair went to his corner, followed by his opponent. Blair then started to run around the edge of the ring again, pursued by a Corporal. Everyone in the audience was laughing, it being a very funny sight. The bell rang for the end of the second round. The Corporal turned and started to walk over to his corner, but Blair ran up to him, hitting him hard in the back, before he had time to turn around. The referee stopped the bout and disqualified Blair. The RSM stated that Blair was a disgrace to his Rifle Company, but he may wish to represent them in any cross-country running event. Blair was booed and verbally assaulted by marines in the audience. One thing everybody in the audience saw was that Blair could move to ensure that he did not suffer any injuries.

During the next two to three weeks Blair and Mansfield were treated like lepers in their Rifle Company. In the dining hall they sat alone, marines were going up to them and insulting each one. They ensured that they went for their meals late, to miss the main body of diners. Both of them had lost their credibility, also they stayed clear of the NAAFI. The night after the boxing tournament in the marines' NAAFI, they had pints of beer thrown over them. They were challenged to retaliate, but sensing the mood to be very hostile towards them they both left, soaking wet and smelling of beer. After a time they were ignored, and both kept a low profile.

*

The Motor Transport Section was always short of drivers, as they worked hard and long hours. Volunteers with a full UK driving licence were sought to apply for duties as Land Rover drivers.

Blair and Mansfield both volunteered, their Rifle Company recommended that they be transferred to the Transport Section. They both thought that drivers just drove, and were not required to do anything else. Little did they realise that drivers work hard and long hours. Their Rifle Company wanted to be rid of both of them, to pass their problem on to someone else. They were both accepted by MT Section, what they did not realise was that drivers start early and finished late.

The Sergeant Major who ran the MT Section ruled with a rod of iron, he was fair, but they were also well looked after by him. He had three Sergeants and eight Corporals under his control, ensuring that drivers carried out their duties and responsibilities correctly. Blair and Mansfield were each assigned a Land Rover and given detailed instructions on how to maintain their vehicles. The first week in MT they were used as cleaners, this involved cleaning the vehicle yard, garages and spare trucks. Also, MT started work half an hour earlier than the main Unit, and at the end of each day drivers had to clean and fuel up their vehicle for the following day's duties. They both found that there was very little chance of loafing and ducking out of work, there was always a Corporal somewhere. They did not mix with the other drivers, most were older marines and a lot wiser. The Sergeant s and Corporals knew that both of them had been passed over to MT as they were not liked, also regarded as poor quality marines. Blair had told the story of his mishap in the NAAFI to Mansfield. Also the background of the saga of the Commanding Officer's driver. Neither one of them wanted to cross his path, so they stayed well clear of him.

Duties also came round quicker in MT as they were always short of drivers and below strength. Four drivers were required each night for duty. Marines in rifle companies did approximately one duty a month where the drivers did, on average, two a week. Also, drivers did less sport than rifle companies, they were required to do three hours of fitness training each week. The MT Sergeant Major ensured that all drivers carried out their fitness training. The vast majority of drivers were a happy-go-lucky bunch. On Friday morning drivers assembled at eight outside the gymnasium to do their fitness training, Blair and Mansfield were absent. The MT Sergeant Major asked, 'Does anybody know where they are?'

One of the drivers replied, 'They have both gone sick.'

At the end of the fitness training, the Medical Centre was contacted and asked for details concerning Blair's and Mansfield's medical conditions. The reply was that nothing was wrong and neither of them had reported sick. The MT Sergeant Major went over to their accommodation and found both in bed at eleven in the morning. He personally tipped them both out of their beds. Both were visibly shocked and immediately started to make excuses. They were given ten minutes to wash, shave, dress and report to the MT main office. When they both reported to the Sergeant Major he was very upset as they had made another marine lie on their behalf.

The previous day 200 tyres had arrived in MT, as most of the Land Rovers and ten Bedford trucks required new tyres to be fitted. After the Sergeant Major had given them a dressing down he told them that they were to work that weekend and change all 200 tyres, on completion of which they were to contact him and he would come over and check their work.

On Saturday morning they reported to the MT office at eight and phoned the Guardroom stating that they were present for work. The Guardroom then phoned them back to ensure that both were where they should be. They worked all Saturday and Sunday, jacking up vehicles, removing wheels, changing tyres and replacing them back on the vehicles. Bedford trucks have heavy wheels, this work is hard and physical, also the day was hot, in the upper 90^0F. The MT Sergeant Major paid them a couple of visits each day, and they managed to complete the tyre changing by late on Sunday. On completion of this extra work they showered, had a meal and went to bed – both were "shattered".

Both of them were finding MT hard, early starts, fitness training, shooting and sometimes finishing late in the evening. Duties were two a week and sometimes driving late into the night, they were missing trips to town, drinking, lying around doing nothing. Also, there was always a Corporal around to ensure that they were maintaining their vehicles. Both did their best to stay out of sight of the MT Sergeant Major, Blair and Mansfield had learnt about hard work and fear in the MT – or so everybody thought.

Two weeks later it was their turn for Saturday duty. With four drivers on, it is relatively easy. Most work is completed by four in the afternoon, then it is just standing by for any emergencies. Both Blair and Mansfield had a few trips to make during the morning, and also early in the afternoon. Once trips are completed drivers stay in the MT duty room, which has a TV, kettle, toaster, armchairs, four bunk beds and a telephone. They are able to relax but must be available for any trips or emergencies. Neither of them liked the idea of having to spend Saturday evening in a duty room, so they decided to take a Land Rover out and visit some bars. The other two drivers who were on duty with them said that they would not cover their duties, or lie. But Blair and Mansfield thought they were safe.

They left at about seven that evening, visiting bars well away from the barracks area. As time passed by the drink went down and driving became more erratic. Whilst parking outside one bar Blair reversed into a parked car, damaging one of its headlights. They realised that damage was caused, but immediately drove off. One bystander noted the Land Rover registration number and reported the incident to the RAF Police. The RAF checked their vehicle records and it was not registered to them. They contacted the Royal Marines and passed the registration number on. The MT Sergeant Major was contacted, he verified that it was one of our Unit vehicles, in the charge of Blair. On Monday morning Blair was asked, 'Where were you, and what happened on Saturday evening?'

He replied, 'I was in the MT Duty Room.' The mileage and fuel on his Land Rover were checked and there were 30 extra miles on the milometer, but Blair said 'I have no idea, I can't account for it.'

The other two drivers were called in by the MT Sergeant Major, who asked them, 'What happened on Saturday night?'

'Blair and Mansfield went out at seven, and returned at around midnight, Saturday,' they both said.

Both had been in the Corps for 15 years, and they were believed. Also, a claim came in for damages to a civilian car, via the Adjutant. The Claimant was told it would be met in full. As the owner saw a chance to have additional repairs carried out, the total claim was for £200.

Blair and Mansfield saw the Commanding Officer on Monday afternoon. They received a fine each of £150 plus costs of the repairs to a civilian car. Both were removed from MT and placed in separate rifle companies. The report from the MT Sergeant Major was not glowing and the RSM had them in his office and bawled them out. But he knew that 14 days extra Guard duties on a day-on-day-off basis would have a punishing effect on them. The RSM ensured that they did not do duties together, and both of them did their extra Guard duties as well as training during the day. At the end of the 28 days they were exhausted, also broke. They were paying off their fines. Everybody now assumed that they would be well behaved now and come alongside.

*

Blair was still smarting from the boxing tournament. He saw the Corporal from Support Company around camp more often now that he was out of Motor Transport, and he wanted revenge and his credibility back. He thought if someone was given a beating by him, then that would raise his status. Also, Mansfield kept telling him that he won his bout, being disqualified gave him credit, as his opponent was knocked out.

There was a good Western showing in the cinema on Sunday night, and on completion of a movie the marines and Corporals would go over to their respective clubs to have a few drinks. Blair and Mansfield saw the Corporal from Support Company (who had beaten Blair in the Boxing Tournament) going over to his accommodation from the cinema. They both followed him. It was very quiet and lonely, as everybody was either in the NAAFI or Corporals' Club. They both followed him into his room, closed the door and set about attacking him. He was beaten unconscious. He was found later by his brother, also a Corporal in the Unit. An

Ambulance was sent for and he was taken to the Naval Hospital on the island. The Corporal from Support Company had several injuries, a broken jaw, loss of teeth, bad bruising to his face, both eyes closed, broken ribs and his left arm broken.

The Provost Sergeant investigated, but no witnesses saw anything and the Corporal was unable to speak, but he wrote down who he thought attacked him. The RSM had Blair and Mansfield in his office and asked them if they knew what had happened to a certain Corporal in Support. They both said that it was nothing to do with them, also Blair said that two independent witnesses would be required to corroborate any statement from the injured Corporal, as that was required by law. The RSM bawled them both out, then said, 'If any firm evidence comes to light I will ensure that you do six months in prison and that both of you are discharged from the Corps.'

What Blair and Mansfield failed to realise was that the injured Corporal had a brother in the Unit, as well as three cousins. All five of them came from Newcastle (making them Geordies) and they were very close. All five of them were a happy go lucky bunch, they enjoyed themselves, mixed well and were always involved in sport. They were well liked by everybody. The injured Corporal was flown home once his health had improved. His brother and cousins had paid him many visits in hospital, also they said, 'We will put right what is wrong.'

One lunchtime on a Saturday both Blair and Mansfield were stopped at the rear of their accommodation blocks by a group of marines, and they were escorted to the 25-metre range. On arrival at the range they were met by four Geordies, also there were about 200 personnel present from various rifle companies as it had been rumoured that something was going to happen to Blair and Mansfield. That old saying, "He that is to be executed is the last to know" is very true. Both of them did not have any indication as to what was going to take place, but rumours had gone around the Unit. Each was told that they were going to fight one of the Geordies, one against one. They could choose which one they wished to fight. Also, there would be no witnesses, it was going to be unlawful, just like the attack on their relation in his accommodation.

Blair then realised that these four Geordies were related to the Corporal from Support, and he was now starting to panic. Immediately Blair asked, 'Why are we being picked on? Neither of us has any desire to fight anybody.'

The injured Corporal's brother hit Blair in the mouth, and he went down. Blair was lying on the gravel, and he told Mansfield to hit his opponent and "take him out". Mansfield knew that he was outclassed, outnumbered, and that this was not his style of fighting "fair". He turned to leave but was stopped by two Geordies. Then all four Geordies laid into both of them, Blair and Mansfield were receiving a good beating when some Corporals, who had been watching, stepped in and stopped the fight. It was pointed out to the four Geordies that the vast majority in the Unit supported their action, but nobody wanted a murder charge brought. Life would be miserable for Blair and Mansfield.

Blair and Mansfield were both covered in dirt and blood, and with noses bleeding and bruising on their bodies they managed to limp back to their accommodation. They spent the rest of the weekend in their rooms. On Monday morning they both reported to the Medical Centre. Both of them had black eyes, which reduced their vision, and their faces were black with bruises and badly swollen. The Doctor gave them three days off, and they were confined to their barrack rooms.

The RSM heard what had happened through the grapevine, but took no action. Both Blair and Mansfield stayed well out of the way for the next four weeks.

In the Corporals Club one of the members said, 'Blair and Mansfield have learnt a lesson which they will not forget.'

I replied, 'Don't count on it, as both have short memories.'

*

Not long after this incident, there was a change over of Corporals and marines in the Unit. The marines coming out from the UK were young and just out of training.

Our Unit was to carry out a Defence exercise in Cyprus. This type of exercise can be hard and tiring. One has to live in a slit trench, patrol at night, carry out watches and numerous other duties, on average a person only has two to three hours sleep in a 24-hour period.

The Unit arrived off Cyprus on HMS Bulwark and were disembarked by helicopter. The Landing Zone was about eight miles from the battle area, which required an advance to ensure that no enemy were in the area. The Unit advanced slowly to the battle area. Once there each rifle company was allotted an area to defend. Slit trenches were required to be dug. It was very dry and hot. When digging trenches everybody was covered in a very fine white powder, as the soil was like powdered chalk. At night intelligence patrols were sent out to gather information, returning before first light. One hour before first light everybody has to stand-to, which means that all equipment is packed and ready to move. Everybody is prepared for an instant move, if required. Also, this duty is carried out one hour before dusk. These are times most favoured by military for any attack, as light is poor and it can play tricks with your vision.

Over the next five days the Unit moved positions three times, which meant that old slit trenches had to be filled in and new ones dug each time the Unit stopped. Also, during this exercise everybody was living on 24-hour rations packs, which provide the correct amount of vitamins and calories for a human body for a day. Everybody found them tasteless and dull, and they tended to make people constipated. During the day large amounts of water are required to be drunk, because it was very hot and dry. There was no shortage of water, however, not like Aden. The exercise went the full five days.

After the Defence exercise our Unit moved to the beach. We camped there and carried out rifle range shooting during the daytime. This was enjoyable, as each afternoon we could swim and relax. During the last two days on the beach Blair and Mansfield sneaked off. They were reported absent by their Section Corporals. This information was passed to the Commanding Officer, also to the Military Police, who were informed that two men had deserted from our Unit.

A Greek Cypriot farmer reported that he had seen a light from a fire in one of his old barns at night, this information was passed on to Cyprus Police. Police arrived in the morning and found

Blair and Mansfield both asleep in a barn, also, the remains of two geese in a corner. An empty four pint jar of KEO brandy, (this drink is good for rocket fuel and lighting fires) was also next to them. The farmer was very concerned about loss of two geese, he wanted to know who was going to pay for them. Cyprus Police handed Blair and Mansfield over to Military Police, who passed them on to our Unit. Our Unit paid the farmer £10 for loss of his two geese, £5 was to be deducted from each one's pay. The farmer had made a good profit on the geese, as he would only have received 50p for them at market.

On completion of the exercise our Unit had two rest days in an Army barracks in Cyprus, and this would enable personnel to go where they wanted and do what they liked. The RSM had a summary charge made out against Blair and Mansfield, which meant that he could work both of them during the two-day rest period. During the day in Cyprus the temperature is in the high 90^0F, also the sun is nice and bright.

Blair and Mansfield were told to report to the RSM at eight the following morning. The RSM had made arrangements for two ten ton trucks to be sent to our Unit, with ten tons of artillery ammunition on board each one. An artillery shell and container weigh one hundred weight, which meant that there were 200 containers on each truck. Both trucks were parked on the edge of the square, one on each corner. The square being 200 yards by 100 yards, and the RSM's accommodation overlooked this area, he had a commanding view. Blair and Mansfield reported to the RSM as ordered, both were clean and smart. The RSM pointed out to them that they were a poor excuse for marines, they spent more time dodging work than doing it, but that was going to change over the next two days. Both of them were taken over to the two ten ton trucks, also they were shown a white marker peg on the far side of the square. They were told that both vehicles, full of ammunition, had to be emptied. The ammunition was to be placed on the other side of the white marker peg, both vehicles were locked so that they could not be moved. The distance from each truck to the white marker peg was 200 yards and the tailboards of the vehicles were four and a half feet above the ground. Once both vehicles had been emptied and the ammunition placed on the other side of the marker pegs both of them were to report back to the RSM. They both started at just after eight. They were allowed a short break at ten for a drink and half an hour for lunch. They finished unloading the vehicles by three in the afternoon. Both of them were soaking wet with sweat and they told the RSM that they had placed the ammunition by the two white marker pegs. He went over to ensure that they had done it correctly. Once he had satisfied himself that all was well Blair and Mansfield were given an hour off for tea and told to report back to him after it. They reported back to the RSM after an hour, then he told them to re-load both vehicles with the ammunition. Once this work was completed they were to report to the Guardroom and the Officer of the Day. He would inspect their work, No way were they to get away with anything. Also, they were required to report to the RSM the following day and carry out the same work again. The first day they finished at 11.30pm and the second day just before midnight.

*

During the return trip to Malta the Unit had two weeks at sea onboard HMS Bulwark. This involved exercises for ship's company. Our Unit stayed out of the way and generally relaxed.

On the day of disembarkation in Malta Blair and Mansfield had to report to the Commanding Officers' Orderly Room for their punishment. Everyone in the unit was expecting them to receive a custodial sentence (detention quarters), but what they received was 28 days "Confined to Barracks" and £200 fine each. Confinement to Barracks is not very pleasant as it restricts an individual's privileges. The routine they had to follow was: -

    A. Early morning call at 0530 hours.
    B. Report to Guardroom at 0600 hours, cleaning toilets.
    C. Breakfast at 0730 hours.
    D. Normal work, with their Rifle Company during the day.
    E. Report to Guardroom at 1630 hours, work in main dining hall till 2000 hrs.
    F. Report to Guardroom at 2200 hours, final muster of the day.

G. Saturday and Sunday work in main dining hall under direction of Chief Cook, cleaning and scrubbing dishes.

The RSM ensured that they both adhered to this routine, as he took a personal interest in both of them. During this 28-day period everything was nice and quiet in barracks.

On completion of their Confinement to Barracks Blair and Mansfield went into town and celebrated. Two weeks later they were very happy and telling everybody about their amazing win at the casino, they stated that they had won nearly £8,000. They were going out every night smartly dressed always finishing up in the casino. Also, they had a lot of Maltese friends in the casino, these were the undesirables of Maltese society, mainly small time crooks, pimps and general thugs, also girls with low moral values. The casino was closely watched by Maltese CID. For the next few weeks they continued to keep to themselves, but still telling everyone about their good fortune. Their luck ran out and they started to lose, and their Maltese friends were not so friendly with them. They started to borrow money from some of the young marines. Both were borrowing more than they could possibly afford to pay back. They carried on going to the casino in the foolish belief that they luck would change, but it did not.

The Unit was paid every Thursday. Most of the Corporals and marines only drew out enough money for a couple of nights out, plus sufficient funds to maintain themselves in basic requirements. Blair and Mansfield drew out all they were entitled to. They did not bother to save any of their pay. The Unit was always paid at 1200 hours on Thursday, just before lunch. One payday, late in the afternoon, several Corporals and marines returned to their accommodation to find their lockers had been broken into. The Ministry of Defence Police were called, but no evidence or fingerprints were found. The following Thursday more Corporals and marines found that their lockers had been broken into, and that money only was taken. The MOD Police were again called but no evidence was found.

The Corporals were discussing the break-ins in the Corporals' Club. Mansfield's Section Corporal noted that Mansfield had a Dental appointment on the first Thursday that the lockers were broken into, and Blair's Section Corporal also noted that Blair had a Medical appointment on the Thursday afternoon of the second break in. One of the Leading Medical Attendants said that the Medical Centre did not see either one of them on the days mentioned. There was no concrete evidence to take them before their Company Sergeant Majors but it was agreed that a word should be had with each one of them.

One morning after breakfast six Corporals surrounded Blair and Mansfield as they were leaving their accommodation to report to their Companies. They were told that there was not enough evidence to report them, but if any more break-ins occurred they would be severely dealt with. One of the Corporals had been in 43 Commando in the early 1960's when a thief was caught, and he told Blair and Mansfield what happened to this marine thief:-

"The Commanding Officer sentenced the marine to 28 days DQ's, and on returning to his Unit he went back into the same Rifle Company. The Corporals and marines in his Rifle Company felt that justice had not been done. One afternoon the marines were told by the Corporal in their company to be in the Company Rest room at six that evening. Just after six, the Corporals came into the Rest Room carrying a marine who had received a very severe beating. It was pointed out that he had stolen from his mates, now he could not be trusted, also, justice had only been done in the eyes of the law. Justice was now to be carried out in a way that would never be forgotten by the marine thief, and all those present. The door to the rest room was of solid four-inch oak, it was very heavy. The marine thief had a hand placed in the doorframe and the door was slammed on his hand. The same procedure was carried out on the other hand. On completion of his punishment he was dumped in the middle of the main parade ground where the Guard found him. He was discharged on medical grounds as he no longer had 100% use of his hands. Also, he never stated to the powers that be what happened.

Blair and Mansfield were told that if any more lockers were broken into they would be the main suspects, and also severely dealt with. They both said that they understood, but they were innocent. After this little talk no other lockers were broken into.

One evening on my way back from supper I saw both Blair and Mansfield talking to a young marine, it looked as if they were threatening him. A few nights later I saw them talking to another marine. He looked ill at ease and very unhappy in their presence. A few of the other Corporals also mentioned that they had seen Blair and Mansfield speaking to marines in a menacing manner. The one common factor was that the marines they were talking to were always on their own. On Monday evening, returning from the Corporal's Club just after ten to my accommodation, Blair and Mansfield stepped out of the shadows. They stopped me, and they were aggressive and threatening. Blair stated, 'You made a fool of me on duty and it is pay back time.

Then Mansfield stated that I had to given them £5 a week or I could end up very hurt. They both pointed out to me that I had nobody to verify any threats made against me. Blair stated that the law required two independent witnesses, and if I tried to report them I would look a fool. I walked away and returned to my accommodation. The Corporal I shared my room with was down in the dumps, not his happy-go-lucky self. I asked him if he had been visited by Blair and Mansfield. 'Yes,' he said, they wanted £5 per week from him. Also, the four marines in the room next door to us had had individual visits from both of them, they were running and operating a protection racket.

I went into the room next door and invited all four marines into my room for a discussion. All four were very unhappy, as they said, 'If any of us report the incidents of threat and protection we will look very stupid, as at no time were any witnesses present.'

I asked all five if they would be prepared to take the law into their own hands to deal with the Blair/Mansfield threat. Their immediate answer was 'How?'

I said, 'I can work out a plan of action, but it will be unlawful and dangerous, also, it has to be kept secret from everyone outside this room.'

They immediately said, 'Let's hear the plan.'

I continued, 'First of all we must all agree to take an oath of silence and secrecy concerning the action against Blair/Mansfield. One of the four marines went to his room and returned with a

Bible. We all in turn swore an oath of silence and secrecy to our future action concerning Blair and Mansfield. I then told them to go away for an hour while I worked out the details of a plan.

I laid out this plan in the sequence of patrol orders:-
- The ground to be covered - was at the rear of the accommodation blocks, where there were 800 yards of rifle ranges leading to the edge of cliffs and the sea.
- The situation - is that we were all being threatened with physical violence if we do not pay protection money every week to Blair and Mansfield.
- The mission - was to strike total fear into the two of them, which they would never forget.
- Execution - I went over the plan in detail, which can be read in the course of events.
- Command and Signals - two teams of three, Armourer Corporal will lead one, I would be in command of the other. They would consist of two marines and a Corporal, this was to ensure that our enemy was outnumbered three to one.
- Service Support - everybody to have a good night's sleep, dress in denims and boots, foul weather clothing as required, plus a Browning 9mm pistol.

Corporal Armourer will draw out six Browning pistols on Tuesday, also book the 25-yard range for that evening. I said that I would sign out sufficient 9mm ammunition.

That Tuesday evening all six of us went to the pistol range and fired off about six magazines each, (a 9mm Browning magazine holds 13 rounds). We left the pistol range just before supper, locking the pistols in lockers within our accommodation block. After supper all pistols were given a good clean and two magazines were loaded by each one of us, in preparation for the morning's work. Late that evening we all met up in the marines' room. I went over the details again and ensured everybody was sure of what they were required to do. I told them that I would shake everybody at five in the morning. One of the marines asked if I was going to get the Guard to wake me. I said, 'No, by having the Guard wake you there would be a record in the Early Call book. Also, there was to be no written record, secrecy was paramount at all times. I would set my alarm clock for four thirty.

The alarm went off at four thirty, I got up and shook the Armourer Corporal. I looked out of the window, it was raining very hard and the wind must have been a force six. I dressed then woke the four marines in the next room. I advised them to wear their ponchos as the weather was very bad. It was still dark, as daybreak did not start till nearly six. We rendezvoused at five by the church at the rear of our accommodation, and split into our two teams.

I was to collect Blair and Corporal Armourer was to collect Mansfield. I led my team into Blair's room, his bed was in the far corner, he shared this room with two young marines. Blair's clothing was on the floor all around his bed. I stood over him. There was a strong smell of alcohol coming up from his breath. I shook him on his shoulder and as he rose I rammed a 9mm Browning barrel into his mouth, knocking out his two upper front teeth. He started to cough, I withdrew the pistol from his mouth. Blair spat his two teeth onto his pillow, followed by a lot of blood. Before he could say anything I told him that he was going for an early morning swim. The other two marines in the room woke up. They were told to forget what they were witnessing and go back to sleep. Blair was now sitting up in his bed looking a little bewildered. I told him that none of us could afford £5 a week, but we were going to give him a free swimming hour. He was told to get out of bed and start making his way to the door, there was no need to dress. He was wearing only his underpants. Blair asked if he could put some footwear on. I said no as he would have a long walk to retrieve any shoes after his swim, as we were all concerned for him. One marine pushed his pistol into the small of Blair's back and told him to start walking.

Both teams met up at the rear of our Church, Mansfield was also wearing only his underpants. The front of Mansfield's chest was covered with blood, which was still running from his nose. The Armourer Corporal said that Mansfield had refused to get out of bed and one of the marines in his team had hit him on his nose with the butt of a pistol. It was pointed out to both of them that legal means had been used to show them the error of their ways, also illegal methods by four Geordies. I explained to both Blair and Mansfield that they were going to go for a swim at the end of the Rifle Ranges. Blair said, 'That's a long way to walk with no footwear on, with the rain and wind is making it cold, and the sea will be rough.' I told them both to start walking, the path to the end of the rifle ranges is compact gravel with lots of small sharp stones on its surface.

We had moved about 100 yards along the path when Blair said that he had something to say. I said, 'We are all ears and ready to take in your words of wisdom.'

Blair then stated that if we let him and Mansfield go he would take no action against us, also, he was prepared to forget the £5 per week from each person present, and he would not report our actions to the Provost Sergeant. One of the marines gave him a kick in his rear and they were both told to keep walking. The rain was heavy, and the wind was blowing very hard. The patrol party had ponchos, plus warm combat clothing. We were dressed and prepared for bad weather. Blair and Mansfield were feeling cold, also their feet had numerous cuts on them now. Mansfield stopped and said that he would forgive all of us and that he would never come near any of us again. Blair said that he would comply with Mansfield's statement, and that all would be forgotten. I pointed to both of them that we were holding all the Aces, and we would decide what to do. They both received a kick in the rear again, plus a pistol pushed into the back of their necks. We arrived at the end of the rifle ranges and the edge of the sea. It had taken about 30 minutes. Blair now became very aggressive, doing his best to intimidate the Patrol Party. For his aggression he was pistol swiped across the face several times.

There was a 15-foot drop into the sea, also 10 feet out there were some large rocks with gaps of 5 and 10 feet between them, to the open sea. The sea was running with an 8 to 10 feet swell, and the wind was forcing the sea against the cliff face and rocks.

Blair and Mansfield were told to prepared to jump into the running sea. Blair said that both of them could be smashed against the rocks or drowned, also it was half a mile to the nearest position to come out of the water.

I said, 'That is the general idea, this will look like a swimming accident, as bodies full of 9mm holes have to be investigated.' Blair and Mansfield got down on their knees and begged to be let off, also, they pointed out that nothing would ever be said about this incident. The Patrol Party fully agreed with both of them.' I pointed out that first of all we had been threatened, then Blair had pleaded, now both of them were begging.

Both of them were told to stand up and jump. Mansfield stood up and jumped, but Blair did not rise. One of the marines pulled him up by his hair and then kicked him very hard in his rear, forcing him to go into the stormy sea. Both were in the sea now and bobbing about amongst the choppy waves. Slowly they managed to go between the rocks to the open sea, but not without severely grazing themselves. Once they were both well clear of the rocks and in the open sea we all emptied our pistols into the water around them. The distance from us to them was about 25 yards, we ensured that all rounds went either in front, over them, or behind. We watched them swimming along for about a further five minutes and then decided to return to our accommodation. The whole business had taken just about an hour, it was now six thirty and daylight.

We washed, changed and all of us went over to the main dining hall at about seven fifteen. On entering the dining hall a big cheer went up, we were met by one of the Corporal Cooks. In the middle of the dining hall was a table with a white cloth on it and six place settings. The Corporal Cook was acting as "Maitre D", and as we sat down everybody in the dining hall rose and clapped. I stood up and thanked them all for their appreciation, also stating that I did not know what all the celebration was for. This caused a lot of laughter. It was one of the best breakfasts I have ever had, the full works. The Cooks served it all to us, "Maitre D" hovered over and ensured that everything was freshly prepared. On leaving the dining hall, the Corporals and marines were coming up to us and shaking our hands. We were overwhelmed by their gratitude.

At nine that morning the RSM sent for me. I reported to him and he told me to take a seat, which was unusually. He then told me that Blair and Mansfield were both seen coming up from a small cove east of the camp at eight this morning, in a state of fear, and with very severe lacerations to their bodies and feet. Both had reported to the Medical Centre then to the Unit Provost Sergeant, asking for protection as they were in fear of their lives. The RSM asked me what I knew, and said that he was aware of the special breakfast that took place that morning.

I said I was not fully aware of all the facts but I could describe a hypothetical situation of what may have taken place. He asked me to give him the hypothetical scenario. I told him that they had been operating a protection racket, mainly on young marines. He then asked if I knew what had happened this morning as both of them refused to tell him anything. I said that I knew nothing of this morning's events. He said he would see the Adjutant and Commanding Officer, as protection was a very serious matter. Also, he was concerned for the future well-being of Blair and Mansfield, no other marines were to get into trouble. The RSM, Adjutant and Provost Sergeant went into the Commanding Officers' office, they were in there for about half an hour. The RSM came out and told me in view of Blair's and Mansfield's past record they were both to be discharged from the Corps that day. The CO said that they would only bring dishonour to themselves and the Corps in the future. Their services were no longer required, a dishonourable discharge. Also the CO was very aware that there would be other attempts on both Blair and Mansfield, it was no longer safe for them to be around any more. It had now been seen that they were vulnerable. The CO, Adjutant and RSM went to the Guardroom to see Blair and Mansfield, who were being kept there for their own safety. Formal notification was given to them, that they were to be given a "Dishonourable Discharge" from the Royal Marines. The Provost Sergeant was told that it was his duty to ensure that all their kit was handed in, plus he was responsible for their safety. Two Corporals and four marines from the Provost Section accompanied each one to their accommodation, they returned all their service kit. Pay and Records completed all forms for discharge, their pay was made up to date. As of midnight that day they would be out of the Royal Marines.

At eleven o'clock they were both put in separate Land Rovers, in the company of a Corporal and two marines. Both Corporals were instructed that they had to see Blair's and Mansfield's flight off from RAF LUQA. The aircraft for the flight home left at midday, the Corporals and marines watched the plane take off before returning to barracks. These two "low-lifes" were the most evil marines I ever met in our Corps.

*

The next three months were quiet and uneventful, that saw me to the end of my tour in Malta. I was to attend a Sergeant's course on return to UK and then join 42 Commando, Royal Marines at Bickleigh.

Some years later whilst walking in Oxford Street, London, I bumped into two Policemen, both of them had served as marines in Malta with me. The normal chat took place, then Blair's and Mansfield's names came up in conversation. I told them that Blair had been sent to jail for seven years for an insurance fraud. A warehouse full of high value goods had a fire in it, the Fire Brigade were called, and on investigation it was discovered that it had been started deliberately. Also, the goods in the boxes were mainly rubbish and of no value. The Police prosecuted Rodney Blair for arson, and the insurance company brought charges of fraud against him. I had read it in a paper a year ago. One of the Policemen said that Rupert Mansfield had been found dead in the East End of London with severe brain damage, he had been involved in an illegal fight. His face had been disfigured and they identified him by his fingerprints. We all agreed that both of them were evil and wicked. Neither one of them would ever learn that there was no easy road to take in life, except the straight and narrow.

Chapter Six
42 Commando, Royal Marines

I successfully passed my Sergeants' course and joined 42 Commando, at Bickleigh, just before Christmas. After Christmas and return from leave our Unit was going on an exercise across the large pond which separates us from America. This exercise was to be carried out with the US Navy and US Marines. The Commando Unit left Plymouth early in January. The main body of our Unit was embarked on HMS Hermes, which was far more comfortable than the old Bulwark. Also attached to the Commando was a company of Royal Netherlands' Marines, they made up 4th Rifle Company. The Unit vehicles were embarked on board a Landing Ship Logistics, Royal Fleet Auxiliary. Hermes sailed up the English Channel to embark its helicopter squadron, Prince Charles was a member of this group. Two helicopters in his flight had a large red band painted around the tail of each aircraft. Once all helicopters had been embarked both ships set off for the Azores.

Once we arrived at the Azores we spent five days going around these islands, which was very pleasant. The weather was mild and warm. Both ships changed course and sailed due North, each day becoming a little colder, and this continued for five days. Then the Captain said, 'We are changing course for the Caribbean.' Everyone was happy for the course change, as we all knew that warmer weather and calm seas lay ahead.

We had been at sea now for three weeks, which is how long it had taken us to cross the Atlantic. Outside the Port of Jacksonville we rendezvoused with the US Navy, all 30 ships of theirs. During the next week we all sailed in convoy under the command of an American Admiral. This training was for the sole benefit of the US Navy.

Now the time came for both US and Royal Marines to carry out their part of the exercise. The ships anchored off the Island of Vieques in the Caribbean. The Royal Marines were to act as enemy to the US Marines. HMS Ark Royal and USS Enterprise joined up to provide air cover for the US Marines. The Americans went ashore in helicopters, taking in men, equipment, vehicles, ammunition and daily supplies in under four hours. There was never any shortage of air support. It took us a whole day to land 600 men and support equipment. The Americans landed 3,000 men plus equipment in less than four hours.

The exercise was for six days, I did a couple of night patrols. Both of them were a big joke, I was to locate and attack the US Marines in their defensive positions. It was easy to find them at night as they were listening to radios, talking and generally having a good time. Each time I showed up with my patrol we were greeted and offered cans of beer, plus hot dogs. We pointed out to them that this was not very professional but they were not really interested. They said that they were all conscripts, just doing their time.

At the end of this exercise my section and I were detailed off to man the helicopter landing/loading pad. There was a total of six of us, which meant we could man three landing spots, one to marshal helicopters and the other man to hook on loads. As it was hot and dry the helicopters blew up a lot of dust, we were all sweating. Dirt and dust settled on us and dried. One of the pilots said we looked like mud men with eyeholes. Prince Charles picked up several loads, and his was the last helicopter to leave the helicopter pad. I had no load for him so I just stretched my arms out and my palms flat up, he understood, waved and flew off. At the end of the day we returned to HMS Hermes by landing craft, showered, ate a good meal and had a long sleep.

Once this exercise was over the Royal Marines organised a barbeque on a beach, and the Yanks were invited. The Unit Chief Cook, Popeye, did an excellent job. Each man was rationed to half a chicken and a pound of steak, also restricted to 11 cans of beer each (which was cold). Everyone had a good time, and it all went off well, thanks to our Cooks.

*

After Vieques we went to the US Navy port of Roosevelt Roads. This port in Puerto Rico is used and operated by the US Navy. The local sports facilities are excellent, plus this island was very interesting to travel around as it is tropical, with well laid out gardens. Also in the dockyard was a US Navy Club, this was packed each night as all ships on exercise were in port, plus beer was cheap. HMS Ark Royal was tied up ahead of us, USS Enterprise was anchored just outside the harbour as she was too large to come alongside. All the ships stayed in port for seven days, then exercise "Rum Punch" had now finished and everyone went their separate ways.

The next three weeks were spent doing exercises with the Dutch Marines on the islands of Curiso and Araber. Because it was early Spring the weather was mild, warm and very enjoyable. The Dutch treated our Unit to a barbeque. The most enjoyable treat at this barbeque was an Indonesian salad. This was made up of special sauces with a peanut base. Everyone had a good time and enjoyed themselves, the Dutch were hospitable.

From the Caribbean we sailed to Fort Lauderdale, Florida, this took four days. The ship was given a good clean so we entered harbour spick and span. For entering Fort Lauderdale the ship's company, both Dutch and Royal Marines lined the upper deck. Then the Ship's helicopters did a fly past after we were secured alongside. Large numbers of people watched us enter harbour, and it was shown on the local TV station. That evening I watched Hermes and the LSL enter harbour, plus the ship's helicopters fly pass on TV, it looked impressive. Both ships were in Fort Lauderdale for seven days. Our Commanding Officer said that the Royal Marines and Dutch Marines could go wherever they wanted, on the condition that they turned up to do their duties, which were their responsibility. Everybody did whatever they had to do, there were no comebacks whatsoever, generally a good time all round. Our CO had faith in his men, we all had a high regard and respect for him.

There is a lot to do and see in Florida, and everybody took advantage of the state with its numerous attractions. Seven of us hired a large American estate car and travelled around Florida, visiting Kennedy Space Centre, Disney World and various other sites of interest. From Florida we sailed North, up the East coast of America to Canada.

*

The Unit was to go ashore at St John, Canada and spend three weeks training. The area we were to train in was the same size as Devon. HMS Hermes arrived at St Johns in early May, and the weather was very cold and misty. We disembarked and dispersed to five separate locations, I was billeted at a camp called "Blue Mountain", although there was no mountain anywhere near it. The camp was next to a small lake, and the surrounding area was low rolling hills. Everybody felt the cold during our first week, but the second week the weather improved, which helped to cheer everyone up.

At the rear of the cookhouse, the Quartermaster had stored our emergency rations. One evening we heard a general commotion going on, on investigation two large bears were rummaging amongst these emergency rations. They were male bears and very powerful, tearing cardboard boxes apart with their claws. Once the tins were on the ground they ripped them open, and on finding tins containing peaches and fruit both bears had a good feast. The CO and personnel in camp stood and watched the bears enjoy themselves. Bears are in decline in this part of Canada so no action was taken against them. After this incident, the following day, the remainder of the boxes was moved into a secure building. In the evening most of our unit used to go down to the landfill site and watch bears rummaging about looking for food. I normally stayed for about an hour, sometimes one or two of the bears would find a fish. They never ate all the fish, just its head. During the week the rifle companies did individual training, sport and lots of shooting.

One Sunday night five of us went into a small town called "ORIMOCKTOE", which was 50 miles from the Blue Mountain camp. It took the taxi two hours to travel there and $50 fare. The roads were mostly single file tracks. In this small town there was one bar, a fast food takeaway and a few shops. There were five of us in the taxi coming in but gradually during the evening we became split up.

At around ten my friend Corporal Roger Haphazard, Royal Marines, and I decided it was time to return to camp. The taxis were parked outside the fast food takeaway, and I went in and ordered two burgers. My friend Roger Haphazard found a one-armed bandit in the corner of the burger bar and he started to play this money-gobbling machine. It was a dollar a game. After five pulls he won $2 but was down three. I told him that we had to go but he insisted he was close to winning the jackpot of $1,000. Anyway, after half an hour he was broke, I had $20 on me and there was 50 miles and a $50 taxi ride back to camp. I explained to my friend that we were now up a creek with only $20 to return to camp, a distance of 50 miles. Roger said that we both had to make morning muster, as he was due his third stripe for Sergeant at the end of that month. I pointed out to him that a bad report for me would put my promotion back a year.

Corporal Roger Haphazard, RM, was 37 years old, he desperately wanted that third stripe to boost his pension. He was close to his pensionable retirement. Roger was very gifted at passing courses, but he fussed a lot and always dropped himself into trouble. He had been a Corporal now for 16 years. If we both failed to attend the morning muster then a special report of absence would be made out against us. A bad report like that could put our promotion back a year or two. I pointed out to him that I was also waiting for my third stripe, once we returned back to the UK. Both of us had to make that morning parade.

I spoke to a taxi driver and explained our situation, he thought it was very funny. Once he had stopped laughing he said he would run us to a bridge which was about 20 miles from Blue Mountain Camp, then we would have to cut across country walking. The taxi driver dropped us off at this bridge and collected his $20 fee, we had a 20-mile walk ahead of us. We knew the area well, as we had done training in this vicinity. There was a full moon and a clear sky. The temperature was minus three degrees, there was a light frost and the air was still. It was just after midnight. I estimated that it would take between five and six hours to reach camp. The area we had to walk over was made up of rolling hills, forests, tracks and two rivers to cross. One river was wide and slow flowing, the other was narrow and deep with a fast current. I told Roger to head east, the moon would gradually fall behind us. Roger said he was worried as we had no map, protractor or compass. I said I did not expect this, if I had known that we were expected to walk back I would have brought them along, I continued, 'Also, you owe me $25.'

Roger said, 'How come, as you only paid $20 for the taxi ride?'

I said, 'If we had gone the full distance in a taxi it would have been $50, and I am doing the navigation back to camp.'

We set off at a good fast walking pace, after four miles we came to the first river, the wide and slow flowing one. Roger said, 'I don't like the idea of getting wet, and it's very cold.'

I said, 'You can turn back and go via the road, arriving in camp around midday, and say goodbye to your third stripe.'

Both of us had slacks, a light pullover and walking shoes on. I said, 'Take your shoes off and tie them around your belt, and make sure they're secure.'

I was the first one to start crossing, and it was cold. Both of us took about ten minutes to cross the river. Once out of the water and in cold air both of us started to shiver. Our shoes were put on quickly then we started to walk as fast as possible to warm up and get our blood circulating. The next three miles was along a track, running straight and flat, which made life easy.

We arrived at the second river, which was half the width of the previous one. The water was flowing fast. I said, 'It's better to keep our shoes on, but ensure the laces are tight as we don't want to lose a shoe with still nearly 12 miles to go.' We walked up the bank towards the direction of flow and I said to Roger, 'We must swim across and with the current, and we should be washed up about 200 yards further down, on the opposite bank.' Roger was worried about the current, also he kept reminding me of how cold the water would be. I pointed out that once we had crossed the river the worst would be behind us, then it was just straightforward walking.

I was first into the water again, it was very cold and the current was strong. I commenced swimming with the current and slowly crossing it. 200 yards downstream I crawled out onto the opposite bank. Roger was still standing on the other bank, I walked up opposite to him and said, 'Make your mind up.'

Roger took the plunge, he was washed up about 100 yards further down from myself. Once out of the water both of us ran for about a mile, this helped to warm us up and to let our clothing drip off.

After an hour and four miles we arrived at the woods, there was a single vehicle track running through, but it had not been used for a few years. The trees were tall and old, some parts of the track had fallen trees across it, which made our going a little harder. After half an hour Roger said that he thought someone or something was following us. I told him that his imagination was running wild and to stop thinking, just concentrate on walking. Then Roger said, 'I think there's a bear behind us.'

I stopped and waited a minute, but didn't hear or see anything. I said, 'It's most probably the ghost of the woods, or small animals moving around in the undergrowth.'

By this time both of us were hungry, tired and fed up. Again I pointed out his folly on the one-armed bandit and the very long walk that ensued, all because of his insistence on winning the jackpot. Now I decided it was time to really spook him and I told him, 'This area is renowned for sightings of the "Canadian Bigfoot", but the sad fact is that people who have seen one have never lived to tell the tale.'

This put the fear of Christ into Corporal Roger Haphazard, then he told me, 'Lead on, and fast.' There were a small number of fallen trees to climb over and negotiate. I tore my trousers and snagged my woolly pullover, and there were patches of soft wet boggy ground to go over. Both of us slipped a few times, covering ourselves in mud and dirt. After one hour we were clear of the woods, and all we had to do then was to stay on the single track running over rolling hills to reach camp.

We arrived at the camp Guardroom just after six that Monday morning to collect our leave passes. Both of us looked a sorry sight. Torn clothing, mud all over us and absolutely exhausted, but extremely glad to be back. Of course Roger had to tell the Corporal of the Guard the whole sad story. Back at our accommodation I informed Roger Haphazard that we were going to be the biggest joke in the camp, also, it would go around the Unit like wildfire. It would take a few months to live this down.

After morning parade we were told that the company was going on a 20-mile march. I thought I was going to die. Luckily the Sergeant-in-charge was told to take all day about it. We returned to camp at four that afternoon; I don't know how I managed to stay awake all day. I had covered a distance of 40 miles on foot in 16 hours, thanks to Roger Haphazard. That evening I went to bed at six and slept till six the following morning, waking up like a new man, fully refreshed. The rest of the time in Canada everyone had a good laugh at our walk across country. It was an experience which I don't want to have again.

*

The time had now come for our Unit to spend our final week in the field, carrying out live firing exercises and night patrols. Everything went well during this week, everybody was tired towards the end and looking forward to returning to camp. The exercise finished on a Sunday morning, and our unit was to host a live fire power demonstration for the Canadian Staff College that afternoon. The whole unit was marched to an area where the live fire demonstration was to take place. On arrival, lunch was served, which was excellent. More praise for our Cooks, well done "Popeye".

A loudspeaker system had been set up and 60 fold-up directors' chairs were set out in rows for the guests. To one side and to the rear was a large hill. The Corporals and marines were told to sit there and observe the following demonstration. The RSM referred to us as the "Crowd on a hill". We had an excellent view as we were raised well up, and we could see over the seated guests. The Generals arrived in staff cars, and Officers from the Staff College in a coach. Our CO welcomed them, outlined what was going to take place, then he sat down with the senior officers.

The live fire power demonstration commenced, with mortars first, then helicopters firing rockets, followed by Royal Navy Phantoms from the aircraft carrier HMS Ark Royal. All was going well and now it was the turn of the Royal Artillery. Eight rounds of 105mm passed overhead, they gave a "Whoosh" effect type of noise. Once you hear the "Whoosh" you know that everything is well and safe. The next artillery round dropped approximately 20 yards in front of the seated officers, throwing up a large amount of soil and dirt. This caused them all to rise together and move back, pushing their chairs over. It was a perfect move, all as one. Once everybody had stopped there was a deep silence, you could have heard a pin drop. They then started to move back to their seats. One of the crowd on our hill then shouted "drop 50". Staff Officers, Unit Officers and Senior Non Commissioned Officers looked up at the hill, - if looks could "KILL". Then our crowd on the hill gave a big cheer and everything went quiet again, with more black looks from unseated Officers.

Once everybody had settled down again the CO apologised for failure of one artillery round, falling short. Also for the behaviour of his men on the hill. The firepower demonstration recommenced, this time ammunition would be fired with live warheads from aircraft. Wessex helicopters came in low, hovered and fired their pods of 2-inch rockets. Watching 15 helicopters fire together at 12 old cars was very impressive. A total of 40 x 2 inch rockets were fired by each helicopter, the old cars had eight jerry cans full of aviation fuel in them, which exploded when hit. This, too, was very impressive, it emphasised the deadly ability of the rockets, giving a realistic appreciation of fire power. Once the helicopters had completed their demonstration it was the turn of the Royal Navy Phantom jets again. They used the burning cars as targets, the first six jets fired two large rockets each at these cars, blowing them apart. This scattered bits of cars and fuel around, and it was far more impressive than the helicopters. The last six jets came in low and dropped bombs full of phosphorous. These bombs were deposited on a small wood. As the fir trees were full of resin they burned fiercely. Once the noise from the Royal Navy jets had died down all was quiet, our CO thanked the visiting Staff Officers for their patience and understanding of earlier incidents. On completion of the fire power demonstration the guests returned to their staff cars, coaches and left.

The Commanding Officer told the RSM to hold all Corporals and marines, and that they had to form a circle round him. The Unit Officers and SNCO's were told to return to their locations.

We knew that our CO had something lined up for us. First of all he stated that the behaviour was not what he expected. Also, it had deeply embarrassed him. For our lack of good manners all Corporals and marines would make their way back to their locations on foot, across country. Also, at nine o'clock Tuesday morning there would be a full Unit parade, in "Combat rig".

The RSM said that as all Corporals were qualified in deep penetration tactics this would be classed as part of an exercise, back to base. The Corporals were told in no uncertain terms that they were responsible for ensuring that the marines returned safely to the locations.

Once the CO and RSM had gone nearly 500 men stood together, extremely unhappy and fed up. Then Marine Robert Thoughtless shouted out, 'This is because of Corporal Roger Haphazard, he is the one that said "drop 50", embarrassing our CO.'

Somebody else then said, 'Let's give Haphazard a good beating.'

Luckily Corporal Michael Sensible stepped forward saying, 'There will be no beatings, it is the Corporals' responsibility to ensure that everybody returns safely. If Corporal Haphazard is beaten up then he will be incapable of walking and a burden on his mates, and awkward questions will be asked by the RSM and Sergeant Majors – possibly followed by a Unit enquiry plus numerous charges.'

All the Corporals got together, it was decided that we would all march to a pedestrians' footbridge approximately nine miles away. This footbridge was over a fast flowing river, from there we would split up and disperse to our locations. Also, the Corporals told all marines to ensure that their water bottles were filled up at the river crossing.

There were approximately 45 of us at Blue Mountain, three Corporals and the remainder marines. It was now three in the afternoon, we estimated that it would be about midday the following day when we got back to camp. Blue Mountain camp was just under 50 miles as the crow flies. Two of the other locations were over 60 miles from our present position.

Corporal Sensible took the lead point, and my group was at the rear. Corporal Roger Haphazard was with me. We stayed well back from the main body as it was not safe for Haphazard. There was a lot of ill feeling and despondency towards him.

We had been going for about half an hour when 20 US Marine Jolly Green Giant troop-carrying helicopters appeared. Their line of flight would take them directly over us. As they started to pass overhead we raised our arms as though we were thumbing a lift. To our surprise the lead helicopter landed. I was nearest to it and the pilot waved me over. The pilot was a Major in the US Marines, and he said, 'What is going on?' I explained the situation to him and he said, 'Where are you going? Show me the location on my map,' and I did so. He said, 'I will radio my other helicopters to pick up and drop the remainder of your unit at their respective locations.' Forty-five of us piled into his helicopter. It only took 30 minutes to reach Blue Mountain Camp. I thanked him for his kindness and all Corporals and marines gave him the "thumbs up" as they left the helicopter.

We all went to our accommodation, showered and changed into clean clothing. The Cooks had laid on a good supper, which we all enjoyed. Chief Cook "Popeye" did not understand why no Officers or SNCO's were present, and this was explained to him. We all had the pick of the food, nice and freshly cooked. I was returning my weapon to the stores when the CO and RSM came into the camp in their Land Rovers, three hours after my return. The CO looked at me and immediately asked, 'How come you've beaten me back to camp? I explained what had happened and his reply was, 'Good, you used your initiative.'

Tuesday morning the whole unit was assembled on the football pitch at Blue Mountain, "present and correct". After all the reports were made the CO told everyone to gather round him. He paid everybody a compliment on their endeavours to return to locations, and also for the good turn out on morning parade. Once he had had his say he dismissed the parade and gave us the rest of the day off. Everybody was still tired from the exercise so the vast majority caught up on their sleep.

*

Once the unit had finished its training period in Canada we all re-embarked on HMS Hermes and returned to Plymouth. It was now early June. During our passage back to the UK Corporal Roger Haphazard was promoted to Sergeant, he ensured that he kept a very low profile. On our arrival back in the UK Sergeant Roger Haphazard was drafted to Lympstone, and he remained there for the rest of his service in the Royal Marines. Our visit to the States, the Caribbean and Canada had been a good time, plus an experience that I would never forget.

Once back at Bickleigh, stores were cleaned and packed away. The unit was to have the last two weeks of June off as leave, then we were to take our turn on "Spearhead" availability.

Chapter Seven
Spearhead

The personnel returned from Summer leave at the end of June. 42 Commando now took its turn on "Spearhead". This means that it is the main Infantry Unit in the British Armed Forces, the first to move to any trouble spot the government of the day wishes to send it to. We were into week two and everything was quiet. All combat kit and equipment was packed, leave was cancelled and personnel were only allowed to go into the local town.

One afternoon the gates to the barracks were closed and all personnel had to assemble on the main parade ground. The Commanding Officer informed everybody that our Unit had to move to Northern Ireland during the next 24 hours. This would be an emergency tour, duration unknown, and the area we were to occupy was not known. The only time out of barracks whilst in Northern Ireland would be on official duty; no trips to public houses, cinemas or shops. Vehicles would be driven to Liverpool during the night. The main body of personnel would be flown out from RAF St MAWGAN the following morning.

Early next morning we arrived at RAF St MAWGAN and then boarded an aircraft for RAF ALDERGROVE, Northern Ireland. Once we disembarked and entered the reception lounge at RAF Aldergrove there seemed to be an air of despondency, dismay and no hope. Northern Ireland is a total experience of different attitudes and outlook on life, compared to everyday events in England. Army trucks were waiting to transport us to various locations. I was told that company Headquarters was going to a camp just outside Portadown. We arrived just after midday, had a meal and moved into our accommodation. The rooms were small, eight bunks in each one, no lockers or cupboards. Our kit and rifles were piled together in the centre of the floor, there was minimum comfort and the main essential was a bed. Washing facilities were adequate.

At two in the afternoon I was detailed off with three other marines as escort to the Commanding Officer's Rover Group. This consisted of two Land Rovers. The Commanding Officer's

Land Rover had a driver, a radio operator and me. The second vehicle had the Regimental Sergeant Major, driver and three marines as escort, to ride shotgun. We all knew that this was a safe, boring duty. But as one of the marines put it, 'We will all see the local countryside.' But we knew that the days would be long with a late finish.

We proceeded down country lanes and then along the border with Southern Ireland. During the late afternoon we paid a couple of calls on two isolated farms, neither of which had a telephone. They were glad to see us, the second farm we called on made us tea and supplied cakes, which was very nice. The CO thanked the farmer's wife. We drove for two hours and made the rounds of our scattered Unit. Three rifle companies were billeted right out in the countryside, in areas known as "Bandit Country". The CO spoke to the Company Commanders, we stayed at each location for one hour. The last location to be visited was the furthest out, here we had a meal and waited for our CO. The journey back took nearly three hours, it was now two in the morning and we were all very tired. The RSM told me to ensure that we all assembled at the Guardroom at 1100 hrs that day.

On day two we arrived at the Guardroom at 1100 hours and waited. At 1400 hours the CO's Rover Group set off and the routine was the same. After we had visited three isolated farms the radio operator received a message instructing our CO that he was required at Army Headquarters, Lurgan. One and a half hours later we arrived, I knew that this was going to be a long wait. The RSM told us to go over to the dining hall and have supper, we should be back at eleven. The CO came out of the Officers' Mess at eleven thirty, he had had a meeting with the General Officer Commanding Troops, Northern Ireland. Before we returned to our location the CO told us to gather round him as he had some sad news to tell all of us. He informed us that two members of our Unit had been injured this day, a Corporal and a marine. The Corporal was going along with his four-man patrol by some vacant, derelict houses. There was an explosion and a large piece of glass flew through the air hitting this Corporal-in-charge. The piece of glass hit his right lower leg, slicing two thirds of his calf muscle off. The second injury was to a marine in one of the watchtowers at our location. A sniper hit him in the head. However, he was alive and in Military hospital.

The Corporal was subsequently given a medical discharge, he could walk but had trouble climbing stairs and running. The marine who was shot in the head lived, and completed a pensionable engagement in the Royal Marines. The sniper's bullet passed in front of his brain, just above the optic nerve. This wiped his memory clean and he had to be re-educated and taught all the basics of life again. The Senior Royal Navy Surgeons and the Royal Marine Generals ensured that he stayed in the Corps and served his full time for a Military Pension. Everybody looked after him.

On Day three the Commanding Officer's Rover group was doing a normal tour of the villages along the border. Whilst driving through a small village two men were seen fighting on the pavement. The Rover group stopped. We all jumped out of the vehicles and apprehended these two men. The two combatants were shocked at the sudden arrival of the marines. They were pulled apart and placed against a wall, and made to spread their legs, then a body search was carried out. Neither one of them had any concealed weapons on their person or anything offensive that could be used as a weapon. Both of them were handcuffed and made to sit on the ground facing a wall. The RUC were radioed and requested to send a vehicle to collect the two men, as there was no spare room in our Land Rovers.

The CO's group had now been waiting half an hour when the Secretary of State for Northern Ireland was passing through the village, returning to Belfast. He stopped and disembarked from his car, much to the annoyance of his Special Branch bodyguards. He approached our CO, who explained what had been happening and confirming that a RUC vehicle would soon collect the two men who had been fighting. The Secretary of State said that as it was a minor incident the two men should be released and the RUC vehicle cancelled. The CO "blew a fuse" and the two of them exchanged words which were not complimentary. The CO then asked the Secretary of State if he believed in Law and Order.

The question received a vague reply and both men were standing in the centre of the road shouting at each other. The

Marines and Special Branch detectives were all facing outwards in opposite directions but everyone heard what was being said. This went on for a few minutes, then the RSM and a senior detective approached both men, and the RSM escorted the CO to his vehicle. The detective guided the Secretary of State to his car and was driven off. The RUC arrived and placed the two men in the rear of one of their armoured vehicles. Both men were charged with a breach of the peace and had to pay a fine.

The CO was unhappy, as he said to the RSM, his chances for a senior staff position were now nil. All Corporals and marines agreed that the Secretary of State favoured the Republicans. His attitude "took the biscuit" for edgy, sullen, state-faced incompetence.

On day four, in one of the villages patrolled on a regular routine by our unit, was a Mini Supermarket and Post Office/Paper Shop. Children of this village were bussed to a nearby town. Men of the village either worked on local farms or at a nearby quarry. The village was predominately loyalist with a small Republican element, but with no history of trouble. The CO's Rover group passed through the village at least once a day. Late in the afternoon one of our mobile patrols was entering the village, travelling along the main road with the two shops. Children were outside the Post Office/Paper Shop, as many of them brought their tuck there after school. Some of the local residents were talking on the pavement and going about their business in a quiet civilised manner. A young girl came running out of the Mini Supermarket, straight towards the leading Mobile Patrol vehicle. The Land Rover braked hard, and the Sergeant-in-charge jumped out and grabbed hold of the young girl. She was in a state of hysteria. The Sergeant managed to calm the girl down then asked her to tell him what the problem was, and that there was no hurry. She was breathing fast, but slowly told him what had occurred:

Two young men had entered the Mini Supermarket carrying a small brown cardboard box, they placed it in the centre of the floor. Once on the shop floor they walked to the door and shouted out that the box contained explosives and would soon go off, then they had run out. The Sergeant asked the girl, 'What direction were they heading in?' She pointed down the road towards open fields where two young men could be seen running out of the village. The Sergeant told his Corporal to take the Land Rover and four marines to capture the two men and bring them back.

During the time it took the Corporal to chase and capture the two young bombers the Sergeant cleared the Mini Supermarket. Marines were placed 200 yards further up the road and also below the shop, to ensure that the area was cleared of all personnel. People in their homes next to the shop were also evacuated and a call was made to Central Control requesting "Bomb Disposal", the Fire Brigade, and extra personnel to help Police the area.

The Corporal brought the two young bombers back and the young girl confirmed their identity. Both of them were cocky and full of bravado, telling the Sergeant that the bomb would soon go off and there was nothing he could do. Also, it was his responsibility to ensure their safety. (Republicans know that once they are caught the law will protect them.) The Sergeant told them that there was something he could do, and had always wanted to do with bombers. They asked him, 'What is that?' The Sergeant said that he was going to handcuff them with their hands behind their backs, then lock them both in the Mini Supermarket. This was a fitting punishment for them. Both of them started screaming and shouting for help, but no-one came forward to offer assistance to save their skins. People standing behind the cordons thought the Sergeant's idea was a good one. The men were carried to the shop by eight marines and pushed in, and the doors were locked behind them. They were both on their knees shouting and pleading at the front door, they could be seen clearly as both doors were clear plate glass. Then the waiting commenced.

After half an hour more marines arrived, followed by Commanding Officer's Rover group. The Sergeant-in-charge explained to the CO what had occurred, also making it clear that he locked the two young bombers in the mini supermarket. The CO congratulated him, and said he had done well. Our CO had no time for Republican terrorists. Bomb Disposal arrived one hour after the two men had been locked in the shop. The Staff Sergeant-in-charge of Bomb Disposal told our CO that his Unit had been working on suspect bombs since five that morning. We pointed them towards the Mini Supermarket, telling them that the bomb was in there together with two bombers. The Staff Sergeant commented that that was very unusual. Then he was told the whole story. The Staff Sergeant explained that normally the bombs go off on average ten minutes after they have been laid. He suggested that there may be a fault in its make up or defective material. While the Bomb Disposal team were talking to the CO and the Sergeant who had locked the bombers in the shop all seemed to be quiet within. The bombers had stopped pleading and were lying on the floor just behind the entrance doors, exhausted. The Staff Sergeant decided to take his team into the shop, saying to our CO, 'I will get the two men to point out the exact location of the parcel bomb before they are released.' This is what happened and the two bombers didn't waste any time showing the Disposal Squad the bomb's location.

Once the two bombers came out of the Mini Supermarket they were led away and placed just outside our cordon. They were by now very subdued, meek and frightened. Their cockiness had gone, they had had a long time within the building to think of their situation and what they had got themselves into. The bomb may not have gone off but the bombers had achieved their aim, "maximum disruption". This incident regarding the Mini Supermarket was one of many carried out in Northern Ireland, and the perpetrators' main purpose was to make the five counties ungovernable, and disrupt life as much as possible.

The crowd had by now built up and were yelling abuse at the two men, although both felt reasonably safe as they knew the Royal Marines would have to protect them. Two marines were detailed off to guard them, and the men knew that they could not run away. They were concerned by the attitude of the local crowd as a lynch mob feeling was building up. As previously mentioned this was a predominantly loyalist village which had not been affected by the troubles. The CO told the Sergeant to ensure that nothing happened to the two bombers, so more marines were detailed off to guard them. They were told to sit and face the wall.

After 20 minutes the Bomb Disposal Staff Sergeant and his team came out of the Mini Supermarket carrying the cardboard box. The Staff Sergeant had a small detonator in his hand telling our CO that it had failed to go off because it was faulty material. The bomb was assembled correctly, everything made up by someone who knew what he was doing. It contained five pounds of plastic explosives, a small travelling clock, a battery, wire and a faulty detonator. The CO told the Staff Sergeant that the two men would be handed over to the RUC for questioning. Everyone agreed that the two who had been caught were only foot soldiers, with very little knowledge of the deadly and destructive ways of the Alpha Males at the top of the organisation. The Bomb Disposal Squad had to place themselves at risk to disarm the explosive device, and they are some of the bravest men in the British Forces.

The cordons were removed and residents told that they were now free to go about their lawful business, in peace and safety. People thanked the Servicemen for their help and expressed relief that the bomb failed to go off. The CO told the Sergeant-in-charge of the mobile patrol to take a short statement from the young girl shop assistant and to collect names and addresses of all who worked in the Supermarket.

The CO's Rover group accompanied the Sergeant's Mobile patrol to RUC Barracks and the bombers were handed over for interrogation. The RUC were very surprised that the bombers had been caught, and as they were being handed over the CO asked them, 'How did you travel to the village.'

They replied, 'We came by bus.'

The RSM then asked, 'What was your getaway plan?'

They were silent for a while as they had to think, then they replied, 'We were going to catch the next bus out.'

An RUC Constable continued, 'The bus only runs once every two hours.'

The bombers had been used by unscrupulous men, who had no feeling for their fellow human beings, and these two young boys had been exploited terribly by the Godfathers in the Republican movement. Both of them were naïve young fools, who had doubtless received instructions concerning this atrocity from intermediaries, to ensure that there was no connection to the Alpha males in command.

Once they had been taken into custody by the RUC, the RSM took the Sergeant-in-charge of Mobile Patrol aside and read him the Riot Act. He was told that if the bomb had gone off a murder charge would have been brought against him. Courts take a very dim view of anybody taking the law into their own hands, and next time he must think and act with responsibility or else his head would be on the chopping block. Thankfully the bomb failed to go off saving devastation and loss of life. 'However,' the RSM said, 'apart from your failure to follow the law you did well.'

Two days later the GOC NI, and our CO received a nasty letter from the Secretary of State for NI concerning the "terrible treatment of the two bombers, clearly showing where his sympathy lay. There was no mention showing concern for the successful outcome. Also, the "Troops Out Movement" had capitalized on the treatment of the two bombers – bad treatment from the Royal Marines. Of course they were supported by other do-gooders and Labour politicians, but the people we spoke to on the streets said that we had treated the two bombers correctly. Decent people want punishments to fit the crime, and the Sergeant-in-charge of the Mobile Patrol was the toast of our unit. We all knew that the Secretary of State for NI had sympathy for Republicans because they have a vote, and he also wanted to appease the Alpha Republican males.

*

Day five started as normal, and at around eleven o'clock I, and the marines in our patrol, assembled by the Guardroom and waited. We departed at around four that afternoon as our CO had been on the telephone conversing with senior officers in London. I knew it was going to be a very long night. We followed the route along the border and made a couple of calls on some isolated farms. The CO always told these farmers to be connected to a telephone, although they all said that there was no need to be on the telephone.

At ten in the evening we left the last rifle company location, but this time we started to drive around small villages and towns. We arrived at a small town, on the eastern side and the lead vehicle stopped in the main square. We all got out and stretched our legs. Suddenly a young girl came running towards us, screaming out that the Police were being killed. She pointed up a side street and I ran up to check. I could hear a lot of shouting and noise, and yelled to my CO that something was going on further up the street. He came running up, accompanied by the remainder of his patrol group. The radio operator had been left to guard our vehicles.

About 50 yards along the street a group of men were beating three Policemen, who were on the ground, rolled into balls to protect themselves. As I approached I witnessed one of the assailants kick a Policemen in the top of his skull, whilst he was rolled up in a ball, trying to protect himself. The force of the kick split his skull and his brains fell out onto the pavement. He died instantly. This was a terrible act of barbarism, murder in the first degree.

We ran straight at the crowd of men with our small Police truncheons and our rifles in our left hand. I ran straight at the man who had kicked the Policeman in the head, and struck him as hard as possible across his right kneecap. He gave a loud squeal as the pain connected with his brain. Leaning forward he cupped his right knee with both hands, the pain was obviously excruciating. As he was now bending forward I struck him across the back of his neck; he then lost consciousness. Our CO waded in with us, and we hit those who were attacking the Policemen as hard as possible. Some of the attackers fell but two managed to escape, they ran up a side street. Using our truncheons we eventually overpowered the assailants. Six of them were unconscious and the other two disabled. One Policeman was dead, due to the kick to the top of his skull, and we covered him with a groundsheet. The attackers were handcuffed and made to sit on the ground (one marine was left to guard them). The two injured Policemen were carried to open ground, and our radio operator requested helicopter evacuation as it would take too long for ambulances to arrive. Ten minutes later two helicopters arrived and flew the two injured Policemen to hospital. Half an hour later three ambulances arrived to remove the injured assailants, who had assaulted and murdered a Policeman. A large number of Police and troops were present in the small town by now. One thing that really struck me was the hatred shown against the forces of Law and Order. These people have the same benefits as those on the mainland, and the same rights. The Senior Police Officer present thanked us all and took our names. We returned back to camp at six that morning, and were told to report to the Adjutant's Office at two in the afternoon.

At the Adjutant's Office there were three Senior Police Officers and four Solicitors. Statements were required. Statements were given to the Police and checked by the solicitors. This procedure did not finish till eleven that night, and by that time we were very tired. Our CO received a letter of thanks from the Chief Constable of the Royal Ulster Constabulary. We heard that one of the other Policemen died because of his brutal beating, and the third one would be an invalid for the remainder of his life. The assailants recovered in hospital and then were sent for trial. The trial took place after we had returned to the mainland, nearly a year later. The sentences varied between 5 and 30 years. The man who had kicked the Policeman's skull in received the longest sentence. The two men who ran away were never caught. The "Troops Out Movement" and do-gooders did not say anything. When the forces of law and order were attacked and injured there was always a golden silence from the do-gooders.

The RSM told me that I would no longer be required on the CO's Rover Group, and the morning after the statements were given I reported to the Sergeant Major, who told me that I would be in charge of a fatigues' party that day, "just cleaning up the camp". He also told me that the marines and I on CO's Rover Group could have the afternoon off. We used this time to catch up on our sleep.

*

That evening I had to report to the Adjutant for a briefing. The following morning I had to take 20 marines to a field, situated outside a small village, and secure this area for a helicopter landing zone. He gave me a list of marines who would be in my party. I arranged for all of us to have an early morning call at four as all of us had to parade outside the Guardroom at five the following day. Everyone assembled outside the camp Guardroom at five. It was the normal routine with everyone moaning and wishing that they were still in bed. Inside the Guardroom were 21 bag rations (sandwich packs), which were for us as we would be out all day. Just after five three Armoured Personnel Carriers arrived. The drivers of these vehicles belonged to the Royal Corps of Transport. The APC's were six-wheeled vehicles used in the desert during the last war. They were slow and hard to drive as they did not have power assisted steering.

I showed the lead driver the area we had to go to, it was 70 miles from our present location. The field to be secured was above a village, next to the border with Southern Ireland. It took three hours to arrive at this location as the APC's were so slow. The marines got out of the vehicles quickly on arrival as we knew we were in "Bandit Country". I placed guards around the edge of the field which was to be the future helicopter landing site. I put a windsock up in the corner of the field and the APC drivers placed a letter "H" in the middle of the field. After an hour 20 troop-carrying helicopters arrived, and disembarked 12 men from each one. As the landing site was well above the village I watched the troops go down and surround the perimeter, securing the village totally. This ensured that nobody could leave or enter without the knowledge of troops. I knew that this was going to be a very long day.

After an hour, three more helicopters arrived carrying 20 Police Officers, they proceeded down to the village to carry out a search procedure. Looking down on the village we watched the Police go from one house to another, carrying out detailed searches of each property doing one street at a time. Three men were brought out of one house and handcuffed, then made to sit down on the pavement, guarded by two Policemen. The procedure of searching all the houses took six hours, there were about 90 homes in the village. The Police returned to the landing zone with their prisoners and several boxes of material. The three helicopters that brought the Police were the first to arrive, they collected their passengers and headed towards Belfast. The soldiers came up the hill slowly and assembled at the edge of the field. It was nearly an hour later when the helicopters arrived.

Once the last helicopter had departed the wind sock and letter "H" were collected and we returned to our location. It was a slow journey as many roads had been blocked off with fallen trees, which was done deliberately to frustrate security forces. It was nearly midnight by the time we arrived at camp.

The marines did not mind going out on patrol, or any other type of duty. The only time any of us were allowed out was on official duty, as it was very unsafe. British forces were prime targets for any type of retaliation, if we were caught on our own we would be murdered. It is hard to believe that we were serving in a part of our own country.

The following two days after the helicopter landing zone guard I worked around camp doing fatigues and having an easy time. The evenings were spent in the NAAFI having a few drinks, and as usual, "putting the world to rights".

*

One morning the Imprest Officer (Pay Officer) sent for me and told me that I was to go to the local bank in our neighbouring small town and collect £2,000.00. The bank had been informed, and I would be escorted by a marine driver and two other members from our unit, acting as bodyguards. We would travel in an unmarked car and wear civilian clothing. I only had a pair of slacks, a blue shirt and a green jumper, and most of the marines had similar types of clothing. We were to draw three Browning pistols and ammunition. We all assembled at the Guardroom at nine o'clock, and a small Ford Escort car came up from Motor Transport compound to convey us to the bank. I got in the front passenger seat and the two bodyguards were in the rear. The driver said he knew the way as he had done this trip twice before.
It took us 20 minutes to arrive at the bank. I went in and the two bodyguards stood inside the main entrance. The driver remained with his vehicle.

I approached the girl behind the counter, showed her my identity card and told her what my business was. She went into the back office and came out with the branch manager. He asked to see my ID, what Unit I was from, and how much I was to collect. I answered all his questions and he was satisfied. He handed me a sealed envelope with £2,000.00 in it. I commented that it did not seem very thick, and he said that it was made up with £5, £10 and £20 notes. I asked if he required a signature, and he said 'No.'

I picked up the envelope, put it in my pocket and walked out of the bank. We all got back into the car and returned to camp. I went to the Imprest Office and handed the envelope over to a Colour Sergeant. He took it and placed the money in the safe. I asked him if he was going to count it, but he said, 'No, as the envelope is sealed and we know who has collected the money.' I returned the pistol and ammunition, then went over to the NAAFI.

On Company Daily Orders, I was to be the Guard Commander in camp for the following two days, starting the next day. This was a 48-hour duty. The Guard assembled at eight o'clock outside the camp Guardroom, just inside the main gate. There was a total of 24 marines, another Corporal and me, as duty Guard Commander. The Sergeant Major was duty Officer of the day, (he was also on duty for 48 hours). A quick inspection was carried out, and I then read out the Guard Orders, which were just over half a page of A4. The marines had worked out their duties themselves and paired off. I put a watch list up and they wrote their names alongside each shift which was their responsibility.

In the evening just before dusk, a foot patrol had to go around the outside perimeter fence of camp, and again just after dawn each morning. I did the evening patrol with eight marines. At the bottom of the fence was an apple orchard. The apples were ripe so we all picked some and filled our pockets; they were excellent. There was a line of oak trees up the hill on the east side of camp and to kill time I decided to take a detour through them. This position also gave a good commanding view of the camp and we could see all movement within it. It would also be possible to draw a detailed map of our camp layout.

The marines wandered through the trees and one of them called to me to come and have a look at what he had found. As I approached the marine he said, 'Look up into this tree.' I looked up and there was a sturdy wooden platform, built high up in the branches. I told them to line out, and to carry a detailed search of the woods for anything suspicious (such as command wire and booby traps).

The search took nearly half an hour, and once I was satisfied that there was nothing suspicious around we returned to the tree with the platform in it. One of the marines climbed up and onto the platform. He said, 'There is an excellent view of the camp, it would make an ideal sniper position,' and 'it has been constructed with four inch sturdy wooden planks.' He came down and we all returned to camp. I rang the Sergeant Major and told him of our discovery. He, in turn, went off to see the Adjutant. Half an hour later the CO, Adjutant, RSM and Sergeant Major came over to the Guardroom; I related exactly what we had found to them. The CO instructed the Adjutant to contact Army Headquarters and ask for the Royal Engineers to cut the trees down.

Just before first light the following morning a Corporal and 20 marines were sent to the location of the trees to guard them. At nine in the morning two trucks with 20 Royal Engineers arrived with two of their officers. I led our CO, Adjutant, RSM, Sergeant Major and two Royal Engineer Officers to the trees. I pointed out the tree with the platform to them. All the officers climbed up into the tree and on to the platform.

The CO was surprised at the commanding view over the camp, and one of the Royal Engineer Officers commented on how well the platform had been constructed. As there were eight oak trees, and the wood was valuable, the landowner had to be contacted. This small exercise was going to be turned into a public relations venture.

The landowner was a local farmer, and he soon arrived. It was pointed out to him that a platform had been built high up in one of his trees giving a commanding view into the camp. He stated, 'I only use this field to graze sheep as it is on such a steep slope.'

The Senior Royal Engineer Officer explained, 'All of the eight trees will have to come down. We are prepared to chop them down and cut them into manageable logs for you, as the wood is of high value.'

The farmer welcomed this and said, 'Then I will organise the wood to be transported to a sawmill.'

The Royal Engineers started cutting down the trees at ten in the morning and they were finished by four that afternoon. All the wood was removed and small branches were burnt by the farmer, who called into camp that evening to thank the CO. He had made a nice profit from his wood. The labour had been provided by the Army and the sawmill had removed the logs. The farmer was very happy about this, also a little richer.

The following morning the guard finished and we were all given 24 hours off. Walking back to my hut I came across the CO, who stopped me and said, 'That was a job well done.' I saluted him then both of us continued on our way. That evening I had to report to the RSM who told me that the following day I would have to set up a roadblock. He gave me the grid reference and road number. It was a "B" road. He also emphasised that every vehicle had to be vigorously searched and nothing left to chance, no matter what direction it was travelling in. The roadblock had to be in place by eight o'clock in the morning and maintained till four that afternoon, after which I was to return to camp. I was to leave the Guardroom at seven thirty the following morning. The roadblock area was only ten minutes away from our camp. The RSM told me that two Land Rovers would be provided and nine marines would meet me at the Guardroom the following morning. Bag rations would be provided.

I knew that the following day was going to be full of abuse, threats and hostility, as people do not like being stopped and searched. All vehicle drivers are always in a hurry and can become very aggressive. Also, roadblocks can be very busy or very boring, depending on where they are set up. In the morning I collected a radio and found the two Land Rovers and nine marines waiting for me outside the Guardroom. I directed the driver in my Land Rover and the other one followed on behind me to the area which had to be blocked off. On arrival the roadblock was set up and signs placed out. The Land Rovers were parked approximately 30 yards apart on either side of the road, with their bonnets pointing across towards the opposite grass verge, staggered. This would ensure that vehicles had to zigzag to pass through, also we would have full control. The marines all knew the drill and procedure.

The road was straight, flat and narrow; we could see about two miles in each direction. I checked the grid reference again to ensure that we were at the right location. The area was very quiet, and there was every indication that the road did not carry much traffic. We all settled down and waited, the hours started to go by. The marines were starting to think that we had been given wrong directions and I checked the grid reference about six times. The whole area was very quiet, the only noise came from birds in the trees. The marines and myself were in two groups of five, gathered round the Land Rovers. We talked, joked and ate our bag rations.

At around two in the afternoon a marine shouted, 'There's a car coming.' Everybody stood straight up and watched the car approach; it was a white Volvo estate. The marine flagged the car down and a woman wound down her window, immediately stating that she wanted to see the person in charge. I was called over. The woman was small, smart, wearing a green tweed suit and had a very expensive pearl necklace around her neck. I realised immediately that she was the type who gave orders and instructions, but did not like receiving them.

She spoke to me and said, 'Who authorised this roadblock, and what is it for?'

I replied, 'My Commanding Officer authorised it, and we are operating under Emergency Regulations.'

The small woman continued, 'I know all about Emergency Regulations but I'm in a hurry, so let me pass.'

I answered, 'Once your car has been searched you can proceed on your lawful business, providing nothing is found.'

She wasn't prepared to co-operate however, and threatened, 'I am a personal friend of the Chief Constable of the RUC, and I am well known to the General Officer Commanding Troops, Northern Ireland.'

I replied, 'It must be nice to have friends in high places but we are still going to search your car.'

She became quite angry and said, 'I want your name, rank and service number, as I will report you to your CO, and I am also a friend of your Company Commander.'

I challenged her with, 'Alright, what is the name and rank of my Company Commander?'

The small woman was completely flummoxed and was silent for a few seconds, so I said to her, 'Once the search is completed we will give you a card with a contact telephone number on it, and I will write my service number on the back.' I knew that this was the only requirement I had to comply with.'

She then insulted me saying, 'You are hoi polloi.'

I said to one of the marines, Go ahead and search the estate car, and ensure that everything is taken out, also ensure you check under the bonnet and the area of spare wheel storage.'

The woman then suggested, 'If you put more marines to the task then it will be done quicker.

I replied, 'The hoi polloi are not in a hurry, everything must be done correctly, this way you will have something to report to your friends in high places.'

The marine carrying out the search on the car took everything out and laid it on the grass verge. He went as slowly as possible. The small woman did not say anything, but if looks could kill we would all be dead now. The remainder of the marines watched in silence and had a quiet snigger to themselves. The marine searching the car slowly placed everything back in the estate, ensuring that nothing was damaged. Then he sat in the front passenger seat and checked the glove box. This took five minutes. Now it was time to check under the bonnet, and this was done very slowly as well. The small woman was glowing with rage, as stated, she liked to give orders, not to receive them.

The searching marine then came to me and said that the search was completed, 'There is nothing in the car that a good vacuum cleaner could not solve.'

The woman heard this. I took out my small notebook and wrote down her vehicle registration number – slowly. This infuriated her even more. Then I took a card and wrote my service number on the back of it. I approached her and handed the card to her. She grabbed it and said in a curt manner, 'Thank you, may I go now?'

I replied, 'Yes.'

She got into her car, started the engine, moved off, drove between our two Land Rovers and vanished down the road. If she had been civil the vehicle check would have been completed in under ten minutes. One of the marines said, 'The only car to come along had to have an obnoxious tart in it.' We had just under an hour to go till four o'clock and in the whole day only one vehicle had come along the road.

The final hour went quickly, and at four we packed up and returned to camp. On entering the camp the CO, Adjutant and RSM greeted us. All of them were laughing. The CO thanked us for our hard day's work and told us about a telephone call from a very bad-tempered woman. He said, 'I was expecting the call so I dealt with it myself.'

*

At around five the Sergeant Major sent for me. He said that as I had had a very easy day just hanging around a roadblock I was to be Guard Commander on some married quarters' estate that evening and for the following few days. A vehicle would collect me from the camp Guardroom at six.

At six an Army Land Rover collected me and we drove for nearly an hour before arriving at the married quarters' location. I asked the Army driver where we were, and he said, 'West, near the border.'

The Army Corporal I was relieving threw his pack into the rear of the Land Rover and said, 'Everything is in order,' then left. When I arrived there were 12 soldiers present, two on the main entrance and two patrolling the perimeter fence. The estate was on the top of a hill with only one entrance. There was a 12-foot security fence all the way round the perimeter and the Guardroom was the first house on the left as you entered the estate. There were 40 houses in total. I walked around the estate accompanied by two soldiers and spoke to a foot patrol and two sentries on the main entrance. They asked me, 'When will we be relieved?'

I answered, 'I don't know.' They had been on duty for three days.

They then told me, 'Food is delivered every second day, and you have to cook it yourself, but how long will we be here?'

Again, I said, 'I don't know.' I was also informed that the previous Corporal had been on duty for six days. This information really cheered me up. I had brought my washing kit and sleeping bag. At eight in the evening three Land Rovers arrived with 12 soldiers. They were the relievers for the present guard. I showed the new guard around and explained their duties. They paired off and told me that they would be leaving at eight the following morning. They were a good bunch of lads.

At eight in the morning a new guard of 12 young soldiers arrived, they were from the Army Pioneer Corps, straight out of basic training. I was told that they were to carry out guard duties for the next two days. I explained their duties then showed them all around the estate. I posted two on the main entrance and sent two off on patrol around the perimeter. A duty roster was made out and everybody settled down. I cooked myself some breakfast, ate and then cleaned up.

At 1130 hours I felt like stretching my legs, so I grabbed my weapon and walked to the main entrance. At the main entrance there was a group of children around the two soldiers. The kids had bullets and rifle parts in their hands. I immediately asked the two soldiers, 'What do you think you're doing?' I told them that they had to assemble their rifles and reload the magazines. I explained to them how vulnerable they were. If any part of their rifle was missing they would face a court martial. Once the weapons were reassembled and the magazines filled I checked both rifles. I then explained their responsibilities and checked that they understood. Both of them said that they did. I checked the sentries patrolling the perimeter fence and told them that on no account were they to show their rifles or bullets to anyone. When I returned to the Guardroom I gathered the other eight young soldiers around me and explained in detail their duties and responsibilities, ensuring that they fully understood. This was their first time on duty in Northern Ireland, also they had just finished basic training. All of them were only 18 years old.

Over the next two days I watched the 12 young soldiers like a Hawk. They settled down after a while. The only thing was that they had to be supervised and told what to do all the time. They were not infantry soldiers. Once they had done their 48 hours, duty replacement soldiers came from one of the Scots regiments. I had been on duty for three nights with very little sleep.

On the evening of the fourth day a Corporal from the Army Pay Corps turned up, but he was only staying for one night. He told me, 'I have very little knowledge of weapons, and I am a nervous wreck.' He was under the impression that we were going to be attacked soon.

I said to him, 'Don't worry, on no account will you go out by yourself. Stay in the Guardroom at all times.' He was more of a liability than an asset and the young Scots were laughing at him. I said to him, 'I will sleep next to the telephone and you can sleep upstairs.' He agreed to this. The night went off without incident and the Pay Corporal left at eight that morning. I carried on with the Scots, they were an excellent bunch of lads.

Night number five I hoped would be my last duty on the estate. The following morning the Scots were relieved by a bunch of soldiers from the Royal Artillery. Five minutes after their arrival a replacement Corporal arrived. He was my relief, but his Land Rover left immediately once he had been dropped off. I showed the relief Corporal around and explained the duty, wishing him all the best. He was also in the dark concerning the duration of the duty, which was the same for all of us. At nine in the morning a Land Rover arrived from my unit to collect me. I had experienced 12 Pioneers and one nervous Pay Corporal.

Once I arrived back at my location I informed the Sergeant Major and he asked, 'Where are the married quarters? and how did it go?' I told him all about it. He had a good laugh about the Army Pay Corporal. He said, 'The young Pioneers should not have been sent there. However, you can have the rest of the day off.' This gave me the chance to catch up on my sleep.

That evening the Adjutant and RSM sent for me, I was told that I was to dig and man an observation point overlooking a village near the border with Southern Ireland. The Adjutant showed me the village on the map, also he pointed out to me a very steep hill at the rear of the village. On top of the hill were some trees and bushes, if I dug a slit/observation trench amongst the bushes I would have a good view, also it would provide natural camouflage to conceal and protect me. I was told that Marine Brown would be my buddy/partner for the exercise. He had been in the Royal Marines 12 years, a good, reliable, steady, dependable man. I was glad to have him as my partner for the next seven days. Both of us were to be flown over and around the village next morning, to enable us to see our future observation area. We were to observe the village and report anything that might be unusual via radio, back to Operations.

The following morning we met the helicopter on a football pitch, I knew the pilot, he was a Sergeant in our unit. It took us just under half an hour to reach the village, we did two circuits around the perimeter. Also, I located high ground to the rear, the Adjutant had been right concerning the observation position. We returned to camp, spending the rest of the day in preparation. That afternoon Brown and I rested in preparation for the nights of work to come. After dark two Land Rovers took six marines and me to a drop-off point about three miles short of the village, the remaining distance was to be covered on foot travelling across country. I checked the area and grid reference the Adjutant had given me, and I found a good point overlooking the village. The extra marines dug a fire/observation trench and dug out a shelter for our rest and sleeping accommodation. The shelter trench was narrow, also, it could only accommodate one of us, but this was our sleeping area for the next seven days. We had to be as quiet as possible. There was no moon that night, but a lot of cloud, and it was dry. No vehicles were travelling in or out of the village to help cover the noise of digging. Everything was still and quiet.

From our observation position we could see over the village and beyond. We counted the streetlights, a total of nine. They were the old-fashioned type, "one light bulb". The fire/observation trench was camouflaged and the shelter dug out well concealed, and behind them were more bushes. The radio aerial was well hidden and concealed in the trees, and it was high up, which was another favourable point. The marines that assisted us left two hours before dawn, and Brown and I settled down.

Just after dawn I placed a location card out for our reference points, we could see right down into the village and identify each house. Each street/road had been given a nickname, also, all radio transmissions would be in code, as we knew Republicans listened into all military broadcasts. We agreed to do six-hour watches during the day and three hours at night. During the first day we both stayed up to watch over the village, enabling us to get the feel and understanding of life below us.

Lights started to com on in some houses at five thirty, the occupants then left their homes at six. We assumed that these people were farm workers. The vast majority of houses turned their upstairs lights on at six thirty, followed by downstairs light five minutes later. Some men assembled at the bus stop just before seven thirty, forming a queue and talking amongst themselves. The bus arrived just after seven thirty, they all departed on this vehicle. Just before eight thirty the children of the village started to assemble at the bus stop. The vehicle arrived and they all embarked, leaving at exactly eight thirty. The remainder of the morning was quiet, some women were talking in the street and a window-cleaner was doing his rounds. Some vans delivered goods, also farm tractors were passing through the village. Just after nine a helicopter from our Unit did a couple of circuits around the village, passing over us once. This was part of a daily routine.

During the first day there was nothing going on, but a small Ford Anglia car kept coming and going continuously, always from one house. The driver was a young man who always seemed to be in a hurry. In the evening I received a radio message telling me that our CO, Adjutant and RSM would pay us a visit. The CO's party arrived at about two in the morning, having approached across country on foot. They also provided us with some fresh food and new night sights. The CO checked our position, stayed for half an hour and agreed that we had a good commanding view over the village.

Day two was just the same as the first day, the Ford Anglia kept coming and going. I reported its registration back to Operations. That evening I was told that it belonged to a Republican quartermaster.

Day three, at about eleven that morning, two large black Ford cars drew up outside the quartermaster's house. Seven men got out of these vehicles and went into his house. Just over an hour later they re-emerged, carrying bags. I radioed Operations, told them what was going on, and also the road they had taken on leaving the village. That night at about one in the morning the Sergeant Major paid a visit. He told Brown and me that the seven men in the two black Fords were all wanted for murder, and that the vehicles were carrying explosives and weapons. The Ford Anglia was not with them when they were stopped at a roadblock set up by the RUC. The RUC had acted on information which I had sent over the radio to Operations, so it had been a very successful outcome. Also, the Sergeant Major told us that the unit had a new Second-in-Command and our Company Headquarters had a new Company Commander, both Officers were Majors. The Sergeant Major also had two marines with him as his bodyguards, and they stayed for half an hour. Their vehicles were parked three miles away, they returned to them across country.

Day four was very wet and unpleasant as it rained most of the day. The Ford Anglia returned, and this information was passed back to Operations. That night nobody paid us a visit.

Day five was dry and sunny, which made life more pleasurable. The Ford Anglia appeared in the afternoon. Several boxes were removed from the car and taken into a house. The Republican quartermaster then left. I radioed this information back to Operations. Two hours later four Army trucks came into the village. Approximately 60 soldiers got out of the vehicles and spread out around the village. Four Land Rovers with RUC also arrived. The soldiers placed a cordon around the village and the RUC searched the houses. The house that received boxes from the Republican quartermaster was searched and numerous boxes were removed and three young men were arrested. The Ford Anglia was not present during this time. The Republican quartermaster's house was searched and I think many residents regretted his presence in the village. That night our Sergeant Major made another visit, also to bring rations and water. We were told that a visit would be made to us by our two new Majors the following night.

Day six at around two in the afternoon I was sleeping in the shelter trench when Brown gave me a wake-up call. I got up and slowly moved into the fire/observation trench, and looked up to see two Royal Marine Majors standing in front of me. They were dressed in Lovat trousers, dress shirt, green jumper, black shoes, and wearing their green berets. They were standing at the top of the hill, against the skyline. I looked down the hill, they had parked two Land Rovers directly below us, and the Ford Anglia belonging to the Republican quartermaster just passed by. The driver of the Ford Anglia could now put two and two together, the reason why seven men were arrested from the village, plus why houses had been searched.

I told both the Majors that they had compromised us and we would have to return to camp. I then radioed back to the Unit telling them that we were evacuating our position and returning to camp, the reasons would be explained later. The senior Major (Second-in-Command of the Unit) said, There is no need to leave, nobody knows we're here.

I replied, 'You have been followed, and you can be seen from the village.'

Marine Brown then added, 'Everyone else visited at night and travelled across country, ensuring they weren't observed or followed.'

The 2 i/c then told Brown, 'I am not used to being spoken to in this manner, and you will be charged with insubordination.'

I told both of them again, 'We are packing up and returning back to camp as our lives are now in danger. You have compromised a good operation which had been authorised from the very top, and as Brown is to be charged I will also be disobeying an order by returning with you. We will both go for a Court Martial, that way everything will be out in the open.'

We packed our kit and filled in the trench, taking our belongings and placing them in the back of one of the two Officers' Land Rovers. Both vehicles had to go into the village to turn around and the Ford Anglia followed us for a short distance.

When we arrived back in camp the RSM was waiting for us, he told me to go into his office and Brown to wait outside. I explained what had happened and how we had been compromised, he wrote everything down. Once the RSM had heard what I said he sent for Brown. Once Brown had finished giving his version, which tallied with mine, the RSM had both of us in his office. He said, 'You have nothing to worry about, this incident would go all the way, to the very top.' We were then told to go away, shower and report to the Adjutant at nine the following morning.

At nine we reported to the Adjutant, and he said, 'I have heard your story from the RSM, but would you both mind going over what happened again?' I told him everything that had happened the previous day, he wrote down all the details. Once he had finished with me he asked Brown to tell his version. Brown repeated exactly what I had said.

The Adjutant said, 'In my opinion you have acted correctly as your lives were at risk. I will inform your Sergeant Major of the outcome.' Subsequently, our Sergeant Major sent for Brown and me, telling us that we had done everything correctly. We had nothing to worry about, and he mentioned that the General Officer Commanding Troops, Northern Ireland, was not at all happy with our two new Majors. The work that had taken place during the past week had proved invaluable, but that the observation point we used could not now be resurrected.

I asked, 'What is going to happen to Brown and me?'

He answered, 'Nothing. The CO was not at all happy about what happened, but he was pleased with the information you both gathered, which proved to be of great benefit to the Security Forces.'

Brown and I were given the day off. We both went over to the NAAFI, had a couple of beers, lunch and a long sleep that afternoon.

*

The morning after my rest day I was told to report to the Motor Transport Officer. He was a likeable man, easy going, friendly, always laughing and joking with his drivers, and liked by everybody. I reported to him in his office. He invited me in and said to me, 'I have a dangerous, unpleasant job to be done.'

'Thank you,' I said, 'what is it?'

He answered, 'I want you to go around all our locations with four trucks and collect empty five gallon jerry cans, then proceed to the main Army stores depot and replace them with full ones. The truck from the HQ location has already been filled with empty jerry cans, but the three other trucks are empty. You will have four drivers and three marines with you.' He continued, 'All the Driver Corporals are out on other duties. Remember, this job is dangerous.'

I told him, 'Two of the company locations are in hostile Republican areas, and most of the petrol cans leak a little. This creates four large mobile fire bombs.'

The four trucks and marines accompanying me were waiting outside the Guardroom. We left our location just after nine that morning. It was about an hour's drive between each location, with half an hour to load each truck. I estimated that we would reach the main stores depot at around three that afternoon. The return journey would be more dangerous. None of the drivers or marines were very happy with the job. One of them said, 'Someone has to do it,' to which the reply was, 'But why us?'

We arrived at the Army Supply Depot just after three thirty. The petrol dump was at the far end of the Depot, by the seashore. The nearest building to it was a mile away. The petrol compound was also surrounded with barbed wire, ten feet high and eight feet deep. The four trucks were unloaded, and the empty jerry cans were placed to one side. An Army Sergeant counted and checked all the empties for damage, stating, 'Your Unit will have to pay for any damaged jerry cans.'

The unloading and checking took just under two hours. 1,240 cans were re-loaded back onto the trucks, the whole area smelt of petrol. There were two large signs displayed, measuring ten feet by six feet, saying "NO SMOKING". Two soldiers spent all their time every day just filling jerry cans up with petrol. We were glad that we did not have their jobs. Once we'd finished loading all the vehicles we filled the trucks' tanks up with fuel. Each truck took nearly 60 gallons, this was equivalent to 12 jerry cans.

This trip to the Army Depot was done on average twice a week. The rear of the trucks were sealed with their canvas canopies, to prevent anybody seeing what was on board. Also, it would prevent an incendiary device entering the rear of the vehicles – we hoped! You could smell the petrol just by walking around outside the vehicles.

We had to go part of the way back through Belfast, to gain access to the motorway system. Just before we arrived at the motorway there was a Police Roadblock. Our vehicles were at the rear, there was about a mile of cars, trucks and vans ahead of us. I realised that we were very vulnerable, just standing still and waiting our turn to go through the checkpoint area. I jumped out of my truck and went up to the checkpoint search area. I asked one of the RUC Constables who was the senior officer-in-charge. He pointed to a Chief Inspector, and I approached him stating that I had four trucks full of petrol at the tail end of the queue. When he realised our immediate danger and the potential for a major disaster he told his officers to stop all oncoming traffic. I was told to go back to the vehicles and lead the trucks straight through, and I did this. As I passed the Chief Inspector a look of terror was still on his face. Four large petrol bombs were now leaving his area.

The first two locations we had to visit were the most dangerous, they were right in the middle of a Republican area. The camps were surrounded by 20 feet of corrugated iron metal sheeting fences. The two watchtowers were 40 feet high, and the lookout positions in each were covered with camouflage nets. This was to enable sentries within to see out knowing that they were not silhouetted. It was now raining very hard, nobody was on the streets, and only a few vehicles were about. When things are getting a bit scary we always pray for rain as all troublemakers stay indoors. I had not prayed for rain, but welcomed it anyway. Once we had left the two locations I felt a great sense of relief. The third location was out in the countryside.

It was now dark. If the truck I was in was hit with an incendiary device we would go up like a Roman candle. The best thing was not to think about it, but just to get on with the job in hand. At the third location we had a meal, unloaded, and proceeded back to HQ. We arrived back just after eleven. It had been a very long day.

*

Two marines on Guard duty came round to the accommodation block informing us that we all had to assemble at the Guardroom at five the following morning. There was to be a roadblock and cordon. No end time was mentioned and I knew that the following day was going to be very long. Early in the morning we all assembled outside the Guardroom at five. There were 80 of us from Headquarters. The CO told us that we were going to place a cordon and roadblock around a Republican estate in West Belfast. We would be joined by one of our Rifle Companies, making a total of 200 personnel. Also, he hoped it would all be completed by nine that morning. The RUC would carry out searches of houses and property. Once we were positioned around the area no-one would be allowed in or out. The RUC would inform our CO when all was completed. The news that it would all be completed by nine AM cheered everyone up. Six trucks pulled up outside the Guardroom and all Corporals and marines embarked onto these vehicles. The CO, Adjutant, RSM, HQ Sergeant Major travelled in Land Rovers. It was an hour's drive to West Belfast.

On arrival we were met by the other Rifle Company from our Unit. They were very tired, having returned back to their camp location the previous night just after midnight from the field. They had had only two hours sleep that night. Their Company Commander was hoping that it would not be a long drawn out day as he wanted his men back in camp to catch up on some rest and sleep. The Police were supposed to be here, and the CO's radio operator received a message from North Ireland Headquarters that they were on their way. We were placed around the outside of the estate, an area of seven streets running parallel with each other. The houses were two up and down, backing on to each other. A truck was positioned at the top and bottom of each street, to prevent any vehicle entering or leaving. Nine marines and two Corporals were also placed at either end of the streets. The remainder of the Unit surrounded the outer perimeter. We were instructed that nobody was allowed in or out. The time was just before six thirty in the morning, it was Saturday and it was also cold and wet. We had our combat clothing, the flak jacket weighed about 30 pounds. Also a web belt, two ammunition pouches and a water bottle, rifle and truncheon. Our headdress consisted of our green berets.

Nobody in the area expected a cordon and roadblock to be placed around their estate on a Saturday. Some people had started to leave their houses for work, and when they approached the roadblocks they were turned back. This caused resentment, and much bad language and abuse was directed at us. We were all hoping the RUC would arrive and carry out their search, then we could leave. One hour went by, then another; it was now getting on for nine in the morning. The milkman and postman were refused entry, and both were very upset. Both stated that we were interfering with their livelihood, and they did have a point. Women were coming up to the cordon and insulting us, although "sticks and stones can break your bones but words can never hurt you". We all hoped that it would stay insults and words. Also, one of their favourite sayings was "you will never go to heaven". What they did not like was a smile back to them from us, and a silent response. This used to throw them into a rage. The RUC arrived just before ten that morning, there were 50 of them. The CO was not at all pleased, he spoke to their senior officer. Also, two representatives of the estate came forward, asking for explanations. The senior RUC officer just showed them his authority to search each house in the area. I witnessed all this. I knew by now that it was going to be a very long tiring day. The RUC commenced searching houses in the street I was guarding, this took them one and a half hours. The weather was getting cold, then it started to rain hard. We had to stand and take it, which meant we were soaking wet.

It was just after 1200 hours, we were all feeling hungry and tired. The other Corporal with me said that he would compile a list, for chocolates and sweets, then go over to the corner shop and purchase the goods. He did this, but when he went into the corner shop the owner refused to serve him. The shop owner was terrified, he said, 'It is more than my life is worth to serve a British soldier.' We all understood, but we were not at all happy.

The Police seemed to be moving very slowly, our Officers and senior personnel moved amongst us trying to cheer us up. At around two in the afternoon a TV crew arrived. I knew this meant trouble. They started to walk around, looking for anything interesting to photograph. But everything was quiet. There was a small group of teenagers, boys and girls, wandering around. One of our marines said that he saw one of the TV crew go up to one of the teenage girls, speak to her and give her some money. The girl commenced walking around, and stopped at our roadblock, and started throwing insults and bad language. We stood in a straight line close together as we thought she was going to try and run through our cordon. The RSM and Adjutant then came along. The TV crew turned their cameras on them. The RSM approached me and asked, 'What is going on?'

I told him, 'The young girl has been put up by the TV crew to stir up trouble.'

The RSM looked at the young girl, then she came forward and spat in his face. She then turned around and re-joined her friends. All of this was caught on camera, the TV crew then left. They had what they wanted, the humiliation of British Servicemen. They also knew that none of us could retaliate against this young girl. Everyone knew that the so-called hard men always used women and young people to do their dirty work, and that the TV crew had wanted something to report.

At five thirty that afternoon the RUC announced that they had completed their search, also that it had been successful, netting two boxes of American dollar bills, six hand guns and a small amount of ammunition. Three wanted members of the Republican terrorist organisation had been found in a secret basement, specially dug and constructed in one house. This find of three suspects had given valuable information concerning future searches. Security Forces knew that property and buildings could be altered to hide personnel, weapons, also documents. The roadblocks and cordons were now removed and people started moving around freely. Some people passed us in silence, others with much abuse. The RUC left with their find and the three suspects. We embarked back onto our trucks for the journey back to camp. It was nice to sit down. We were all cold, tired, wet, hungry and miserable, plus our shoulders were aching from the weight of our flak jackets.

Once we arrived back in camp the CO welcomed all of us, telling the Corporals and marines that they had done well. A special supper was laid on at seven thirty that evening. Everyone piled their plates up high with food. Mugs of hot tea and food were enjoyed, consumed and appreciated. Once personnel had finished their supper there was a move into the NAAFI. The NAAFI staff, all one of him, could not pull pints fast enough. We all sat in groups of eight and ten. Now it was time for a good moan, much abuse was expressed concerning people of the estate and the TV crew.

The HQ Company Clerk and the Orderly room Corporal were also sat near us. Someone yelled at them to come over to us, and they did. Both of them were asked what our two new Majors did, and where had they come from. The HQ Company Clerk was the first to answer. 'Our new Company Commander has come from the Ministry of Defence, London. He has been there for the last eight years. He is now an expert on Law. During his time in London he studied Law and gained two degrees, his last one was a Master's. He was posted to London on promotion to Captain.' He went on to say, 'Today he has re-written Company Orders and Guardroom Instructions, and he has made it plain to the Sergeant Major and Junior Officers that no Corporal or marine is to speak to him directly.'

I dare not write down the comments that followed from Corporals and marines, but Marine Brown then gave a good fitting nickname to our Company Commander, "Major INCOMPETENCE". Also, the Company Clerk said that our Sergeant Major and Junior Officers detested him. We all agreed that he was doomed to fail. Also, it was pointed out by Brown that we should all keep our places, as "PEASANTS". This nickname given to our new Company Commander stuck, and went around the Unit like wildfire – "Major Incompetence".

The Orderly room Corporal then spoke up in regard to the new Second-in-Command, 'He has come from Commander-in-Chief, Naval Staff. He doesn't like fieldwork as he regards it to be very uncivilised and uncomfortable.' We all agreed with this. The marine in the Orderly room had taken our new 2 i/c a mug of coffee, he was told to take it away, as an Officer could only drink refreshments from a cup with a saucer. It was very uncivilised to drink from a mug. A cup and saucer was brought over from the Officers' Mess for the new 2 i/c. He spent most of his day on the telephone, avoiding leaving the camp. He had not put his combat clothing on yet, only dressing in Lovats, all nice, clean and smart. We were all now of the opinion that this man was another blunder waiting to happen. His nickname was "Major BLUNDER". One of the Corporals asked, 'What have we done to be cursed with these two idiots?'

As it was now getting late the majority of men started to leave the NAAFI, for a good night's sleep to prepare for tomorrow. I was to be Guard Commander over the next three days.

*

I went over to the Guardroom at seven thirty, dropped off my kit and then spoke to the out-going Guard Commander. The routine was that the Guard fell in for inspection at eight, orders were read out and they were briefed on anything that may require special attention. The out-going Corporal told me to look at the revised Guard orders, they had been re-written by the HQ Company Commander. I picked them up, they were now six pages of A4. They listed what the two sentries on the main gate had to do, and there was a list of questions to be asked of drivers wanting to enter camp. The duties and responsibilities of the Watch Tower Look Outs were there and what the Wandering Patrol had to be aware of. I then read the most controversial paragraph of all. This concerned what action had to be taken if a proxy bomb is delivered in a vehicle via the main gate. Briefly, it was as follows:

"When the Guard Commander is informed that a proxy bomb has arrived at the main entrance he is to go to Motor Transport section and sign out a Land Rover. This vehicle is to be driven to the main entrance and a towrope attached to the car or van with a suspect bomb in it. The suspect vehicle is then to be towed to the bottom of the camp and the Company Commander informed, via the Sergeant Major. The Company Commander will ring Bomb Disposal. The Guard Commander is then to question the Sentries on the Main Gate, to ascertain from where the suspect vehicle and bomb originated".

The out-going Guard Commander said, 'The Company Commander has no idea about a proxy bomb, everything happens too quickly. He thinks he is in a office in London, where everything happens slowly.'

I also pointed out that it would take nearly half an hour to read out these orders, and there would be some questions from the marines. There was no allowance made for common sense, all marines had done Guard duty three or four times before. Normally the Guard is in the Guardroom ten minutes after eight, and the old Guard gone by eight fifteen.

I asked the outgoing Guard Commander who the Duty Officer was for this duty. His reply was, 'HQ Sergeant Major.' I knew he was a dependable man, with lots of common sense.

I fell the Guard in at eight and reported, 'Present and correct,' to the Sergeant Major. He stood the Guard at ease and told me to read the Guard Orders out, and I did this. It took 25 minutes. On completion of these orders being read, questions from marines started coming fast and furious. The Sergeant Major came forward and told them all, 'Use your common sense.' The Company Commander was standing behind him, and he did not like this comment at all. The Second-in-Command of the Guard, another Corporal, had made out a duty roster. The marines paired off, settled down, and then started their duties. There were two on the main entrance as these two gates are 20 feet high and eight feet wide. On a windy day they are very difficult to open and close. Also, there is a 20-foot corrugated iron sheet fence around the perimeter and four 40-foot watchtowers, one positioned at each corner. The relief Guard Commander and I agreed that we would do six-hour watches, also alternate patrols around the perimeter of the camp.

The first two days went by nice and quietly. On day three at about two thirty, the Sentries on the main entrance came running into the Guardroom shouting that a bomb had been delivered in a van and was about to go off. I pressed the general alarm button, grabbed my rifle and evacuated the Guardroom. The Guard ran to the bottom of the camp, logic told everybody that this was the furthest point from the main entrance. Also, the General Alarm could be heard by everyone in the camp, and personnel left their offices and buildings, joining us at the bottom of the camp. Major INCOMPETENCE arrived, and he immediately asked, 'Who is the Guard Commander?'

'I am,' I replied.

'Then why haven't you carried out my written orders concerning the Proxy Bomb?' he demanded.

I replied, 'It is going to go off at any moment, and it's best to be as far away as possible from the blast area, and I hope to return home alive, not in a box.'

He said, 'You will face a charge of disobeying a Written Order.'

To which I replied, 'The written order will be presented at my court martial, and fortunately I will be alive to argue my case.'

The marines started to pass remarks amongst themselves so that he could hear them, then Marine Brown went up to him and said, 'The Land Rover is over there, you deal with the suspect vehicle. Lead by example.'

Then another marine said, 'If you bring the vehicle to the bottom of the camp and it explodes, it will completely destroy the barracks.'

The RSM heard what was going on and told everyone to be quiet, then he approached the CO, saying, 'Bomb Disposal have been contacted and are on their way.'

Major INCOMPETENCE then said, 'That was my job.' The CO was listening to what was going on, and he called the two Sentries over from the main entrance forward and asked them what had happened.

They answered, 'A small van drove up to the main gate, it stopped and the engine was turned off, whereupon the driver got out and shouted "There's a bomb onboard, it'll go off in 40 seconds." Then he ran off. We both ran into the Guardroom to warn everybody, then the Guard Commander raised the General Alarm.'

The CO said that everybody was to stay at the bottom of the camp and wait for the all clear from Bomb Disposal, and he told both Sentries that they had done the right thing.

Two hours later a Staff Sergeant from Bomb Disposal reported to the CO stating that the vehicle was now safe. He explained, 'The bomb was a milk churn device with a home made mix of sugar and weed killer in it. The fuse had been lit, but failed to connect with the detonator because it had been crimped incorrectly.'

The CO then told the RSM, 'Everyone can go back to their duties, and I want to see the Guardroom Orders as soon as possible.'

I collected them and handed them to the Adjutant, who said, 'These have increased in volume.'

The driver of the van turned himself in to the RUC. His family had been held hostage, forcing him to deliver the vehicle and bomb to the camp. The Police went to his house where they found his wife tied and gagged. His baby son was in a cot, requiring a nappy change and a feed. The couple required a few days off to recover after their ordeal. It again showed what scum the Republicans were.

At six that evening our Sergeant Major came into the Guardroom with a big grin on his face. The case against me had been dropped, on orders from our CO. Major INCOMPETENCE had had a grilling from the CO, and had been told that he had to get out of camp and see what was going on outside it. Also, the Guardroom Orders written by Major INCOMPETENCE were now out of date, and we were to revert back to the original one. The following morning we all left the Guardroom at eight fifteen, feeling a sense of relief. One less duty to do.

*

From the Guardroom I went over to my barrack room, which accommodated eight personnel. I wanted to have a wash and shave, then go over for breakfast. I gathered my washing kit and proceeded to the bathrooms. There was a sign at the entrance saying, "Closed for cleaning and Unit 2 i/c inspection". I asked the marine who was doing the cleaning what it was all about. He said that the Unit 2 i/c still thinks that he is on a ship. All accommodation, offices, stores and the dining hall have to be ready for his inspection by ten thirty this morning. I returned my washing kit and then went over to the dining hall. The old guard were all there, not washed or shaved, like myself, and fed up. The Cook Sergeant-in-charge of the kitchen/dining hall wanted to know why we had not washed or shaved. One of the marines told him what the problem was, and he told us all to go and help ourselves to breakfast. He also informed us that Support Company were returning back to barracks that morning, having been in the field for the last five days. They would want a wash, shower and to be able to clean their kit, and they would be very tired.

I had my breakfast and then went back to my room. I shared the room with seven other personnel, it had four sets of double bunk beds. Our kit bags and webbing was piled up in the centre of the floor. Rifles were hung on the ends of the bunk beds. I had now to wait until the Unit 2 i/c had completed his inspection rounds. One of the marines said, 'Major BLUNDER is making his presence felt.'

Just after ten I could hear a commotion going on outside. Members of the Support Company were going into bathroom, all 200 of them. Their Company Commander and Sergeant Major were having a stand-up row with our Unit 2 i/c. I heard the Support Company Commander, also a Major, point out to the Unit 2 i/c that this was an operational unit, now on active service. Personnel were coming and going at all times of the day, "this is not a ship". Also, he was going to see the CO. Major BLUNDER did not even attempt to stand his ground. He did not like to be spoken to in this manner, especially in front of other ranks, by a fellow Officer. It is very unusual for Officers to argue in front of the men. The Support Company Commander was a good down to earth Officer, who always looked after his men. Both Officers went off to see the Unit Commanding Officer. I wish I had been a fly on the wall in the CO's office. The only information that was relayed back to us was that the Unit 2 i/c had resigned at his own request. This meant that the CO had taken the side of the Support Company Commander against the Unit 2 i/c. Major BLUNDER left that afternoon and caught a flight to London, as of midnight he would not be a serving officer in the Royal Marines. One down, one to go.

That evening whilst we were all having our supper the Adjutant and RSM came into the dining hall. The RSM asked for silence as the Adjutant had an important announcement to make. He said, 'Late this afternoon by the dock, a Sergeant from the Quartermasters' Department and a marine driver were shot. The vehicle they were travelling stopped at a red traffic light and three gunmen, from the opposite side of the road, shot the Sergeant and Driver whilst the Land Rover was stationary. The gunmen used a small low fence to conceal themselves. When the vehicle stopped they stood up and fired two or three bullets each. Both our personnel were killed instantly. The three gunmen then stepped forward to admire their bloody handiwork, but were not aware of the fact that there were two marines in the rear of the vehicle, who both disembarked quietly and shot all three gunmen dead as they approached the Land Rover. The three were dressed in standard Republican dress, black balaclava, black trousers and green jumper.'

The day after, I was on the petrol run again, and that afternoon whilst at the Army Stores Depot I went over to the NAAFI shop and bought a newspaper. On page three was a small article concerning the death of two Servicemen in Northern Ireland and the death of the three Republican murderers. The article was brief and to the point, an accurate report with no gloss on it. I was disappointed that news of the two Servicemen murdered in the course of their duty only warranted a small article on page three. I showed the paper and article to the rest of our boys and they too were very unhappy that we did not receive greater attention. It was very late at night by the time we returned back to barracks, so I was unable to hear the views and feeling of other Corporals and marines.

The following day I was on bank run, collecting the normal £2,000.00 for our Imprest Office. Whilst out I bought papers for the boys, as our NAAFI hadn't received any.

At lunch time in the dining hall it was pointed out to everybody present by one Corporal that five left wing Members of Parliament had asked, 'Why had the three Republicans not been arrested, rather than shot?' Also, they wanted to know if the two marines that shot the Republicans had followed the procedure of challenging before opening fire. They reasoned that the three murderers should have been arrested, this would have enabled them to stand trial and have their case heard by a Judge and Jury. They did not understand that the situation was fluid. The article in the tabloid news (toilet) paper supported their view that the gunmen were murdered by Armed Servicemen. There was no mention that the Services were doing a difficult job under hostile conditions, and there was no concern for our two murdered colleagues. This Sergeant and marine were not warned that they were going to be shot whilst peacefully going about their business. Everyone ate their food and left the dining hall.

It is with honour that everyone contributed a day's pay for the families of the Sergeant and marine who had been murdered by Republican thugs. The Sergeant had a wife and two young children. The young marine driver supported his mother, he was single. Our CO authorised that two days pay could be taken out of personnel's pay over a four-month period. The CO down to the youngest marine in the Unit contributed. All the members of the Unit showed their sorrow for the loss of two comrades in a practical way. We all cared deeply for our fallen comrades, but consideration had to be given to their next of kin too. Life goes on, the sun rises in the morning and sets each day.

*

That evening after supper some of the Corporals and marines went over to the NAAFI to enjoy a pint and talk. We all gathered around a large table. The talk was obviously about the two tabloid news (toilet) papers. We all felt that we were doing a good job, but with no support from our elected left wing Members of Parliament. Also, why did the opposition party not challenge these left wing MPs? There were only derogatory comments passed about the Labour Party, which were as follows:

- In 1935 Labour stated that they would not fight for King and Country.
- Also, they supported Hitler as his party was called, NATIONAL Socialist's (NAZI).
- They only changed their opinion after the invasion of Poland.
- Labour will allow and support a fifth column in our country.
- Labour hate: Freedom of expression, Respectability, Nationhood and common sense.
- Labour talks but fails to act.
- Labour are incapable of organisation in any form.
- When Labour is in government costs rise and standards drop.
- They do not understand how a budget works, live within your means.
- Labour thinks there need be no limits when taxing the public.
- Labour governments end in a financial mess, the country has to pay for their blunders.
- Ask a Labour supporter why he votes for them. The supporter's standard reply is "Because I am working class". If you ask what their policies are, the standard answer is "I don't know".
- Labour leadership is always weak and Government Departments under them are in chaos. No leadership from the top, and no original ideas from any of their MPs.

There are many others, but I will end there as this could go on for ever. Even now, three decades later, Labour are now in office but not in full control. They now call themselves "New Labour". They have altered their policies somewhat but still perpetuate envy. There is hatred of anything that is decent, respectable or to do with self-responsibility. The Prime Minister says that he dislikes the forces of Conservatism, emphasising his hatred of decency and self-reliance. The Prime Minister, Mr BLAIR, likes to stand in front of a TV camera with a big smile on his face, his hands level with his chest, palms pointing inwards, always emphasising the phrase, "believe me, I am a straight forward sort of guy". I am not sure if he is trying to convince the public or himself.

He has brought a hollow peace to Northern Ireland, giving the Republicans everything they wanted. Republican prisoners in the Maze have been released, also Loyalist thugs. The Republicans still have their large stockpiles of weapons and explosives. Any sensible person would have ensured that weapons were handed over first, then prisoners released. The Prime Minister has been taken for a fool, but that is no surprise.

The Republicans are now in government in Northern Ireland, but still up to their old tricks of smoke and mirrors. They cannot sit in the Houses of Parliament, Westminster, as they refuse to take the oath of allegiance to our Queen. Our Prime Minister is working on ways to change that, he wants them in Parliament as he knows they will support New Labour, he puts himself first, then his political party next, the country comes last; it is "power at any price".

Giving support to the Republicans he has ordered another inquiry into the events of Bloody Sunday, 1972, this is more appeasement. This investigation is costing the taxpayer millions, and lawyers are growing rich, as it greatly benefits them. One of the principal Alpha males in the Republican party, also a main player in the Northern Ireland Assembly, has been called forward to answer questions put to him by Lawyers at this inquiry. The man has refused to answer questions, as he says, "my first loyalty is to Republicanism, and I will not betray old friends and colleagues". This person has shown clear and total contempt for decency. Also, the Royal Ulster Constabulary has been reduced in size and re-branded, "The Police Service of Northern Ireland" again to appease Republicans.

The Prime Minster's wife supports the Palestinian so called "struggle against forces of Law and Order implemented by

Israel". New Labour lawyers describe Republican and Islamic terrorism as "political violence". They have never had to clean up after their acts of violence.

New Labour has total contempt for the Crown and any form of Law and Order. Republicans have made a big show of informing the daughters of Mrs Jean McConville where the remains are of their mother. In December 1972 the mother of ten was taken from her home in West Belfast and never seen again, removed by Republican thugs. She was interrogated in Belfast before being taken to South Armagh, where this decent woman was shot in the head. Her crime, according to the Republicans, was that she comforted a young dying British soldier. She was a decent citizen, hopefully by now a Christian burial has been given to her.

The following article is included in this book, with kind permission from *The Daily Mail,* published on 29th May, 2003.

FURY AS MP LAUDS THE IRA

A Labour MP caused outrage yesterday by claiming that the murderous campaign of the IRA should win "honour and praise". John McDonnell claimed it was terrorist "bombs and bullets" that brought peace to Ireland.

The left-winger brushed aside atrocities at Warrington and Enniskillen to praise the IRA as freedom fighters.

The relatives of victims expressed horror at comments, and Conservatives called on Tony Blair to condemn his backbencher.

In a speech to Republican sympathisers in London, the Hayes and Harlington MP said, "It was the bomb and bullets, and the sacrifice made by the likes of Bobby Sands that brought Britain to the negotiating table".

Colin Parry, whose son Tim was killed by an IRA bomb in Warrington in 1993, condemned Mr McDonnell, "He makes it sound like Tim and others were legitimate targets. How can a 12-year-old boy be a legitimate target?

There has been no condemnation concerning the comments of Mr John McDonnell by our Prime Minister. One must not upset the Principal Alpha Male Republicans, as they may withdraw their support. This New Labour MP has shown his total contempt for Forces of Law and Order. The only body to hold Law and Order in any esteem are Ulster Unionists, the forces of Conservatism, hated by our Prime Minister, Mr Blair.

The New Labour Home Secretary has withdrawn many Police from our streets, crime is out of control. Also, the Forces of Law and Order are immersed in a sea of bureaucracy, turning decent Policemen/women into pen pushers. New Labour government believe in statistics, forms and performance tables, which ensures that Police are kept off the streets, although left wing Chief Constables welcome this approach to modern day policing. Thugs, burglars and drug peddlers are protected by the courts. Any person who protects himself from a mugger is prosecuted by the Police. The Crown Prosecution Service has now been re-named the "Criminal Protection Society". Police have been very successful in pursuing motorists and prosecuting them. This is New Labour policy to get the Green vote.

Border controls have been dismantled, this is to allow large numbers of foreign invaders into our country. By allowing a large influx of foreign invaders New Labour hope to destroy the British character, culture, and its traditions. Also, in the future these foreign invaders will vote for New Labour. It's "goodbye Great Britain". One thing the Prime Minster said, which is very true, is that "Conservatives will never revoke any Laws or Acts of Parliament that Labour pass whilst in office." New Labour likes to use our Armed Services to promote Prime Minister Blair "as a World Statesman" but they do not appreciate them. Left Wing politicians have free speech, do-gooders have total freedom to wreck our society and scavenging legal aid lawyers fleece the taxpayer.

My grandfather told me the following verse, also it is known to many servicemen:

It is the soldier, not the reporter,
  who has given us freedom of the press.
It is the soldier, not the poet,
  who has given us freedom of speech.
It is the soldier, not the student activist,
  who has given us freedom to demonstrate.
It is the soldier, not the lawyer,
  who has given us the right to a fair trial.
It is the soldier, who salutes the flag,
  and whose coffin is draped by the flag,
who permits the protester to burn the flag.

*

We return now to our story in Northern Ireland. The Sergeant Major told me that I and three other marines would be accompanying the CO in his Rover group. I did not mind this duty as it was peaceful, apart from two incidents mentioned earlier on. We did the normal country roads, farms, and visited other unit locations. Some of the farms that we had visited on previous occasions still did not have telephones. The CO always emphasised the advantage of a telephone considering the isolation that they lived in. We all knew that change was slow and in the future. The seven days passed with no incidents, just routine.

After the CO's Rover group I was in charge of fatigues in camp, there were eight of us. At lunchtime whilst in the dining hall the Company Clerk came round telling Corporals and marines present that they had to be outside the Guardroom at two o'clock. The dress required was flak jacket, combat clothing and rifle. A rifle magazine with 20 rounds had to be in combat jacket pockets. We asked him why this was but he only said that Major INCOMPETENCE had told him to tell us, so we were all in the dark. We returned to our accommodation and dressed as required. At the Guardroom there were 30 of us, no-one knew what was going on. A Land Rover pulled up with Major INCOMPETENCE in it, and behind him were two trucks. He told one of the Corporals to load the personnel into the trucks and then both of the vehicles were to follow him. We found it a bit difficult to understand, but Major INCOMPETENCE was dressed in full Lovat uniform.

The vehicles travelled for nearly an hour, then stopped outside a cemetery. We looked around the surrounding area and immediately knew that we were in a Republican part of NI. Major INCOMPETENCE told everyone to disembark from the vehicles. The drivers were told to park up a side street. Normally the drivers and vehicles are not left alone in a Republican area like this, but we all assumed that this Officer-in-Charge knew what he was doing.

Once we had disembarked Major INCOMPETENCE told all of us to form three ranks, as though we were on a parade ground. We all knew that would make us an easy target for any sniper. Also, we noticed that there were no Senior Non-Commissioned Officers present. One of the Corporals asked Major INCOMPETENCE, 'Where is the radio operator?'

'You are to follow orders, not question my command,' was the reply.

We did not fall in as ordered, but spread ourselves along either side of the road. Major INCOMPETENCE realised that we were not going to do exactly as he said. He then told us, 'Proceed to the cemetery and stand on one side of the gates.' Once we had all arrived there he said, 'One of the Republican gunmen (that shot our comrades) is going to be buried this afternoon, and we are here to show the Republicans that we cannot be intimidated.' We all stood to one side of the cemetery gates, with a six-foot steel wire mesh fence behind us. There was no way out, only in, to the cemetery. We also knew that our presence at a Republican's funeral would be provocative, just like a red rag to a bull.

Major INCOMPETENCE walked up and down in front of us and 15 minutes later people started to arrive. They saw our presence outside the cemetery gates. We could see that our being there was provocative to the gathering crowd. They gathered together and then proceeded to approach us. Major INCOMPETENCE told us to stand firm as if nothing had happened. It was obvious to all present that he had never been in a tight spot anywhere since joining the Unit. This was his first time on the streets in Northern Ireland, and his dress, bearing, and manner was going to really upset these people.

Then the bad language started, and fists were shaken at us in defiance. I knew it would not stop there. Major INCOMPETENCE walked up and down in front of us, turning round and staring at the crowd, and they did not like this behaviour. There was an explosion heard in the area where our three vehicles had been parked, then smoke rose up. The three drivers came running down by the side of the cemetery fence, followed by a small group of young men. They immediately said, 'The vehicles have been set on fire, and we've had to leave because of the attack.'

The whole area was now filling up with Republican supporters. A half brick came over the top of the women and children, just missing Major INCOMPETENCE. He turned round to the crowd and said, 'Who threw this brick?' The crowd just laughed at him. Then more stones and bricks flew in our directions. We did not have any shields so we had to dodge the thrown missiles.

I saw a TV crew just to our right, about 30 yards away, filming us and the action. Two of our group had been hit with bricks and they were unconscious. Major INCOMPETENCE then froze, as he did not respond to any of our questions. The Corporals told the marines to pick up the injured personnel and carry them into the cemetery, behind the wire fence. Just before we left our present position I ran up to the TV crew, placing my arm around the shoulders of the man-in-charge. I turned him round so that he faced the crowd, and his cameraman followed suit. I immediately turned round and ran back to my colleagues. The hostile crowd saw the TV crew and turned their anger on them. They were pelted with bricks and stones, and the cameraman dropped his camera and ran. One TV crewmember collapsed after being hit with a brick, and once on the ground he received a beating from the crowd. The TV crew were the same ones that had been at the roadblock and cordon some weeks previously. They were now part of the news, instead of recording it.

We all went into the cemetery, closing the gates behind us. We then asked Major INCOMPETENCE what he was going to do. By now three personnel were unconscious, plus many more had cuts, and bruising to their faces and heads, as green berets do not protect a person from stones and half bricks. Luckily for us, one of the residents in the area had telephoned the RUC. Half an hour later a large number of Police and troops turned up. It did not take long for them to disperse the crowd and bring the situation under control, by the weight of numbers.

There was a full Army Colonel in command, he wanted to know who was in charge of our party. Major INCOMPETENCE went forward like a puppy with its tail between its legs. Three Ambulances had to take our injured away, a Corporal and a marine had each lost an eye. The Republicans had been firing ball bearings at us from catapults. Several personnel were kept in the Military hospital for a week. The TV crew were also removed in an Ambulance, to a civilian hospital.

Major INCOMPETENCE was taken to Army Headquarters, Northern Ireland, for an in-depth inquiry. The Major had acted on his own, without any intelligence reports, and with no approval from above. He had provoked trouble for no reason. Two men had each lost an eye, several others were injured, and three vehicles were destroyed. We returned back to camp at about six that evening, feeling very tired and fed up.

At nine that evening the Adjutant sent for me. I went over to his office, knocked on his door and went in. He had a big smile on his face. He told me, 'You, and a marine driver, are to be outside the Guardroom at five tomorrow morning. You are to take the Headquarters Company Commander to the docks at Belfast, for him to return to the mainland on the eight o'clock ferry.' Major INCOMPETENCE had resigned his commission, at his own request, rather than face a court of inquiry followed by a Court Martial. He had fallen out with the General Officer Commanding Troops, Northern Ireland, and the Commanding Officer of his Unit. Major INCOMPETENCE's career was now over. During his short time in the Unit he had only left camp twice, and each occasion had been a disaster. He had taken the coward's way out and resigned at his own request.

I arrived at the Guardroom at four thirty in civilian clothing, and a small blue Ford Escort was parked outside. The driver was in the Guardroom drinking a cup of tea, he was also in civilian clothing. I was offered a mug of tea, which I accepted. A few minutes later a marine arrived with some luggage, accompanied by our out-going Company Commander. We loaded the vehicle up. The Company Commander sat in the front passenger seat, and I made myself comfortable in a rear seat. It took us just over an hour to arrive at Belfast docks. We stopped at the passenger terminal and carried our out-going Company Commander's luggage in for him. We said 'Farewell,' but he did not reply. During our journey to the docks nobody had said a word.

*

As we commenced our return back to camp, all was well leaving Belfast. We travelled about five miles along the motorway, then came to a Police checkpoint. We stopped and produced our identity cards. We explained to the Police where we were bound for. They told us to take the next turn off and stay on a back road for the remainder of the journey. We left the Police roadblock and did as instructed, travelling along and admiring the countryside. Just as we went round a bend in the road, the back of our vehicle was thrown sideways. The driver turned the steering wheel in the opposite direction to correct his line of drive, and he put his foot hard down on the floorboards. We took off like a "bat out of hell". I heard a loud explosion and saw large lumps of earth falling on the vehicle and road.

We travelled at high speed for about four miles and then pulled over. I could smell something in the vehicle which was off-putting. I wound down my side window and asked the driver if he was alright. He said that all was well but he had "filled his pants and wet himself". Both of us were as white as sheets. We both got out of the vehicle and had a good laugh, staying put for about five minutes. The driver said that he was feeling better now, so we returned to camp. I told him to park the vehicle up and then have a shower. I reported what had occurred to the Adjutant, also showed him on the map where the incident had taken place. The Adjutant informed Army Headquarters and they sent a helicopter up to check the area.

The Adjutant sent for the driver and me just before supper, and informed us that the explosion had been a command detonation. The Army had located the spot where a person had sat to observe the road. He had to press a button to set off the explosive device. If we had been half a second earlier, the full force of the explosion would have caught our vehicle. The explosive device had been buried in the side of the embankment. The Commanding Officer came into the Adjutant's office and asked the driver if he had washed his pants yet. We all had a good laugh, the CO told both of us to call into his office on our way out. We left the Adjutant's office, I knocked on the CO's door and entered. The CO told us both to be seated, he went over to a filing cabinet and produced three glasses, plus a bottle of Hine brandy. Two large measures were poured and a small one. The two large measures were given to the driver and me. He told us to enjoy the brandy, and it would give us a good appetite for supper. He also emphasised how lucky we had been that morning. The brandy was most enjoyable, and it did give us a good appetite for supper.

*

Twenty marines and four Corporals were detailed off by our Sergeant Major to guard and assist the Police at one of their barracks. On the mainland it is known as a Police Station. Apparently the local Republicans had been targeting this Police Barracks, causing trouble and accusing the forces of law and order of all kinds of misdemeanours, which was normal for them. We were all told that it would be a seven day duty, start mid morning, finish late evening, commencing on Wednesday till the following Tuesday. Nobody was looking forward to this duty as we all knew the days would be long and boring, just waiting for something to happen. Everybody reasoned that only fools, madmen, and possibly Republicans cause trouble to a Police Barracks.

Two trucks delivered us to the Police Barracks, which was in a small market town between Belfast and the border. The front of the Police Barracks was covered with scaffolding, which extended 12 feet out from the main building. This scaffolding went up to the eaves of the roof, with corrugated metal sheeting bolted on to the outside of it. Also, the scaffolding was extended right over the roof and strong wire mesh placed on top of it and secured. The metal sheeting was an extra safeguard, and the wire mesh was to help to stop a mortar bomb. The main disadvantage was that electric lights had to be on at all times within the building. Cameras were also positioned on each corner of the building, which were monitored at all times.

The Chief Inspector-in-charge of the Police Barracks welcomed us all. He told us that over the next few days there were going to be demonstrations in the area, and the Police did not have enough manpower to control large numbers of people in any one area, as there was so much trouble going on in Northern Ireland. We were shown into the canteen, meals would be provided, and coffee and tea was available all day. The first two days were totally uneventful, the only highlight was a visit made by our CO and RSM. Friday was now upon us, and the Chief Inspector informed us that a delegation was expected late in the afternoon. A petition was to be presented, which also meant that there would be a demonstration. He required all of us to be just inside the main entrance, if needed we would be called forward.

The petition was presented and a crowd gathered outside. All outer doors to the Police Barracks were locked, barred and bolted, except the main entrance. The person who delivered the petition was outside, using strong words against the Police. The main speaker had not arrived yet, but a small crowd were being fired up. The crowd became restless and bored. Stones then started to be thrown at the Police Barracks, which caused a lot of noise, but no harm. One good thing about this Friday was that heavy rain was forecast for late in the afternoon.

The main speaker arrived, accompanied by three minders. As normal the Alpha Republican male and his bodyguards were better dressed than the local people in the area. The speaker clambered onto the roof of a van, which had been placed in position for him to address local inhabitants. The bullhorn was placed to his mouth, then he started to denigrate the forces of law and order. The man had been shouting for about five minutes when the sky became dark with clouds, the wind built up, then it started to rain like stair-rods. The crowd dispersed very rapidly. The speaker and minders were soaking wet. The speaker, who was wearing good quality expensive leather shoes with nice flat smooth soles, started to descend from the roof of the van. The roof and bonnet of the van were now wet and slippery, his footing slipped and he made an excellent swallow dive onto the hard surface of the road.

He landed face first and lay motionless for a couple of minutes, soaking up the heavy downpour of rain. His minders helped him to his feet. His face was covered with blood, also, there was a tooth on the ground. Whilst being assisted up, he was saying something to his minders, which we all knew would not be very complimentary. The minders had to support him back to his car, as he was very unsteady on his feet. We watched all this on the TV monitors, it was a shame that there were no video recorders around in those days. The speaker's vehicle was parked a few streets away in case of trouble, to ensure his car would not be damaged. The Chief Inspector was glad of the rain, and as he said, 'A good downpour does wonders to quieten and disperse crowds.' The remainder of the day passed quietly and without incident.

Saturday was now upon us. The Chief Inspector said, 'This is normally quiet as the public houses are full, and all the women are playing Bingo.' Late in the afternoon some youths started to throw half bricks and stones at the Police Barracks, causing an annoyance. The Chief Inspector told us to round up the teenagers and bring them in, as he wanted to give them a lecture on good behaviour. Nobody in the area was aware of our presence within the Police Barracks. The youths then became more troublesome and aggressive.

All 24 of us gathered just inside the main entrance, minus our webbing and rifles. We only had our combat clothing, flak jackets and a small truncheon to protect ourselves. On the count of three the main entrance was thrown open, we all burst out, and the youths froze as they did not expect this. A few turned to run, bumping into each other. There was complete chaos amongst the main body of troublemakers. We gathered up about 15 of them and escorted our captive teenagers into the Police Barracks. The Chief Inspector gave them a lecture on good behaviour. Then they were held in the cells for four hours before being released.

Once outside the Police Barracks they started shouting bad language, and also shouted that they had been badly treated, which was not true. The story of these youths being detained by the Police reached the nearby public house, frequented by Republican sympathizers. The elder brothers and fathers all arrived in mass, just after the pubs closed. Their shouts and abusive language was directed at the Police. The Chief Inspector instructed us to parade in front of the barracks, which we did. Our presence had the desired effect of quieting the crowd and slowly they dispersed. Half an hour later we returned back to our camp for a good night's sleep, after a more interesting day.

Sunday could often be a very bad day as the public houses were closed, the local troublemakers had time on their hands, and there was no Bingo. Mid afternoon a large crowd gathered outside the Police Barracks, and stones and bricks were being thrown, causing a lot of noise as they hit the corrugated sheeting. The action went on for about an hour, and the Sergeant on duty took four Police Constables out with him. The local Roman Catholic Priest arrived and managed to calm the crowd down. As he was addressing the crowd a large rock hit him on the head, rendering him unconscious, then more stones and half bricks followed. Two Police constables were also hit and their colleagues tried to help them, but they were set upon by the mob.

We could see what was going on via the TV monitors, all of us assembled at the main entrance. We gathered in a tight bunch and charged into the crowd, using truncheons as our only weapons. The men and youths around the Police were the first to be hit, some of them ran away, the remainder fell, injured, to the ground. The Police were helped up, and they managed to make their own way back into barracks. The Priest was carried into the barracks by marines and eight arrests were made. The Priest was taken to hospital, he was kept for 24 hours, receiving many stitches in his wound. We all knew that if we had not gone out to help the Police they would have been kicked to death. Nobody from our Unit wanted that.

Monday was a Bank Holiday. The Chief Inspector was expecting demonstrations and much trouble. The local Republicans were spreading rumours around the area of Police brutality against their youths, also saying that the Roman Catholic Priest had been arrested. The Republicans knew how to distort facts and turn them into fiction. As trouble was expected the Chief Inspector requested additional help from our Unit. Eight Corporals and 40 marines were sent to the barracks. We were all equipped with brown motorcycle style safety helmets, shields and truncheons. The Commanding Officer and Regimental Sergeant Major accompanied us.

Early in the afternoon a large group of women and children gathered outside the Police Barracks, shouting insults. After half an hour the local Republican rabble-rousers arrived, and about 100 men accompanied them. One stood on the bonnet of a car and addressed a crowd around him, for the first ten minutes he talked, then he turned his venom on the Police Barracks, also pointing. Shouts of Police brutality followed. Stones then started to fly from the men and youths behind the women. Slowly the women and children were being pushed towards the Police Barracks, while stones kept coming and hitting the corrugated sheeting. The CO ordered 20 marines to parade in front of the barracks with their shields and safety helmets on, which had a subduing effect for a few minutes. Then the stones started again. The women and children at the very front were being hit by stones coming from the rear, falling short of their intended target, and four of them collapsed.

The CO could see the crowd advancing forward and that the women would be trampled to death if nothing was done. The order was given for the 20 marines to advance 15 paces, and for each step forward they gave a beat on their shields with their truncheons. The crowd stopped and eight marines ran through the front rank, picked up the unconscious women and took them into the Police Barracks. Then the cry went up that their women had been arrested, not "rescued". More bricks and stones were thrown at the Police Barracks. All the Corporals and marines were now paraded in front of the main entrance. The barrage of stones and bricks became more accurate, but our shields, safety helmets and flak jackets protected us.

Then two youths ran to the front of the crowd and threw petrol bombs at us. The bottles landed in front of our cordon, the splash washed up onto three marines' trousers and set them alight. Two Policemen ran out with fire extinguishers and managed to douse the flames. The three marines were carried into the Police Barracks, all of them with burns to their legs. The bricks and stones kept coming, interspersed with the occasional petrol bomb. There was a loud sharp crack and one Corporal fell to the ground, being hit in the upper shoulder with a bullet. The pistol shot came from just behind the front row of women, and a young man was seen on the TV monitors to turn and run to the rear, then he disappeared up a side street. The CO ordered two ranks of ten with shields to form up, and the remainder of the men were to be behind them.

The line marched forward nine paces, beating their shields with the truncheons in unison. Once they stopped, personnel behind burst through the front rank and flayed into the crowd with their small truncheons. The crowd was dispersed and chased up side streets and alleyways for nearly 100 yards. Once everybody was well away the Corporals ordered the marines back to the Police Barracks.

Whilst we were returning two explosive devices were thrown over a wall. We were in a narrow alleyway with high walls on either side of us. Both devices were made up with a quarter pound of plastic explosives, detonator, short fuse and several large nails embedded inside. All of us started to run as both explosive devices went off within seconds of each other. One Corporal had a six inch nail embedded in his shoulder, which protruded into his lung. One marine had three nails in his back, he was picked up by us and carried into the Police Barracks. One other Corporal had a nail embedded in his leg, which jammed his leg in a straight stiff position, causing much pain and discomfort.

Once inside the Police Barracks the Police surgeon rendered medical assistance. The Corporal with the nail in his leg was one of the first to be attended to. The Police doctor just pulled the nail out, and immediately, feeling and life returned to his leg. The nail had trapped a nerve and locked his leg straight. The Corporal was given an antibiotic injection, no stitches, and was OK. The Corporal with a nail in his shoulder, together with the marine wounded in his back, were taken to the Military Hospital and operated on. Both of them, together with marines who had burns to their legs, were returned to the mainland. Sadly, the marine who had wounds to his back was to be given a medical discharge from the Corps.

We maintained a presence outside the Police Barracks for the next two hours, and once night closed in, personnel were withdrawn inside. That afternoon we had saved four women from being crushed underfoot, three marines suffered burns, one wounds to his back, and one Corporal with a nail in his shoulder. Plus another Corporal with a gun shot wound. I considered myself to be very lucky, as both bombs were near me.

The following day 40 of us were stationed at the Police Barracks, but no demonstrations took place, it was a very quiet period. The "Troops Out Movement" printed an article accusing the Police and armed forces of beating up four helpless women. Also, a peaceful demonstration was harassed and broken up. There was no mention of petrol bombs, shooting or bricks thrown. Again, another one-sided damaging allegation against the Forces of Law and Order.

*

After the Police Barracks duty the Adjutant told me that I was to man a roadblock to the north of the small town in which we were presently located. Another roadblock would also be in position at the southern entrance to the town, both would be in place for two days. The northern entrance had a road made up of dual carriageway, which was four miles long. I was to place the roadblock three miles up the dual carriageway in the southbound lane. My party would consist of fourteen marines and four Land Rovers. We had to man this roadblock from six in the morning till six in the evening. I was given a list of names of marines who were to accompany me. I went round the camp and told each one individually, they were not at all happy. Road checkpoints generate a lot of hostility from drivers and passengers of vehicles. Also, this town were in was a stronghold for Republicanism. We expected the worst.

We all assembled at the Guardroom at five thirty in the morning and collected our bag ration. The day was cold and windy. The position where the roadblock was to be set up was flat and exposed to the wind. It took us ten minutes to reach the position as there was no traffic about at that time of day. The warning signs were placed 200 yards north of our position, and one Land Rover was positioned facing towards oncoming traffic with its headlights on "dipped" as it was still dark. Two other Land Rovers were positioned 60 yards south, staggered with a gap between them, only allowing one vehicle at a time to pass through. I split the marines into three search teams of two, this way we could keep traffic queues short; also it was hoped to sweeten drivers up with quick checks. The remainder of marines were guards and lookouts. We were to look out for weapons and explosives. We all knew that nothing would be found as people in this town would soon be aware of our checkpoints. We were told that the average flow into the town was about 40 vehicles per hour. This could be coped with.

At about six thirty the first vehicle approached our checkpoint, it was a milk truck. A quick search of the cab and underside of this vehicle was carried out. The driver was friendly and understanding. Around seven fifteen the traffic started to build up, but not enough to cause queues, as our three search teams coped well. The main flow was from eight till nine, then it eased off. I estimated that we were receiving about 20 vehicles an hour, passing through our checkpoint. We received the normal amount of threats and abuse but we did not answer back. If they were very abusive the marines then took a long time searching their vehicles.

Later on in the afternoon Dr Ian Paisley drew up in his car with driver and bodyguards. He was like a breath of fresh air. He asked, 'What is going on.' He was told that it was a vehicle checkpoint, carried out under Emergency Regulations for

Northern Ireland. Dr Paisley said, 'I welcome any search of my vehicle. Go ahead. Also in the boot are some crates of beer, please take two for yourselves to enjoy this evening.' We found two crates of beer in his boot, and he said, 'Go ahead, take two out for yourselves to enjoy this evening.' We found the beer in the boot of his vehicle, two crates were removed immediately and placed in the back of a Land Rover. We thanked him for his generosity and understanding.

Whilst the search of his vehicle was going on he went round and thanked each marine individually for the work they were doing in Northern Ireland. He shook hands with every one of us. Before he left, Dr. Ian Paisley came over to me and stated that the British Armed Forces were doing a splendid job under hard conditions, with little help from the government in power. It was a nice change to be welcomed, rather different from the hostile reception we received from most drivers. The gentleman went on his way, waving as he left us.

We were now getting fed up and tired, also the daylight was fading. The vehicle headlights were turned on to prevent any cars or trucks running into us. At six we brought in the warning signs and embarked in Land Rovers for our return journey to camp. We were all glad to be going back to camp at the end of a long cold day. Once we arrived back in camp the Sergeant Major was there, he told us to park the Land Rovers up and all of us had to go into the Guardroom. We all went into the large front room of the Guardroom, there were two men dressed in smart civilian clothing. When they turned round I recognised one, he had been my Company Commander in Malta. He saw me and came over and shook my hand. He told all present that he was the new Second in Command of the Unit. I knew that he was a good down to earth Officer, and reliable. The Sergeant Major introduced the other gentleman as our new Company Commander, he welcomed us back into camp. Also, he said that he knew we had had a long tiring day, he would not detain us. I saluted him, then we all left the Guardroom, split the crates of beer up amongst ourselves, then went off to prepare for the following day.

We left the Guardroom at five thirty in the morning and set up our roadblock in the same place. The day was cold with heavy rain. Drivers in vehicles that were stopped thought it was a big joke, us in the cold rain and them in nice warm cars. We ensured that they stood in the rain while their vehicles were searched. Also, if there were any passengers in their cars they joined them. The day went slowly, we had our ponchos on, but rain still managed to penetrate our clothing. At times it rained very hard, but mostly it was a steady downpour. Mid morning four Land Rovers drew up. The CO, the new 2 i/c and the Company Commander disembarked. The CO asked how things were going, and told me that there were two large flasks of hot coffee in the rear Land Rover. I told the marines to go two at a time and have a cup of coffee each, they welcomed this refreshment. I was the last one to go. After my coffee I returned back to my post.

A large sand/gravel truck then arrived and stopped at our checkpoint; the new Company Commander said that he would carry out the search of this vehicle. He approached the vehicle, and the driver wound down his door window and shouted abuse at him. When the Company Commander was directly below the driver's cab window the truck driver put his head out and spat in his face. The driver was told to dismount from his cab, he thought that he was going to receive a beating, but the Company Commander wiped the spit from his face then climbed up into the cab and drove it onto the hard shoulder. The truck driver was told to release the locking catches on the tailboard and stand well clear. The load of sand was then tipped onto the hard shoulder and the truck body was lowered back into position. Just behind the cab was a shovel, and as the Company Commander disembarked he took the spade down, he went to the driver and told him to start shovelling the sand back onto his truck. He didn't know how to react, but he obeyed his instructions.

He was overweight, bald and had a very large stomach. Also, he had not washed or shaved for a few days. I went over to him and said, 'Now's a good opportunity for you to get in shape.' Then the Company Commander said to him, 'Watch your Ps and Qs in future, and refrain from spitting.' The keys to the truck were handed to me and the driver was told that he would have them returned once all the sand was back on his vehicle. The CO's group left after about an hour.

Both new Officers were well liked and respected, in later years they finished their careers as Generals in the Royal Marines. The story of the sand/gravel truck driver went around our Unit, it was something good to relate.

At around six it was time to pack up, the sand/gravel truck driver had just over a quarter of his load left to shovel onto his vehicle. He was sweating and also very unhappy. We all went over to him and I told him, 'We have your name and address and the sand has to be cleared up,' then we gave him his ignition keys. We left and returned back to camp, leaving the sand/gravel truck driver still shovelling his load back onto his vehicle. The end of another day, tired, wet and miserable.

*

Two days later I had to take a Corporal and a marine to the docks in Belfast, as they were returning to the mainland. This involved two Land Rovers and six personnel. We left camp very early and travelled to Belfast docks, arriving just after six. We said goodbye to our mates, they went into the passenger terminal, then we all proceeded to a small café in the docks and had tea.

The return journey took us part of the way through Belfast, there was very little traffic around at this time, as it was still very early. We turned into the main road, which was wide, and full of prestigious buildings. As we approached a large hotel a man ran into the road, waving his arms at us. We pulled over. He came up to my vehicle and said, 'A suitcase bomb has just been delivered to the hotel.' I got out of my vehicle then told the driver to go 200 yards up the road and park in the centre with headlights on full. I told him to stop all vehicles and people approaching the hotel or entering the area. He would be accompanied by a marine riding guard in the rear of the Land Rover. I then went to the rear Land Rover telling the driver to park 200 yards to the rear, stopping everyone from entering the area. I told Marine Brown to come with me.

I asked the man from the hotel who he was, and he said that he was the Night Receptionist. He also told me that there were about 60 guests and staff within. I asked him to show me where the bomb was and he took me back into the hotel entrance lobby. Just by the reception desk was a large suitcase standing upright. He said that a man had come in, put the suitcase down, told him that it contained high explosives, then turned round and run out of the hotel entrance.

I saw a red fire alarm box on the wall, Brown also saw it. He went over and smashed the glass cover, setting the main fire alarm off. Guests and staff started to come into the hotel lobby, they were told to run out into the road and away from the building, there was no time to explain why, all would be revealed later. The Night Receptionist then told me that everyone had left; then we ran out of the front entrance. As Brown and I were running away from the hotel a young girl was running towards us. Brown and myself grabbed her under her arms, lifted her up and ran with her between us. She was facing towards our rear.

As we got near our Land Rover there was a loud explosion. We could hear glass and debris flying around in front of the hotel and onto the road. We lowered the young girl to the ground, whereupon she told us that she had left her handbag in the hotel. Then she started to cry. Brown put his arms around her telling her, 'The shops are full of handbags, whereas healthy, fit, beautiful young females are hard to come by.'

We were all as white as sheets, a little shocked. The guests and staff stood together, frightened, shaken, but safe. One of the marines had gone to a public telephone box, phoned the Police, and instructed them to inform the Fire Brigade and Ambulance. Five minutes later the Police arrived followed by the Fire Brigade, and a Senior Police Officer took control of the situation. Flames and smoke were now coming from the hotel, it took the Fire Brigade nearly two hours to get it under control. Luckily, the Ambulance was not required, by clearing the building there were no casualties. The Police arranged for hotel guests to be billeted in other hotels in the area.

The Senior Police Officer asked me, ''What happened here?'

I said, 'When I heard about the bomb I cleared the hotel building of guests and staff, and set up the roadblocks, the man who can help you most is the Hotel Receptionist.

We had been in the main road for nearly three hours now, and the Police asked us to accompany them back to one of their barracks to make our statements. Once we arrived at the Police Barracks the Inspector-in-charge asked which Unit we were from and where we were billeted. He said that he would ring the Unit and put their minds at rest concerning our whereabouts. We were all given tea and a hot bacon sandwich. We gave our statements, and one of the Police Sergeants told us some interesting stories concerning Republicans. We returned back to camp late that afternoon.

One of the stories told to me by the RUC Sergeant concerning Republicans was this:

As you know, they do not like Police or any form of law and order. Their main aim in life is to attack, disrupt and destroy forces of the Crown. This story concerns a helicopter, a good idea and poorly thought out plan. One of their bright sparks, an Alpha male, thought it would be a good idea to bomb a RUC Barracks. It was decided that this mission would be carried out, but they needed some form of air transport. They could not legitimately hire an aircraft or any form of air transport. Then this "bright" Alpha male decided to hi-jack a helicopter.

The Yellow Pages were checked for leads relating to hire firms that had helicopters, and four companies were found. The "boys" were sent out to watch and study each helicopter hire firm. Three were found to be moderate sized firms, and they operated from Belfast's main airport, "Aldergrove". The fourth firm was a small one-man operation, which was carried out from a small airfield North of Belfast. The small 4-seater helicopter was owned by a gentleman whose main income was from carrying fare paying passengers to Liverpool Airport and the Isle of Man, and ferrying people around the counties of Northern Ireland, as well as doing surveys for the Ministry of Agriculture. The airfield was observed for nearly two weeks, so that information could be gathered on routine and methods of work by this one-man operation. It was observed that in the late afternoon the helicopter had maintenance carried out, mainly by its owner. Sometimes an engineer would arrive and do a full maintenance schedule and survey, to comply with air transport regulations. At the end of each day the aircraft would be fuelled up and stowed in a small hangar. The Republicans followed the owner home at the end of each day, and also observed him leaving his home early each morning.

The Alpha males decided that a bomb with 70 pounds of explosives in it would be dropped on a RUC Barracks near the border with Southern Ireland. The RUC had several observation posts near the border, which were causing a considerable amount of trouble in the area for Republicans. This exercise would show forces of the Crown how vulnerable they were. A milk churn was obtained and filled with fertiliser compound, which is very volatile, also an electric timer and detonator were fitted, with an anti-handling device. This would ensure that once the timer was set, it could not be switched off or tampered with.

The helicopter pilot left his home early each morning and drove eight miles to his airfield. As he parked his car four men jumped him, wearing balaclava hoods, he immediately knew they were Republican thugs. He was now instructed to take his aircraft out of the hangar, which he did. Once out of its hangar and on the landing pad, a small white van drove in and parked with its rear doors towards the helicopter, which had four seats and two large doors. It accommodated one passenger in the front and two others in the rear seats, and there was very little room for anything else. The pilot was told to take his place behind the controls, while the milk churn was loaded on. He had to move the front passenger seat forward to enable the milk churn to be loaded onto the aircraft. Once the bomb was loaded and wedged behind the front passenger seat the man who had the duty of setting the timer sat in the rear next to it.

The pilot told the Republican thug-in-charge of the hi-jack party that only two passengers, the milk churn and the pilot could fly in the aircraft as there was not enough power or room to carry five men. The Republican-in-charge said, 'I will sit in the front passenger seat next to the pilot and give instructions as to our target destination.'

The two men who were to remain behind said that they were looking forward to a trip in a helicopter, and now they were going to miss all the fun and excitement. They were both told to wait for the return of the helicopter.

The Republican-in-charge had the keys to their vehicle, which would take them all back home after the bombing mission. They were very unhappy, as this was their highlight of the week. The front passenger sat in his seat and the pilot told both Republicans that they must have their seat belts on, as it was standing instruction from the Ministry of Transport. Also, he told them that he had to ensure the front passenger door was securely closed. He reached across and gently checked the door, but unbeknown to the front passenger, he also pushed up a small locking pin under the door handle, which locked the door securely from inside. Both passengers agreed that they had to follow safety instructions. The pilot thought to himself that they were like all passengers, but these were hi-jackers, about to use his aircraft for a criminal offence.

The helicopter took off, the pilot was told not to use his radio, then he was given instructions to fly towards the southern border. Once the aircraft had been airborne for ten minutes the exact location was given, and the purpose of the hi-jack. The rear seat passenger asked the pilot to inform him when they were near the intended target, giving two minutes warning.

The pilot asked him, 'Why do you need two minutes warning?'

'To set the timer,' was the reply.

The pilot knew that the milk churn could not be thrown out of the helicopter whilst airborne, as it had been placed in the rear with great difficulty. He decided to check the area below for an emergency landing, and to keep this information to himself. Two minutes from the drop zone the pilot informed them that they were near the target. The man in the rear seat said, 'Timer set.'

The pilot saw a field directly below, and as he put his helicopter into a steep emergency dive he told the Republican next to him, 'I am not going to die with you two fools.' Then the penny dropped with the two Republicans as they realised that the milk churn could not be taken out of the helicopter.

The front seat passenger shouted to the man in the rear, 'Switch the timer off.'

'It's impossible, it's fitted with an anti-handling device,' was his reply.

The helicopter landed in a field heavily, the pilot threw off his harness, pushed the door open and dived out, ensuring that he kept low because of the turning rotor blades above him. He crawled away from the helicopter; and once clear of the blades he stood up and ran as fast as possible. He came across a shallow ditch and threw himself into it. The two Republicans left behind were frantically trying to open the passenger door, but could not.

The explosion happened just a few seconds after the pilot fell into the ditch. He felt a change in air pressure above himself. The explosion destroyed the helicopter and killed both Republicans. Once the debris had stopped falling the pilot stood up and made his way to the RUC Barracks, which they had intended to destroy. He told the Officer-in-charge what had happened, and informed him that two Republican thugs were waiting at his landing pad for the safe return of the helicopter. The police arrested the two Republicans, who gave a large amount of information to the RUC. Both sang like canaries. The exercise had cost the Republicans a great deal, and for once the forces of the Crown benefited.

The pilot received a commendation from the Chief Constable of the RUC, also compensation was claimed under a scheme operated for terrorists' acts of violence in NI. The pilot owner now operates out of Belfast main airport, for security reasons. The Republicans came off very badly, thankfully. The good guy won for a change.

*

Our Unit was spread out over a large area and many minor incidents occurred which were of no real importance, but silly and stupid. One thing all services have in common is waiting. Sometimes in barracks, and sometimes in the backs of trucks or on street corners. The waiting is normally for an event, an attack, or just to be addressed by somebody in an important position.

One of our Medical Assistants told the boys in the NAAFI about an incident that took place one morning:

The Unit Doctor, a Surgeon Lieutenant, Royal Navy, was waiting at a street corner to be collected and taken to Musgrave Park Military Hospital, to visit one of our injured personnel. With him were three members of his staff, and four marines. They ensured that they stood well back on the pavement so that no passers by were hindered or inconvenienced. The group of servicemen were talking amongst themselves, cracking jokes and not bothering anybody. Two local men came along the road, both of them were loud and boisterous after leaving a public house. One of the men was very large, with a big pot belly, and the other man was of average build. Both of them had one thing in common, they stank of stale sweat, tobacco and drink. They were not drunk, but happy and in full control of themselves.

They approached the group of servicemen, at first both were polite and amicable. Both of them stated that they had served in the Royal Navy doing their National Service. The large fellow saw the badge of rank on the doctor's shoulders and started to abuse him. The marines and medical staff tried to calm the man down, and advised his mate to take him away. The large fellow became more aggressive and abusive, also telling everyone present that he hated Officers as they had done him a mischief whilst he was in the Royal Navy. One of the marines told him to go away, as his big mouth would land him in trouble. The big fellow then tried to get through the cordon of personnel around our Unit doctor, to have a go at him, but he was blocked. More insults followed.

The Unit Doctor was a man of six foot four inches, well built and liked by all ranks. He was very fit as he took part in all physical training and played rugby for the Royal Navy/Royal Marines. The doctor was by now becoming very annoyed, as the large fellow continued with abusive insults towards him. The doctor told the personnel that he would remove his insignia of rank from his shoulders to allow the big fellow to have a go at him. The big fellow now became silent. The doctor removed his insignia of rank, handed his personal weapon to a member of his staff and stepped forward. The large fellow was stiff with fear as his accomplice told him to sort the officer out. The large fellow now realised that his bluff had been called. He just stood there, and went as white as a sheet. Then he turned and ran down the road. His accomplice was told to follow him. The doctor, his staff and the marines then had a good laugh, all ended well, no harm to anybody, except the pride of the big fellow.

*

One night, a patrol from our unit, working in the southern part of the town we were billeted in, was shot at. The shooting took place just before midnight, and this raised concerns with High Command. It was thought that the Republicans now had sophisticated night sights, which would enable them to shoot soldiers from a distance, during darkness. The Corporal-in-charge of the patrol reported that the shooting happened as they were passing along a white painted wall. The shot came from a side street, which led on to a main road. On investigation it was discovered that the wall, which was 30 feet long and eight feet high, had been painted white the week before the shooting happened. The wall ran along the side of a pavement on a main road. Also, at night this area is well lit by three streetlights.

It was assumed that the three painters who painted the wall worked for the local council, as they had placed warning notices out. Also, they wore white overalls and had all the necessary equipment for a professional paint job. They had been friendly and chatted to passers by, and were also courteous to our passing foot patrols. It had taken them three days to paint the wall, which is the right speed for local government workers, they had made a good professional finish to their work. From the side street a sniper would have a good shot at a silhouetted person wearing dark clothing against a white backdrop.

During the day there was a constant flow of traffic using the main road, but after eleven at night – none. At night you could not see up the side street as there are no streetlights in it. During the day the side street did not offer any cover from view. It was assumed that the sniper was 150 yards up the side street, positioned in the centre, firing straight into the main road. The shot was nearly successful, missing a marine target by half an inch at head height. A bullet indentation was left in the wall.

I was told that I was to take a four-man foot patrol out, and the Unit 2 i/c and new Company Commander would accompany us. We left just after nine in the morning, and the two Officers were dressed the same as ourselves. We walked around the northern area first, also meeting the regular foot patrol in that section. The Officers had a friendly talk with the Corporal patrolling the area, then we proceeded to the southern part of the town. It took us a further half an hour to arrive at the white wall. Both Officers inspected the area closely. They commented on the excellent standard of paintwork finish to the wall. A truly professional job. They could see how a person wearing dark clothing would be silhouetted against a white background. We returned back to camp at midday and the 2 i/c told me to report to him later that afternoon.

At four I went over to his office. He told me that at midnight I was to take a painting party out. It would consist of my four-man patrol, six marines with long poles, rollers and trays. Also, one marine would bring a .22 rifle along and shoot out the three streetlights. A Land Rover would follow along behind with 20 gallons of black matt paint.

Just before midnight the painting party met at the Guardroom. The painters had overalls on, and were carrying a paint roller on a six-foot pole and a clean roller tray. The Land Rover arrived with the 20 gallons of black matt paint in four drums. We all set off and arrived at the white wall just after midnight. The three streetlights were shot out and rendered useless. The wall still reflected some light from it as there was a full moon out that night with a clear sky. A person would still be silhouetted against the wall on a bright moonlit night. The marines placed the paint trays on the pavement and the Land Rover driver filled them up with black matt paint. They started opposite the side street where the shot came from and worked in either direction away from this point.

It took about two hours to paint the wall, also the pavement had a generous amount of matt black paint deposited on it. The paint was oil based, it would take a long time to dry, and the weather was cold at this time of year. We returned back to camp, some of the marines that had used rollers had just about as much black paint on themselves as the wall.

In the morning the local council was informed of our action, also requested to place barriers next to the wall to prevent people getting paint on their clothing. The local council had not been informed the previous day as they could not be trusted to keep our painting party secret. It was assumed that there were some Republican sympathizers amongst them. The whole operation had been a success.

*

Two days after our painting venture six of us in two Land Rovers had to rendezvous at a grid reference, which was a road junction, four miles from the camp, with the Royal Ulster Constabulary. We had to be at the road junction at five in the morning. We left the Guardroom at four thirty, to ensure that we arrived at the rendezvous point on time. To our surprise the RUC were waiting for us when we arrived at four forty five. There were 12 of them in two Land Rovers. I reported to the Officer-in-charge, a Chief Inspector. He told me to follow his vehicles as we were going to search a farmhouse, about five miles away from our present position. Our two Land Rovers tagged on behind the RUC, and after half an hour we turned off the tarmac road onto a farm track. The farm track was hard, it did not appear to have had many vehicles using it as there had been a lot of rain previously, which would have rendered the surface soft and boggy. All four vehicles drove into a courtyard which had a lot of weeds and grass growing in it. It was obvious that this was not a working farm.

In the courtyard there was parked a brand new Range Rover, outside the main entrance to the farmhouse. The Chief Inspector asked me to conduct a sweep of the surrounding farm buildings. These were disused sheds and two barns next to the farmhouse. We searched all of the building very carefully, always aware of booby traps. The farm buildings were mainly full of old machinery, rubbish and a few bales of straw. It took us just over an hour to search and check the buildings. I informed the Senior Police Officer that the buildings were safe and clear.

He then instructed his officers to follow him; one of them carried a battering ram to break down doors. They were just about to break the door down when it opened. A man stood in the doorway, he was dressed in a very expensive silk dressing gown. He immediately demanded to know, 'What is going on?' The Chief Inspector handed him a search warrant, which gave the Police authority to search and make arrests. The farmhouse was very old, large and dilapidated. It had been built in the days when families were large, and when many people worked on one farm.

The Senior RUC Officer said to us, Police drivers will remain outside and guard vehicles in the courtyard, and you can guard this man in the house.' We all moved into the kitchen; the Police searched it but nothing was found. The kitchen was very large with a flagstone floor, an old sink with one cold water tap over it, and two Welsh dressers against a wall. Against the far wall was an old wood burning stove and oven, it was rusty. It was obvious that the farmhouse had been vacant for many years. In the middle of the kitchen was a large oak table with ten wooden chairs around it. Next to one of the Welsh dressers was a newly installed electric power point. The Chief Inspector split his men up into four search teams, they then left the kitchen to carry out their work.

The suspect pulled up a chair and invited us all to sit down, which we did. Everyone was seated and quiet, nobody said a word for about half an hour. Then the suspect said, 'Water and electricity is laid on, and there is an electric kettle, teapot, milk and mugs in the Welsh dresser.' One of the marines got up and did the honours of making tea. The suspect did not have a Northern Irish accent, he was cultured and polite. Whist we were all drinking our tea he started to talk. He was not aggressive or full of hatred, which you normally receive from Republicans. He made three statements to all present which were:
1. The Republicans would win the battle as they were prepared to carry out atrocities. If caught, none of them would ever fact the death penalty.
2. English politicians were afraid of public and world opinion, especially from the USA. They lacked backbone and determination.

3. The cost of maintaining a large amount of troops, together with an increased Police force was detrimental to the economy.

We all agreed that he was right, even the present Secretary of State for Northern Ireland showed more concern for Republicans than Loyalists. We sat there for a further two and a half hours, then one of the Police Constables came in. The Constable asked me to take the suspect up to his room so that he could dress. I and one marine escorted him upstairs, his bedroom was at the end of a long corridor. He said, 'This farmhouse has nine bedrooms, two attic rooms and six large rooms downstairs.' His room was small and contained a single bed with sleeping bag, a wardrobe, a chair, a washbowl and pitcher of water. Also, an electric cable had been run into the room, this was for an electric heater and lighting. A great deal of preparation and planning had been done to accommodate this person with basic comfort. He washed and opened the wardrobe. In it hung a good quality suit and a very expensive Crombie overcoat. He dressed, then we all proceeded back downstairs.

The Police were all sitting in the kitchen drinking tea. On the table were five cardboard boxes sealed with special RUC tape. The suspect saw the boxes and said, 'I see you have found the money.

The Chief Inspector replied, 'Yes we have. It will be counted back at the Police Barracks.'

To which the suspect answered, 'I can save you the trouble, there is $250,000 there.'

The money was raised in the USA as the Yanks think that Northern Irish people are fighting for freedom and justice. A large amount of money was raised by educated people in Northern America, but they all have one thing in common, Irish ancestors. They have an image of their kinfolk fighting evil oppressors.

The Chief Inspector then told the suspect, 'We have been after you for a long time, as you are the main Republican paymaster and banker.'

The suspect replied, 'I will be free within 24 hours, it is not a crime to have US dollars.'

Once we were outside the Chief Inspector told me that they had located this man by chance. His Range Rover had been seen twice going along this road, but never made it to the end. Just before dark the previous day his vehicle was followed from a distance, and it was seen taking the farm track. A helicopter flew over the farm and it was confirmed that the Range Rover was parked in the courtyard. The rest is now history. I mentioned that the suspect had no accent and was told that he had attended the best public school, and that he was a fully qualified Chartered Accountant. But his loyalty was misplaced.

We all got into our respective vehicles, two Policemen were in the Range Rover. The suspect under arrest was in the rear of a RUC Land Rover. The Police proceeded to Belfast and we returned to camp.

*

On Company orders I was detailed off for another 72-hour guard, commencing the following morning. At nine in the morning the Sergeant Major came over to the Guardroom and told me to be ready at ten o'clock to take a patrol out. The patrol would have in it the new 2 i/c and Company Commander. Three marines and I were to go around the perimeter of the camp and then up to where the trees had previously been. All of us proceeded as planned, then up the hill. Ten minutes later we were at the tree stumps at the top of the hill. Even without the trees there was still a good view into the camp, but now there was nowhere a person could take cover from, or hide.

Both Officers admired the view, the 2 i/c asked, 'Which tree had the viewing platform in it?' I pointed to the middle stump. Both agreed that whoever put up a platform knew what they were doing. From our present position all movement within the camp could be seen, from the main entrance down to the motor transport compound at the bottom of the camp. One of the marines then pointed out to both Officers that we had been expected to tow a vehicle full of explosives from the main entrance gate to the bottom of the camp. The 2 i/c said that this would not have been a good idea. We also pointed out that if we had placed a vehicle at the bottom of the camp we would have helped the Republicans to achieve a good result. We all returned to the camp and I settled down to the routine of Guard Commander. The remainder of the first day passed quietly, so did the second.

On the third day I went for an early supper at four in the afternoon. Returning back to the Guardroom everyone takes the direct route between accommodation huts. Outside the Unit Padre's hut there was a young Red Setter puppy, about ten weeks old, tied up. The Padre had purchased the dog about four weeks previously. The puppy was only tied up outside his hut when the weather was good whilst the Padre was away on his duties. I stopped and patted the dog, giving him some affection and tickling his neck. The young dog always enjoyed attention, and he was very friendly. I was with the puppy for about a couple of minutes, then it was time to return to the Guardroom.

I proceeded on my way and turned right at the end of the hut. Just as I had gone two steps around the corner there was a loud explosion. I froze as I was unsure at first where it had come from. Then there was the sound of glass and stones flying around. I turned around and moved to the corner of the hut and looked down the route I had just taken. There was a hole in the ground, about a foot deep and two feet across. Glass and pieces of wood were lying all over the area between the huts. Then I noticed the dog lying on its side, it looked alright at first. When I got close to it I saw a large sliver of glass had gone into its neck. It was motionless. Checking the puppy close up I knew that it was dead. The Unit Doctor checked it later and said that it was a clean kill. Apart from the death of the dog no-one was injured. Again I was lucky. If I had stayed with the dog a few more seconds I would now be a statistic. The following day carpenters and glaziers repaired the damage to the huts.

The explosive device had been launched from a mortar on the back of a truck. The vehicle had been placed 300 yards north of the main entrance, between some residential houses. The vehicle used had been stolen, it was the type of open-backed truck which carried commercial sand and gravel. It had been taken from a builder's yard two weeks previously. On the rear body three mortar tubes, made out of four-inch steel pipes, had been set up on a crude wooden framework. This type of amateur mortar is very dangerous as they sometimes explode on launch or blow up within the tubes. Also, it was impossible to predict with accuracy where the bomb would land. Only one of the tubes was successful in launching its mortar bomb. The other two had failed due to poor wiring.

The houses nearest to the truck had two front room windows damaged. No concern had been shown for occupants of the properties nearby. One witness said they had seen the gravel truck stop, two men jumped out of the cab and one climbed onto the rear body. He had been on the back of the truck for nearly a minute then he jumped down. Both men ran down the road to where a car was waiting for them. Once they were on board the vehicle it sped off in the direction of Belfast. Just as the car left there was a loud explosion, followed a few seconds later by another, down the hill. The one down the hill missed me but killed a dog. Bomb Disposal made the mortar vehicle safe, then it was taken away for inspection and examination by the RUC. Everyone knew that this was more handiwork carried out by the Republicans. Thankfully it had not fully succeeded. The Padre was upset at the loss of his dog, everybody in the camp now started to call Republicans "Dog Killers".

I completed my guard duty. The following morning I was required to do the bank run, which was uneventful and completely successful. After a Guard everyone had the afternoon off to catch up on their sleep.

*

At around three in the afternoon six of us sleeping in our room were shaken awake by the Petty Officer Medical Attendant. He told all of us to get dressed and assemble outside the Guardroom. I asked, 'What is going on?'

He just said, 'You will be informed once you are at the Guardroom.

We all dressed, and everyone was moaning. We proceeded to the camp Guardroom where all the Unit's Senior Officers were also present, plus all Medical Staff. There was a total of 40. The RSM told us to bunch together as the Unit Doctor was going to speak to all present. The doctor said, 'There has been a bomb at a bus station which has caused damage and devastation. We are going to help clean up the area.' Four trucks arrived, together with six Land Rovers. Everybody embarked and we left the camp.

The small market town we were going to I knew well, as we passed through it very often. The people living there were all Loyalists, and were friendly and polite. The town was clean and well kept. Once a week was market day. There was also a cattle market which was open twice a week. The farmers in this area were all Loyalists.

Today was market day and farmers' cattle market, which meant that there would be lots of people in town. So far this town had been spared all the trouble; no incidents, shootings or rioting. The Republicans had now caught up with the innocent inhabitants of this small town. As we approached the town Ambulances were passing us, heading for hospitals in surrounding areas. As we approached the bus station it started to become obvious that some terrible event had taken place. Some buildings we passed had tiles dislodged from their roofs and windows broken. Further in there were other buildings with walls collapsed, and debris all over roads and gardens.

We stopped near the bus station. Large areas were cordoned off by Police. Firemen and Royal Engineers were working to make buildings safe, and more Ambulances were leaving the area. A Senior Police Officer spoke to our CO. They liaised for about five minutes. We all disembarked from our vehicles, waiting for further instructions, then our CO told us all to gather round. We were not addressed by the CO but by the Unit Doctor, who told us that two large suitcase bombs had been placed at the bus station about two hours ago. So far nearly forty people had been taken away in Ambulances, severely injured, some of them would not live. Also, there were other people still left behind in the debris of the bus station. They were all dead. He did not know how many dead were still in the bus station.

The medical staff then distributed surgical gloves to us, and we were given plastic bags. A marine asked, 'What are the plastic bags for?'

The doctor replied, 'The people you are going to recover will be in bits, not whole bodies.' We then realised what we were actually going to do. It was a shock to all of us.

We slung our rifles over our backs and entered the devastation of the bus station. There were three buses still smouldering after having fires extinguished by Firemen. The first thing we smelt was the rancid smell of burnt flesh. It turned our stomachs. A few of the boys vomited – nothing to be ashamed of. We paired off and commenced the horrible task of recovering body parts. I found a complete arm, still with a watch on its wrist and rings on the fingers. It belonged to a woman. Once we had a body part in a bag it was placed on a stretcher. Once the stretcher was full of body parts it was then placed in an undertaker's van, which was driven to a hospital mortuary. Hospital Pathologists had the terrible task of trying to make a body match up, and of identifying the individual. We had to pick between debris to recover some of the body parts. Really small pieces of human flesh would be eaten by birds. We stayed for nearly an hour and a half when the doctor came round saying, 'It's time to go.' We were told that many people had died at the bus station. How do we know? Well, it was done on a head count, recovered from the devastation. We returned back to camp, not many went for supper that evening. Everyone felt demoralised and totally drained of energy.

Republicans always favour the bullet and bomb. Southern Europeans prefer a knife. A bullet is always in the back or fired by a sniper from a distance. The bomb is either a suitcase or mortar, and explosives are hidden in drains and sometimes delivered by proxy. Leaving a suitcase full of explosives at a bus station, then walking away, shows how sick and sad Republicans are. Republicans do not like close quarter battle. It takes more nerve to stick a knife into somebody, as the assassin has to get close up.

That evening I went over to the NAAFI to watch the evening news on TV. Someone said, 'Where are the Labour MPs who support Republicans? We don't hear any condemnation from them, just silence.'

*

The Sergeant Major sent for me stating that I would be on duty for the next couple of weeks at the Army Military Hospital. I would have three marines in my team doing a duty on, duty off, each day. The three marines who were to accompany me shared the same room as myself. The duty would run from eight in the morning till eight the following day, followed by a day off. This duty was considered safe, boring, uneventful, and it was in the warm. Also, we would have two meals in the hospital, lunch and supper, plus tea or coffee whenever we required it. I spoke to the three marines, also pointing out what our requirements were whilst on duty. We had to control the one and only entrance in, by an electric switch. We were responsible for all weapon security, and nobody was to take any weapon past us. We had to search all non-military personnel entering the hospital, and any parcels which might be delivered had to be checked and signed in by the Store Sergeant. On no account were we to accept any store or parcels.

The following day we set off to the hospital. The Corporal I relieved was glad to leave. He had been doing this duty for four weeks. He said, 'It gets boring and tedious as nothing ever happens.'

All four of us said, 'Good, that's what we want.'

We decided to split the 24 hours into four six-hour shifts. To decide who would go first we flipped a coin. I lost. The two marines on the opposite shift said that they would like to start ton the second set of watches.

At first it was very quiet, then at around nine thirty visiting military personnel started to arrive. They were mainly coming to see injured soldiers from their Units. They proved their weapons (showed that they were unloaded and safe), and we put them into the rack and gave them a numbered disc. We were able to see who was approaching by a TV camera, this was in the early days of CCTV. The electric door control switch was clicking every five minutes, allowing people in and out. Around one o'clock everything went quiet after a very busy morning. There is not much to tell but there are four events worth mentioning.

The first evening the marine and I were sat at the main entrance desk talking. It was very quiet. At around nine three young soldiers who were patients approached us, and wanted to know if we were going to make any coffee. We said it was about time we had a cup. I went and filled the kettle up and my mate said that he would make the coffee as I was hopeless. Whilst drinking coffee the normal questions came from the young soldiers, asking what unit we were and how long had we been here? We answered all their questions, all three were very young. I said that it was now our turn to ask questions.

Soldier number one was from the Royal Engineers. He had been shot through both hands whilst driving a truck. The bullet had passed through both hands, shattering bones and cutting tendons. He said that from now on he would only have limited use of his hands, and it had been his ambition to be a carpenter. He was going to be returned to the mainland and await discharge into civilian life. He showed us his wounds. We could see where the bullet passed through both hands. He was 19 years old, likeable and friendly.

Soldier number two had been shot twice in one shoulder by a sniper whilst on duty outside a Police Barracks. He said that he was very lucky to be alive, his Commanding Officer told him that the sniper was aiming for his head. He was from an Infantry regiment, and he too would be discharged into civilian life. He had been in the Army since he was 14 years old. He too was worried about leaving his regiment, as he had no skills.

Soldier number three had lost an eye in a bomb blast. A splinter had pierced his right eye. He said he was happy to be alive as three of his mates had died in the blast. He was from the Pioneer Corps. A bomb had gone off whilst they were guarding an Army barracks in North Belfast. Damage to the building was minimum. All four of them had been close to the bomb, and this young soldier was only 18 years old. He had only completed his training three weeks ago. It had been his ambition to make a career in the Army, but Republican thugs had ended that.

All five of us continued to talk. We were laughing and joking when a fourth young soldier came limping over to us on crutches. I asked how he was. He said that he was still in pain. One of our marines then asked him what had happened. The three young soldiers had gone very quiet. The fourth soldier said that he had been shot through both feet. I asked how that happened. He said that he had done it himself. Then there was a deadly silence from the marine and me. Nobody said a thing. After a couple of minutes soldier number four turned around and went back to his ward. One of the young soldiers said that he was from Ward One, which only had personnel who had self-inflicted wounds in it. The soldier with self-inflicted wounds was only 18. He would be discharged from the Army, "Services No Longer Required". Eventually all three soldiers went back to their wards, and we had completed our first day's duty.

A few days later the Secretary of State for Northern Ireland was making a visit to the hospital. The Army Medical Corps Sergeant Major told me that he would like a full presence of security staff at the main entrance. All visiting press had to show their identity cards, and their bags had to be searched. If anybody failed to comply then they were to be refused entry to the hospital. One marine and I would be outside the main entrance and carry out the checks. As each person was cleared we would give a thumbs up sign to the TV camera and the marine inside would release the electric door locking mechanism. Medical staff would direct visitors to a side ward to await the arrival of the Secretary of State.

Everything was going well, press reporters and cameramen were friendly and obliging. They complied with our request for identification and submitted to searches willingly. Everything was going very well. Then two dirty, scruffy individuals arrived. First of all they tried to brush past us. I asked them to step to one side and produce some identification. They just said 'Press.'

The marine said, 'You will have to do better than that. Identification please.' Then the abuse and insults started. We both replied, 'You had better watch your Ps and Qs, bad language is offensive.'

They became more aggressive and abusive. One of them brushed past me, I grabbed him by his collar and pulled him back. He told me, 'You have assaulted me, I demand your name, number, rank and Unit.' He was told in no uncertain terms where to get off. The main door then opened as the Sergeant Major came out, both of the men then tried to force their way past us. I hit one of them and the marine also struck him. He went out like a light. The Sergeant Major said, 'The Secretary of State's car is approaching, what are we going to do about this man lying on the ground?' The marine and I picked him up and placed him in bushes on one side of the main entrance, and I told his sidekick to keep his mouth shut.

The Secretary of State arrived in his chauffeur driven Jaguar car and the Medical Sergeant Major opened his door and escorted him into the hospital. Half a minute later the bedraggled individual emerged from the bushes, brushing himself down. The driver and security staff accompanying the Secretary of State noticed the character emerging from the bushes, and the police driver asked me, 'What's going on?' He told me that he was a Sergeant in the Metropolitan Police, and two other bodyguards were from the same force. He said, 'These so-called reporters are well known to the Police. Both of them work for an organisation which functions under the name of "Troops Out of Ireland". It is funded and supported by Republicans and left wing politicians.'

Both of the so-called reporters went up to the three Policemen and stated that a crime of violence had been committed against one of them. The Police asked them to explain in detail what had happened. It took them about five minutes. Once they had finished with their explanation of events the Police asked them for names of two independent witnesses. Their reply was 'One of us and the Sergeant Major in the hospital.'

The Policeman then said, 'No serviceman will bear witness against another. You'll have to do better than that.'

The marine next to me said, 'I took part in this so-called assault. Both reporters failed to comply with our request for a security search.'

The Police Sergeant spoke to both of them saying, 'Is that true?'

Both reporters said that they were attacked without provocation.

The Sergeant then said, 'You two usually do all the antagonising and provoking. I suggest that you both leave, or you will be charged with wasting Police time.'

Both of them started to abuse the Policeman, and one of their ranks said, 'You had better be careful of what you say as there are a lot of witnesses around.' Then they were told to clear off. We watched them walk along the road, away from the hospital.

The Police Sergeant then came up to the marine and me and shook our hands. He said to us, 'Both "reporters" are well known trouble makers. They are always trying to gain access to government buildings and establishments. I wish I'd been here when they tried to gain entry to the hospital. They'll go away now and write a very uncomplimentary article about the Royal Marines.' In fact we saw it about a week later, in one of the left wing rags.

Police were not allowed into the hospital as they were armed. If they entered then their weapons had to be handed in. Only our security team were allowed weapons within the hospital. If anybody was seen with a weapon they would be challenged, and if there was no positive response, then he or she would be shot.

We started up a conversation with the Police, one of whom could tell good yarns. Sadly I have a terrible memory concerning jokes and normally forget them about five minutes after I've heard them. Anyway, after about five minutes the marine asked all of us if we would like a cup of hot coffee. The Sergeant said, 'I thought you'd never ask!' A few minutes later five mugs of hot coffee were being enjoyed.

The weather was now becoming very cold, but it was dry. The three Policemen said that they knew our Commanding Officer, and they knew that he didn't get on with the Secretary of State. They also told us that our CO would like to go into the trouble areas and deal with problem people, but that the Secretary of State would not allow this. He only wanted restraint and appeasement. There was a lot of friction between them. However, most Commanding Officers were of the same opinion as our CO, but he was more forceful, he always bettered the Secretary of

State, who often became tongue-tied and flummoxed in any argument with our Lieutenant Colonel.

After an hour the Medical Sergeant Major came out to warn us that the Secretary of State would be leaving in a few minutes. The Police driver started the car engine up and two bodyguards prepared for his arrival. The Army Medical Lieutenant Colonel escorted the Secretary of State to his car. They wished each other 'Goodbye,' and then the car drove off. I never saw this Secretary of State again, but I heard a lot about him.

One afternoon at around four o'clock a nurse came to the front desk and told us to prepared for the arrival of three casualties. We immediately responded with the normal questions: 'What has happened?' 'Where was it?' 'Who were they?' and 'From which Unit?'

The nurse replied, 'I don't know; only that they'll arrive within the half hour. The Medical staff assembled at the main entrance with three trolleys. The Lieutenant Colonel, a Major and Sergeant Major also arrived. Ten minutes later two Ambulances approached, accompanied by six Land Rovers belonging to the RUC. The Lead Land Rover stopped by the front door and a senior RUC Officer got out. He came into the hospital. He asked me, 'Who is the senior person?' The Lieutenant Colonel stepped forward. The RUC Officer said, 'I have an unusual request. The two Ambulances have three Republican informers in them. They have been shot and it's not safe to place them in a civilian hospital.

The Senior Medical Officer said, 'It's an unusual request but I'll look at the three men and have it clarified higher up as to their status, and whether they can remain in a Military Hospital.

The three wounded men were brought into the lobby, and both surgeons started to inspect their injuries. The three stretchers they lay on were covered in blood; I could see blood running out of the wounds of one of the injured men. The Medical Officers examined the wounded men in detail, inserting their fingers into the entry points of the bullets to see if they could feel them, and find how deep the wounds were.

All three of them had been shot three times at close range, in their chests. The surgeons then gave priority of operation, but one was already dead. Only one of them was worth trying to save as the other one who was alive would be dead within half an hour. The Sergeant Major told the Ambulance staff to put the two dead or dying back into their vehicles, and the Police helped to carry them out. There was a lot of blood on the hospital tiled floor, and one of the nurses came over with a bucket and mopped up the mess. The third man was taken into the operating theatre, but he died on the table. The Republicans had a full 100% success rate in this execution.

As mentioned before, the Unit Officers visited the hospital to visit their injured staff. The Marine with me said, 'There are four Land Rovers approaching, belonging to the Royal Military Police.' They parked just down from the main entrance. There were eight RMP's wanting to enter the hospital, all Majors. The door lock was released and they entered.

I called them over instructing them, 'No weapons are allowed beyond this point, we will look after your pistols and return them to you as you leave.' They agreed to this. The first Major took his 9mm Browning pistol out of its holster. He pulled the body mechanism back and fed a live round into the firing chamber, all the time talking to a colleague. The barrel was pointed at my stomach. I shouted as loud as I could, 'STOP!' Then he stopped talking. I pointed out to the Major that he had fed a live round into the firing chamber and the barrel was still pointing at my stomach. He froze and went as white as a sheet when he realised what he had done.

I told them all to go outside, and to prove their weapons were safe, which they did. We took their weapons in and gave each one a metal numbered disc. The Major who had nearly shot me was very apologetic and I accepted his apology. I realised how lucky I had been. If he had pulled the trigger I would have died within an hour. Also, it would have been the end of his career.

We completed our two weeks security duty at the hospital, it had been a little eventful. During this time we had witnessed soldiers being brought in with some very severe wounds. Sadly, some of them did not recover. Some of the ones that did recover, and were returned to the mainland, would live with a disability forever.

*

The four of us who had done Hospital Guard for the last two weeks now had to take our turn doing Street Patrolling. All Corporals and Marines carried out this duty for a period of four weeks. Nobody looked forward to or liked this patrolling of streets on foot. The duty was for 24 hours, doing three four hour patrols, and another team would also be working the area, as our opposite number. Each team would relieve the other throughout the 24-hour period. There would always be a presence in the area of one of our foot patrols, plus Land Rovers with additional personnel cruising round to support men on the ground. Our dress would be combat clothing and flak jacket, and we also carried an SLR (Self Loading Rifle) with 20 live rounds in its magazine, and a truncheon. Our rifles had to be strapped to our wrists. Also, we would be issued with plastic hand ties. Wearing a flak jacket for long periods always made our shoulders ache, and it slowed us down when we needed to run. I also had a small radio so that I was in constant touch with the Operations room.

 The area to be patrolled consisted of six streets approximately 500 yards each in length, running north and south. At the rear of the houses ran a service lane with a small backyard. The service lanes were full of dustbins and rubbish. All the houses were old, built in the 1870's, consisting of two rooms upstairs and a kitchen and living room downstairs. None of them had bathrooms, the toilet was at the rear in the back yard. The front door opened directly onto the street. The washing was hung across the street. A new estate was being built on the other side of town and this area was due to be demolished the following year. At the Southern end of the street ran a main road, which had a large public house, and three shops, a baker's, an off licence and a fish and chip shop. At the Northern end of the streets was a motorway to Belfast. The public houses opened at ten each morning and closed at ten pm. It was normally full by 11am, staying like that till closing time each day. The fish and chip shop opened at 11am and closed at midnight. This shop was used by all local women as a meeting and gathering place.

On the first day I reported to the Operations room at seven thirty for a briefing. I was given a list of codes and nicknames of streets to be patrolled. Also, I had to radio in every 15 minutes, in code. We were told that there was nothing specific happening in the area but to be careful of large numbers of young men. If a large group of young men appeared in the area I was to inform Operations immediately, they would then send the Rover groups in. Groups of young men would try to overwhelm the military, their main aim being to take a service weapon, and the Republicans would like to capture and execute any serviceman. It was hard to believe that these people were once our fellow citizens.

We arrived in the patrol area before eight, slowly walking up and down the streets to familiarise ourselves, two of us would walk on either side of the street, watching each other's back, observing up and down the street at all times. We all knew the area, after travelling around in the CO's Rover group. It was still quiet, a few people were going to work. At around eight thirty children started to leave their houses, going to school. Walking along the main road by the shops women were commenting to us that we were the new boys on the streets. They all knew who were in each patrol team and were fully aware of any changes. Just before twelve we started our return trip to camp, passing our relief on the road. We told them that all was quiet.

At 3.45pm we all set off for our second patrol of the day. Once in the area I radioed Operations telling them that my patrol was on station. Five young girls approached me on my side of the street, pulling up their skirts showing that none of them wore any knickers. They asked us if we would like to go with them to a derelict house and have some fun. I said, 'No thanks,' after all we did not know where they had been, plus we would be susceptible to catch some unmentionable disease. This was a regular approach and we were fully aware of what was planned in this honey trap. Once you arrived at the derelict house you would be ambushed and murdered. The five young girls moved off. By now there were a large number of children playing in the streets. As time got nearer to eight o'clock the streets became quiet. We were now looking forward to returning back to camp for supper, also to the luxury of removing our flak jackets.

The last watch, midnight till four in the morning, was the quietest of all. We did see a few men on street corners but once they saw us approach they all vanished into the night. We returned back to camp at four, showered and then went to bed. The first day's duty was quiet and uneventful. 'Good!'

Our second day patrolling this Republican area started on a Saturday afternoon. Once we arrived in the patrol area, going up and down the streets, we had a large number of small children surround us. They wanted to know our names and where we were from. Also, they asked where the other patrol had gone. We explained what they wanted to know but did not give them our names. These young children stayed with us as we slowly patrolled the streets. Their clothes were dirty and of poor quality, but they were friendly. Most of them had jam and dried food around their mouths. We gave them a nickname for each of ourselves, never revealing our real identity.

As we started to walk along the main road with shops and public houses on it there were a large number of teenagers around. Some of them shouted abuse, and the young girls were still saying that they were available. We ignored their abuse and comments. The fish and chip shop was full, people were standing on the pavement eating their food. The off licence was doing a brisk trade, people were leaving with bottles of cider. The public house was full, all the local men were in there. As the afternoon wore on it became colder and daylight started to fade. We were glad to return back to camp, rest, tea, and to prepare for the next shift.

Moving out for our second shift of the day we had to pass a disused derelict factory. Going by this factory a number of stones were thrown at us by a gang of youths. They were in the factory compound and the fencing was still up and secure. One of the gates was open, and we closed it, keeping the youths within. I then radioed for back up. A few minutes later a Rover group arrived, I told the Corporal-in-charge what had happened. He took five marines into the old factory compound with him, and re-emerged ten minutes later with seven youths. All the youths had their hands tied behind their backs. He asked me to radio for a truck to collect the troublesome teenagers. All of them were between 15 and 19, and the Rover group Corporal said that he had been after two of the youths for a long time, as they were suspect delivery boys for Republicans. All of them were taken to a RUC Barracks. Five of them were released after a couple of hours but two were kept back for further questioning.

As we patrolled the streets in the evening the children gradually went indoors. There were a good few men around, most of them unsteady on their legs. They had spent the day drinking and were now returning home. This was for two main reasons, either they had enough drink inside them or they had run out of money. We started to move down the main road; it was nine thirty. We wanted to be clear of the area before the public house closed as we knew that we would be prime targets for all the local drunks. As we approached the off licence I noticed two men with balaclavas covering their heads and faces, in the shop. Their backs were now towards us and I could not see what was in their hands. One of the marines said, 'The counter assistant is doing something by his till.' We positioned ourselves, two either side of the off licence door, well back so that we could not be seen from within.

A minute later two men emerged from the off licence. Both of them had handguns in their hands, one was carrying a bag. I shouted, 'Stop, drop your weapons and put your hands up high.' They both dropped their handguns and the bag.

Both of them were very surprised at our presence and started shouting as loud as they could, 'Don't shoot, don't shoot.' We picked up both handguns and the bag of money. Both men were placed against the wall and searched, and their balaclavas were removed.

As we were putting plastic cuffs on one of the men a large group of young women came running at us from the fish and chip shop. One of the men saw his chance and ran off. The women surrounded us and tried to free our prisoner, also shouting, 'Don't shoot him,' several times. There were about fifteen of them around us, we formed a tight bunch close up to our prisoner, ensuring that our backs were to the wall. The women were trying to kick and punch us, also shouting at us to release their man. I radioed for urgent immediate assistance.

By now some of the men had started to leave the public house. We had to use our rifle butts, hitting some of the women on their shoulders and arms. The screams increased from the women, who were now being joined by men, most of whom were drunk. One of them pushed his way through a group of women and tried to grab one of the marines, and he received an uppercut from a rifle butt. Now the crowd was building up around us and the suspect under arrest was trying to get away. Two marines kept him pushed back against the wall; they gave him a hard blow to his stomach with their elbows; this quietened him down for a little while. The women were now becoming more aggressive as they had been joined by drunks from the public house.

We were beginning to think that soon we would be overwhelmed when suddenly they all started to run away. Once we could look round I noticed a Rover group had arrived, some of the marines were laying into men with their truncheons and the women were screaming. After a few minutes the situation quietened down and sanity returned. We still had our prisoner, the handguns and a bag full of money. During the attack my radio had been broken. The Corporal-in-charge of the Rover group radioed for more back-up, as he considered the situation very hostile. The prisoner was put in the back of one of the Land Rovers, and the handguns and money were put into another vehicle. They were guarded by two marines. I went into the off licence to see the counter assistant, he was told that two men had been caught but one escaped. He said that no robbery had taken place, and I was wrong. He was trembling and very afraid. It was obvious that the robbery had been carried out on behalf of the Republicans.

The public house was now empty and a large group of men and women were gathered at the fish and chip shop. They were shouting abuse, and saying that the prisoner was being held against his will and fitted up by marines. They were calling out to him by his name. He was one of the local residents in the area. The crowd was full of drink and Dutch courage and the women were doing their best to stir up the men against us.

Another Rover group arrived; a Sergeant was in charge of this one. He radioed Operations and asked for a strong force to be sent to the area. The CO's Rover group arrived five minutes later. As the crowd were all by the fish and chip shop a cordon was formed around them. The four women that attacked my patrol were recognised, also the man who received an uppercut to his jaw. I pointed them out to the CO. They were extracted from the crowd, handcuffed and placed in the back of a truck. The remainder of the crowd were forced to disperse in different directions. The CO told me to take my patrol and go with the truck to RUC Barracks. Four women and one man were to be charged with obstructing justice. The armed robber followed in another Land Rover, and the counter assistant in a separate vehicle. Once we arrived at the RUC Barracks the women started to become abusive and violent, but it was not a problem as they were handcuffed. The man who attacked us was fast asleep. He was woken, and gave no trouble. The Desk Sergeant alerted the duty Superintendent, and all six prisoners were placed in cells. The marines and I gave statements; this took us till early Sunday morning.

Four women and one man were charged with assault, and the armed robber faced more severe charges as he had been in possession of a handgun. The CO arrived at the RUC Barracks just after two in the morning. He handed two handguns and a bag of money over. Both handguns were high quality Colt .357 Pythons, brand new. The CO left a large number of marines patrolling the Republican area, they were withdrawn the following morning around nine. The area was now considered safe and back to normal.

The counter assistant gave a statement on condition that he was moved to the mainland, and this was arranged. He passed on a large amount of valuable information concerning Republican activities, as well as names and positions within their organisation.

Four women and one man went before a Magistrate. They all received two months in jail for obstruction and assault. The armed robber received five years in prison. Four members of the patrol gave evidence at all the court trials. However, jail to Republicans was like an award for achievement, there was no stigma attached to it.

A few days after the armed robbery of the off licence, two reports from the "Troops Out Movement" published a story in a left wing rag. It accused the Royal Marines of beating women, and of planting weapons on young men, together with false charges of robbery from an off licence. More distortion of truth and propaganda from the Republicans. Britain did not need enemies, with so-called "citizens" such as we had in Northern Ireland.

Another day, another duty. We all left camp just after seven thirty so that we would be in our patrol area by eight. The morning was cold and, for the moment, dry. Some people were leaving for work, and at around eight thirty children would leave their homes for school. We continued to patrol our six streets and the main road. The whole area was very quiet, there were no young men on street corners. At around eleven the sky darkened and wind came in from the west. Just before eleven thirty the rain started, and within five minutes it was once more coming down like "stair rods". We all moved to the west side of the street, taking shelter against the front wall of a house, under the eaves. As the wind was coming from the west, with us against an east-facing house we were having some protection from the heavy downpour. To my left was a front room window, on my right the main entrance to a house.

I had been standing there for a few minutes when the window was raised and a woman's voice said, 'Please listen, and don't look around, just raise your left hand if you understand.' So I did this. She continued, 'I live here with my husband and three teenage boys, and about three weeks ago my husband was given a beating, and he's off work and at home. The reason for this was that he did not want to pay protection money to the Republicans, they call it "contributions to their cause". The Republicans want my boys to do small errands for them, but I won't allow them anywhere near them, and they collect their protection money on Thursday nights. They have look-outs watching for the Royal Marines foot patrols, and thy are using the "Cause" for organised crime and extortion.' She pointed out, 'Most people in this community want nothing to do with crime or the Republicans, but we are victims as well now, and if anyone speaks out against them they can expect a severe beating or worse.'

The window was then pulled shut again. The marine on the other side confirmed that he had heard every word said. Once we returned back to camp I went to the Operations rooms and told the Duty Officer what the woman had said. Also, I gave him her address. He said, 'The CO will be interested, and from now on the area will be saturated with foot patrols and Rover groups, Thursday evenings as well as every other day.'

That evening it started to rain "stair rods" again. We were in a back lane between the houses, many of which were boarded up and empty. In the rear of one of the empty properties was a large coalbunker with a fold down lid. We looked inside it. There was nothing inside – but space for four young men to take shelter from the rain. We all got in, the lid was pulled down and a piece of wood put under it so that we could see out. The rain continued to pour; nobody was around. We had been inside for nearly 15 minutes when I receive a radio message from our CO to meet him at a rendezvous point, codenamed "Westminster". This was the corner of the fifth street and the main road. Our present position was inside a coal bunker, between the first and second streets.

We all got out as quickly as possible then ran to the corner of fifth and main. The patrol waited, ensuring that our backs were hard pressed against a wall, so that we offered minimum silhouette for any sniper. We had been there about five minutes when the CO's Rover group arrived. The CO got out of his Land Rover and came over to us. He said, 'I have to tell you that I'm leaving the Unit this coming weekend, having served three years in this Commando Unit.' He shook my hand and wished me good luck for the future, then he spoke to each marine in the patrol individually. Before he left he also said, 'You should all be home in Plymouth for Christmas.'

He was going to an administration posting at the Ministry of Defence, London; and he was promoted to full Colonel. That would be his final rank in the Royal Marines, as above that level it is up to politicians to approve. He had clashed with the Secretary of State for NI many times. We all agreed that he had been a good CO, firm, fair and straight, and would be a hard act to follow. As it was now after eleven thirty we decided to start our slow return back to camp.

As we came near the first and second streets along the main road, four gunshots were heard. I immediately radioed Operations and asked for a Rover group as back-up, and told them the direction from which the shots had come. We proceeded to the first and second streets, then started to go up a dividing alleyway at the rear of the properties. The rear yards of the houses were checked to ensure that there was not a trap set for us.

About 100 yards up the alleyway we found two young boys. Both of them were unconscious and unrecognisable. They had received a very severe beating, also, both of them had been knee-capped; that was the four shots we had heard. Their faces were covered with blood and both eyes were closed. We checked their airways to ensure that they could breathe. I radioed Operations and told them an Ambulance was required. As the alleyway was too narrow for a vehicle, we carried them down to the main road. They were gently placed on the pavement in a semi-prone position to ensure that they could clear their mouths if they vomited. In the future they would be walking with stiff legs, and slowly.

The Rover group arrived, the Sergeant-in-charge told us to make our way back to camp; he would see them into the Ambulance. Both the young boys had been punished by the Republicans for failing to carry out some crime. Also, it was a clear message to any other boys, to obey the rules and instructions given to them.

We did our third patrol and finished at eight in the morning, there was nothing to report. The following day before proceeding out on patrol I had to report to the Operations room. The Duty Officer handed me an arrest warrant, to serve and apprehend a man in his early 20s. The man was tied in deeply with Republicans, and was also wanted for arms running and other illegal activities. The Duty Officer also told me and my patrol members to expect trouble from his family. His mother was a very keen supporter and campaigner for the "The Cause". She would do everything possible to stop her son's arrest, and would try to frustrate us once the man had been arrested and in custody. I was to radio for a Rover group to collect him. The Duty Officer made it sound like an everyday event, it was decided that we would make the arrest our first priority.

The man lived in Fifth Street, we arrived at the house just after eight. Two marines went round to the back door as we knew it would not be straightforward or easy. I waited a couple of minutes to ensure that both of them had sufficient time to be in place. I knocked hard on the front door, then the upstairs window opened. A large overweight woman looked out. Immediately she saw two Royal Marines standing outside her front door bad language poured out from her foul mouth. I replied 'We have heard it all before. We have a warrant to arrest your son.' She then went in, and a minute later re-emerged at her window with a chamber pot; the contents missed both of us and landed on the pavement. Next the pot was thrown at us; this also missed. I could hear movement inside the house, someone was coming downstairs in a great hurry. We both pushed hard against the front door, which opened easily. The young man was pulling on his coat and trying to insert a key in the back door lock to make his escape. I allowed him to go on. He could not understand why we both watched him leave through the rear door. Once outside he was grabbed by two marines, plastic cuffed and brought back into the house. I showed the man our arrest warrant and he agreed that it was him.

We all thought that everything was alright now. His father came downstairs in his pyjamas threatening all of us, also using normal bad language. His mother was close behind him, and she went into the kitchen. The father immediately tried to attack the marine nearest to him, but as he was only just five feet tall and very slightly built there was no strength or power in him. One marine grabbed him, and made him sit down. He tried to get up and continue his attack. I told the marine to plastic cuff him, which he did.

The mother came rushing out of her kitchen with a large frying pan. She hit the nearest marine across his back. As we were all wearing flak jackets the blow had no effect but to annoy us. She then tried to attack all of us, also swearing that she was going to save her son and husband. The frying pan was being used as a weapon and she took another swipe at a marine but missed, and received a punch on her nose, which caused it to bleed. She dropped her frying pan then started to accuse us of assaulting an innocent woman. I made her sit down and told her that she would be plastic cuffed if this behaviour continued. Also, I told her and her husband that they were now under arrest, in the name of our Queen and her Majesty's Security Forces.

The front room was small and it had seven people in it. One of the marines went into the kitchen and came out with a tea towel. It was given to the mother so that she could nurse her bleeding nose. I told her to go upstairs, to dress and bring some clothes down for her husband. One of the marines would go up with her but stand outside her bedroom door. Once dressed she returned downstairs with clothes for her husband. His plastic cuffs were removed to enable him to dress. The mother was plastic cuffed, just as her son was; hands behind back. Once the husband was dressed plastic cuffs were placed back on him. By plastic cuffing them with their hands behind their backs it was easier to control them, and they were reluctant to offer trouble.

By now there was a small crowd of women outside the front door, shouting and attracting more people to join them. There was no telephone in the house so I used my small portable radio to tell Operations that the arrests had been made, and that the parents were apprehended for "Obstruction". I requested a strong force of marines as the situation might get out of control. We ensured that the front door was kept closed but abuse from outside was getting louder and more vicious. The son and husband sat very quietly but the mother continued to threaten us. She said that we would all regret this day. She was told to "shut up".

A few minutes later two trucks and four Land Rovers arrived. A Sergeant was outside the front door and in control. He had dispersed the crowd of women and placed marines up and down the street. I was told that it was now safe to bring the three arrested people out. They were brought out and placed in the back of three separate vehicles. The Sergeant said he would ensure that they were delivered to the RUC. Also, he had been instructed to leave six marines behind to guard the house as it was suspected that there could be weapons hidden within it. This was unusual as most weapons are stored at farm and in the countryside. Later that day a search team removed the floorboards and found six handguns buried below them. The whole house was taken apart as these people supported death and destruction of Her Majesty's Security Forces.

The son received three years in jail. Both mother and father were locked up for 28 days each, for obstruction. And now additional charges were brought for concealment of illegal weapons in their house.

The morning had started badly and I knew that other events would go wrong this day. You get a feeling for these things after a while. As the morning wore on more people were coming out of their houses. Most people were quiet and well-behaved, but there was always a small hard core of troublemakers. Some men jeered at us, always from the other side of the road, never close up. Women who favoured the Republican "Cause" would shout insults at us as they passed by.

The day before, one of our Rifle Companies had been successful on a roadblock near the border with Southern Ireland. A truck had been stopped with half a ton of high explosives concealed in its cargo of goods. Also, three big Alpha males in the Republican movement, in the top management ranks, had been arrested by the same Rifle Company. It had been put around that informers gave information to the Security Forces. This was done to cast doubt and suspicion amongst them. At the best of times they did not trust each other, and these two incidents helped to sow the seeds of doubt.

As we were now in Sixth Street and the time was nearing midday, it was decided that we would start our slow return back to camp. Turning the corner of Sixth Street onto the Main road, we saw six young thugs kicking a man lying on the ground. He was rolled up in a ball. All of us took out our truncheons and ran to the group of men. They did not hear our approach. The next thing they knew was when two of their group collapsed onto the ground after being struck on the back of their necks. The other four turned and started to attack us, but they did not have aggression or the ability to fight with determination. One of the thugs managed to break loose and run away. We had five of them, and they were immediately plastic-cuffed and searched.

Once the search of their persons was completed they were made to sit cross-legged facing a wall, with their backs to the Main Road. Two marines stood over them as guards, although in the present position they were in it would be hard to try and stand up to run away. One of my marines and I now turned our attention to the injured man, lying still on the cold pavement slabs. He was still conscious but in pain. His face was swollen and there was blood running from his mouth and nose; he was going into shock. His dentures lay on the pavement broken. All he said to me was, 'No money.' He was in his late 50s, medium build. I went up to one of the thugs facing the wall and asked what he meant. The reply was, 'He will not pay for our Cause."

I answered back, 'No protection money for you scum.' I radioed for an Ambulance and more marines as this situation could get out of hand. Operations told me an Ambulance was on its way, although the Rover group would be a little late as there was trouble in other areas. The Ambulance arrived after 15 minutes. Also, my relief showed up with his patrol. Now there were eight of us here, which gave me more confidence. My opposite number told me that there had been a lot of trouble in a small town some 20 miles away, riots, property set on fire, and punishment beatings.

The five prisoners were now starting to get restless and a small group of men and women were gathering on the opposite side of the road. One marine went up to the prisoners and told them, 'If any attempt is made to rescue you, you will all be shot.' Two of the prisoners then started to panic saying that they were only following orders.

I then said to the two, 'Would you be prepared to give us some information about others if we spare your lives?' Three was mad panic amongst them now, begging not to be shot. We told them that that depended on them, and both of them said they would give information. It was hard to believe that they actually thought we would shoot them. This was a successful case of "Brainwashing" by the Republicans. Two of the other prisoners then started to abuse them stating that it was only bluff. The two who offered to talk were now white with fear, more afraid of the Republicans than of the Security Forces. I then told them that if they did give the RUC any information both would be well rewarded. Both "would be informants" were now between a rock and a hard surface. The Republicans showed very little concern for their own people. We all knew, as members of HM Security Forces, that if we ever fell into their hands we would be tortured to death.

A group of women now came up from the Fish and Chip shop joining others on the opposite side of the Main Road, staring at us and talking amongst themselves. None of the men came out of the nearby public house. It was nearly one o'clock now. Then a Rover group arrived; all of us were glad to see more marines. Once women saw the arrival of the Rover group they dispersed. The prisoners were put into the back of the Land Rovers and taken to an RUC Barracks. My patrol then made our way back to camp, and once we had returned I reported to the Operations room. The Duty Officer said all of us were required to make statements concerning recent events. That afternoon statements were given and passed on to the RUC.

My second patrol of this day started at four o'clock, meeting my opposite number on his way back. He told me that there were groups of young men looking for trouble, also giving the normal abuse from a distance. We proceeded, and as we came to the First Street some stones were thrown at us, by a group of teenage boys. They ran up the street and dispersed in alleyways, leading to rear backyards. We decided to let them go as no damage had been done, but they would be kept in mind if we should come across them again. Normal behaviour came from the teenage girls, which we were used to by now.

There was a young man in his early 20s, who always abused us from a distance. Also, he sneered and thought we were a big joke. He was entitled to his views, however, we all decided that something should be planned for him before our stint of patrolling was finished. Also, he was given the nickname of "Laughing Boy".

There was a feeling of restlessness in the area this evening, as though everybody was expecting something to happen. As we walked around a corner the young stone throwers were standing there, they did not hear or see us coming. Once they realised that we were upon them two managed to run off. But we had three of them, then they said, 'We were only playing and joking with you.'

One of the marines answered, 'If a stone hits us in an eye and we lose it then that would be no joke.' The three teenagers were searched, there were no weapons concealed on them. Then one of our Rover groups arrived on the scene. The Sergeant-in-charge stopped, got out and asked what was going on. It was explained that these three teenagers were persistent "stone throwers".

He said, 'The general cure for stone throwers is a long walk in the nearby countryside.' All three were made to remove their shoes and socks, which were placed on a window ledge. The teenagers were put in the rear of the Land Rovers and the Sergeant said, 'They will be dropped off about 12 miles away and forced to walk back on bare feet.' As it was dark now it would take them a long time to find their way home. Also, the weather forecast was for heavy rain that evening, a fitting punishment for young idiots. The Sergeant's Rover group left with three teenagers. We continued on our foot patrol.

By a motorway, which was north of the six streets, a team of Royal Engineers were carrying out some repair work. We stopped and had a chat with them. Their Sergeant asked if one of his young privates could return with us to our camp, as he had a bad cold. A vehicle from his Unit would collect him that evening. I said, 'OK,' as it was nearing the end of our second shift. The young Royal Engineer was told to stay between me and the marine bringing up my rear. We commenced our journey back to camp; it was nearly eight o'clock in the evening.

We were walking along by the side of a low wall when I heard an explosion behind me. Turning around I saw the young Royal Engineer was lying on the ground. We all ran to his aid, but the explosion had blown all the flesh off his thigh, exposing his femur. Flesh from his thigh was blown across the road, together with much blood. A marine cradled the young Sapper in his arms, who was saying that his leg was "on fire". We took our water bottles out and emptied the contents on the upper part of his thigh.

Then the young Sapper started to become delirious, talking to his mother. We all did our best to reassure him but he was fading fast. Blood ran onto the pavement from severed arteries. I am not ashamed to say that all of us had tears running down our cheeks. I radioed for an Ambulance but this Royal Engineer died in the arms of a Royal Marine. All of us felt useless and very upset at the loss of the life of this young man. The Ambulance arrived, and his body was placed on a stretcher and covered with a blanket. The blanket covered his whole body, including his face, that told all of us present that he was dead. A Rover group arrived, we were all told to go and sit in the back of the vehicles. The area was cordoned off for examination to ascertain where the explosive had come from. The Army would send a specialist team to investigate this terrible incident.

The Land Rovers dropped us off at camp and I reported to the Operations room. The Duty Officer said that statements would be required. I replied that we would all give statements in the morning, and he said that was OK. We all went over to the NAAFI. One of the marines went to the kitchen and brought back eight bacon rolls. All our webbing, flak, jackets and rifles were placed in the corner. I phoned the Guardroom and asked if the wandering patrol could come over to the NAAFI at 2330 hours to ensure we were all awake, ready for our last patrol of this 24-hour duty. It was my turn to buy the round; we had a pint and a couple of bacon rolls each, nobody felt like eating a meal. We had a couple of rums after the beer; nobody felt like talking. All of us fell asleep in the chairs, and at 2330 hours the wandering patrol woke us up. We prepared ourselves and went over to the Operations room.

The Duty Officer said that the explosion had been investigated. A brick had been removed from the wall and a small amount of plastic explosive and a radio-controlled detonator had been placed in the cavity. Then a piece of coloured paper covered the brick cavity to shield the explosive device from view. The person who activated the explosive device sat in a building watching as we approached. The small bomb went off just as the young Royal Engineer was directly opposite it. This was a real concern to the Security Forces, as the Republicans now had means of radio controlled detonators and equipment. Work would now commence on blocking radio signals. Also, the Royal Engineer's next of kin had been informed of his tragic death.

Again I thought how close I had been to this bomb, a couple of seconds earlier it would have been me. There go I, but for the grace of God. We all proceeded to the patrol area, meeting our opposite number returning. They said it had been a bad evening, stone throwing, abuse and threats. One of the marines in the opposite patrol had a young girl of about 12 come up to him and spit in his face. All the women from the fish and chip shop were watching, they clapped after this little incident. We said 'Goodbye' and proceeded on our way.

Going up Second Street we meet two of the young stone throwers who had been given a ride into the nearby countryside. Both were afraid that they would receive a beating from us. They were soaking wet and their feet were very sore. We asked them, 'How are things?'

They replied, 'We were dropped off in a country lane and it took us nearly an hour to find out where we were. Then it took four or five hours to walk back here.'

We continued, 'Will you be throwing stones at us or any of our Patrol in future.'

'No,' they replied, quite firmly. We explained to them that we do not beat people up as we are trained, disciplined and responsible individuals. It was our job to keep the peace not disturb it.

'But why do you hate us so much?' we asked.

They answered, 'Because you are English, Church of England and working for the Queen to suppress our community.'

I responded, 'Only I am English, two of the patrol are Welsh and one other a Scotsman. One of us is Roman Catholic. Your kinfolk receive the same protection and rights as everybody else living in the United Kingdom.'

One of the young boys said, 'I would like to join the Royal Air Force, but if I did my parents would have to move as they would be victimised by people in the area.'

I answered, 'Just work hard at school, and in any case all residents in this area are going to be moved in the next two years.' Both of them went into their homes and we continued our patrol, going up and down the streets. We were all glad to return at four, tired, demoralised and fed up.

Later that morning my patrol gave statements to an Army investigation team concerning the death of the young Royal Engineer. His body was taken to his home town for a family funeral.

The five young men caught beating up the elderly man received six months in jail each. One of them did give Queen's Evidence against the others. He served his jail sentence in England and stayed there after his release.

*

Whilst I was carrying out my street patrols other events were taking place within my Unit, some good, others bad. First of all the bad event will be explained:

15 miles away from our camp was a small town by the border of Southern Ireland. The town was only patrolled by Rover groups, which consisted of three Land Rovers, with six personnel in each vehicle. The RUC would not venture into the town, their presence was seen as provocative, and it antagonized the local population, which consisted of farmers and large numbers of unemployed men. Farmers hated the Armed Services because our Royal Engineers were always blowing large holes in roads that crossed into Southern Ireland. Many of these farmers had fields across the border. Also, the large holes in the cross border roads made it harder for Republican terrorists to move about. Unemployed men blamed Protestants for the lack of job opportunity in the area, but they were all doing casual work on the side for cash in hand, paying no taxes. The unemployed ensured that they claimed all benefits possible, even ones they were not entitled to. Many of the farmers used them as a cheap source of labour, tax payers were subsidizing employment requirements in the area.

There were two large public houses in the town, their turnover of beer and spirits was extremely high for such a small population. All marines who had patrolled the area referred to the local population as "parasites". They fed off the taxpayer and hated any form of authority. Everybody said, 'People living in the area are mad, bad and Republican.' Large areas of the town had boarded up houses; many properties had been torched by Republicans. The empty properties once belonged to Protestants, but they were forced to move by bigots full of hatred. A small number of Protestants remained, but the vast majority had been driven from their homes. There was always some sort of trouble in the area, punishment beatings, riots, and more often, our patrols stoned.

One afternoon a Rover group was patrolling in the town. The lead vehicles slowed down and stopped as all four tyres were flat. The driver got out and examined the tyres, and all of them had nails in. The nails had been positioned in soft sand and the first vehicle to pass over them absorbed them into its tyres. As the tyres are tubeless it took a couple of minutes for them to deflate. Just as the marine driver was examining his vehicle a large group of young men appeared from behind a wall. All of them had half bricks in their hands which were thrown at the driver and his vehicle. The driver was hit on the head and other parts of his body, and was rendered unconscious. Other personnel in vehicles jumped out and picked up their injured colleague using the disabled Land Rover as a shield. The other two Land Rovers drew up alongside and the injured driver was placed as quickly as possible in the rear of one vehicle. The remaining personnel squeezed in, half bricks were being thrown fast, and with accuracy. The Sergeant-in-charge decided it was better to withdraw and leave the damaged vehicle where it was. The crowd was too big, too many for 17 Royal Marines to handle and control.

Later that day a Rifle Company went to the area, everybody expected the Land Rover to be burnt out. When they arrived the vehicle was in the same spot, in one piece. Local thugs had vented their anger by smashing all the glass fitted to the vehicle, windscreen, headlights, rear taillights and instrument panels. Both front seats had been taken; if the idiots had looked under the seats they would have found two fuel tanks full of petrol, each of which contained ten gallons of petrol as the vehicle had been fully fuelled up before leaving camp; only one match would have been required. The Land Rover was loaded on to the back of a recovery truck and taken to a Royal Electrical Mechanical Engineers workshop and returned a week later as good as new. The Royal Marine driver spent a week in the Military Hospital and made a full recovery.

Event number two was also by the border with Southern Ireland, but this turned out well for us, in more ways than one. A delivery truck going down a narrow country lane was hi-jacked. The driver always took a short cut along back roads, as this saved him time. The driver knew the area well, as he lived locally. He was stopped and told to walk up the lane, and his vehicle cab was set alight. The vehicle was positioned 100 yards down from a sharp bend, completely blocking the lane. Six Republican terrorists now formed an ambush party, three on either side of the lane. One group of three looked down on the other group opposite them, they were totally exposed. The group opposite had to stand up and look over a high wall, they ambush position had not been selected with care or understanding, which highlighted their lack of military skill and poor leadership.

The truck driver walked approximately two miles back and stopped a Royal Marine mobile patrol, he gave them exact details of the hi-jacking, pinpointing precisely on a map where it took place. The Sergeant-in-charge of the mobile radioed back to Operations and asked for a helicopter to reconnoitre the area. This was arranged and the Rover group was told to await the outcome of the reconnaissance report.

15 minutes later a unit helicopter flew over the lane and located the hi-jacked truck. The ambush party stood up and the three terrorists on one side crossed the lane and jumped over the wall, joining their other colleagues. They all then started to run across and down the field, heading for a gap in the hedgerow. What they failed to realise was that the lower section of the field was a large bog, and as they got nearer to the gap in the hedgerow and lower down, the ground become soft, which made running very difficult. They kept going, then one of their group sunk up to his waist in soft, boggy, wet, cold soil. His pal tried to pull him out but he also became stranded. The other four then tried to help

them, but as they closed in the ground became softer and two more started to sink. They tried to get out but the more they struggled the deeper in they went.

By now there were four stuck in the bog, and the other two decided to try and rescue their colleagues. Their rifles were laid on the surface and used as stepping-stones. This did not work, and they also sank and joined their colleagues. The unit helicopter made some low passes over them which forced the six to duck and sink further into the bog. The helicopter pilot informed Operations and the mobile patrol of the position and predicament of the terrorists.

It was decided by Operations to despatch an additional 30 marines to assist the mobile patrol and 45 minutes later they all arrived. They proceed, together with the mobile patrol, to where the six terrorists were. The hi-jacked vehicle was found in a narrow lane, its cab had been burnt out. The field where the six terrorists were stranded was located and the marines formed a line across the field and slowly moved to the bottom, where they found the six terrorists up to their armpits in soft cold bog. They were all cold, wet and totally demoralised. First they asked for help, then they begged for it. The Sergeant said, 'Why should we help you all as your aim, just over an hour ago, was to shoot and murder us. Where are your weapons now?'

They replied, 'At the bottom of the bog.' All the marines stood around the bog looking at these idiots and would-be murderers.

The Sergeant then said, 'We will have to help the idiots, we are duty bound to do so.' So two marines were sent back to collect ropes from their vehicles. They returned 20 minutes later as they were not in any hurry. The six bog dwellers were pulled out, one at a time. It took six marines to pull each one out as the mud had a firm hold, and this took nearly an hour. None of the terrorists were in a fit state to walk, as by now they were suffering from hypothermia too. Stretchers were brought from the trucks and they had to be carried up and out of the field. They were placed in the rear of the trucks; it was becoming very cold now. The incident had taken a good four hours to resolve, as caution was the order of the day. All six were dropped off at a local hospital and guarded by the RUC. I don't know what happened to them.

All six terrorists were in their late teens. It was good that they had very little knowledge of military skills, as their chosen area was poor. Also, no escape plan had been worked out. Their poor planning, lack of knowledge, and lack of military skills had saved the Royal Marines from death. The day after this incident a special team of Royal Engineers was despatched to dig up and retrieve all the terrorists weapons from within the bog.

The truck was towed away, an insurance write off. Its cargo was five tons of baked beans, and the gentleman at the insurance head office also wrote these off, and they were given to our Unit. Needless to say we had them for breakfast, lunch, and supper. Subsequently, our Unit was no doubt responsible for enlarging the hole in the ozone layer; this was caused by sheep in the Southern Hemisphere and Royal Marines in the North!

Members of our Unit checked the daily newspapers to see what had been written concerning both events, the stone throwers and the six terrorists; there was no news. We all agreed that if we had shot the stone throwers and terrorists it would have been front-page news. Republicans with help from the "Troops Out Movement" tried to paint a picture of six young men wrongfully arrested by Royal Marines. They said, "Six young men were found in a field with no weapons and driven into a bog, they nearly died from hypothermia". The Secretary of State for Northern Ireland always ensured that criticism of Republicans was kept to a minimum. All Corporals and marines believed that he thought the Services were expendable, but Republicans had votes, so they must be appeased at all cost.

*

It was a Saturday, and our patrol had the first set of watches. We left camp and proceeded to our six streets. We passed and acknowledged greeting with the patrol returning to camp, who were looking forward to their beds now their 24 hours of patrolling was complete. We were all going very slowly as there were only a few people around early in the morning. As we turned into Sixth Street a large black car was parked 50 yards up from the corner. We recognised come as local inhabitants. The car was gleaming and highly polished. There were also three other men who did not come from the area. Their dress was immaculate and very expensive, two were in their late 20's and the third man was in his 50s. From where we were it looked as though small sacks, about six inches by four inches, were being handed over to the three well-dressed men and placed in the car boot. The small bags were bulging out and we had no idea what was in them. I radioed Operations, giving them the registration number of the vehicle and a description of what was going on. One minute later a reply came back that the vehicle and occupants were to be apprehended immediately. None of the people around the vehicle were aware of our presence, we still had the element of surprise.

On the count of three we all ran as fast as possible to the car. Five local inhabitants ran up the street and away, but we were not interested in them. The three well-dressed men did not know what to do. The older man made some sneering remarks concerning the Royal Marines. All three were made to spread against the wall of a house so that we could search their persons. I held the rifle of a marine carrying out the search, the other two covered the suspects with their rifles; we ensured that they could not run away. The older man was declared clean, then he was plastic-cuffed. The two young men had handguns in shoulder holsters, and these weapons were removed.

They were asked if they had authority to carry weapons, to which they replied, 'Yes.' I asked them to produce that authority, but both of them stated that their weapon authorisation document had been left at home. They were told that permits and authorisation documents had to be carried on their persons if in possession of a personal weapon, and that 'No permit meant illegal possession of a firearm.' They were plastic-cuffed.

The older man started to speak to me again saying, 'I am high up in Security Services and you are making a big mistake, you will be lucky to still be a Corporal by the end of today.'

I answered, 'When you are at a RUC Barracks you will be checked out, and if you're in the Intelligence Services you will be released.' He became very abusive and foul-mouthed. I continued, 'If I had any soap with me I would ram it down your mouth, so watch your Ps and Qs.'

The two young men were very quiet. All three were made to sit cross-legged on the pavement with backs to their car. I checked the boot of their car, and found that it had 40 bags of money in it. I estimated that each bag contained about £20, in coins. A mobile arrived and took all three men away. A marine drove their car away with the bags of money in its boot. My patrol continued, going up and down the six streets.

Later that morning I saw "Laughing Boy" just ahead of me, with two of his friends. He was not aware of our presence in the street. Earlier, I had obtained a small brown envelope from the Unit Registry Office, folded some old newspaper sheets up, and placed them inside the envelope. We all ran as quietly as possible, and I caught up with "Laughing Boy". Putting my arm round his shoulders I thanked him for all his help apprehending the three men this morning. Then I took out the brown envelope and placed it in his inner jacket pocket. He didn't say a thing; his surprise was total. Once "Laughing Boy" realised what I had done he turned white with fear, shouting at me to go away. He then turned round and ran for all his worth, with two friends close behind. We heard later that a man was found in an alleyway, badly beaten up. At times it is better to use the enemy to do your dirty work for you. I never saw or heard any more of "Laughing Boy".

Going along the main road near the public house we realised that something was going on. We crossed the road and moved opposite, where there were about eight men having a fight. Each group of men had supporters in the crowd of onlookers, cheering them on. Some of the crowd noticed us across the road and left. I radioed Operations and told them what was going on, and they said, 'Observe, don't interfere.' This was a good fight, then a group of women came up from the fish and chip shop. The women split into groups supporting their men. One woman went in to help her man, then others moved in, until they were all fighting each other. Hair was being pulled out and finger nails were going for each others' eyes, and they were making a lot of noise. The fighting carried on for about five minutes, then both sides got tired and went their separate ways. They were all grown up adults who knew right from wrong. It was evenly matched. The women were really nasty, and even more vicious than the men. Once they had all gone there was blood, hair and a couple of teeth on the pavement. We decided to award nine points for the women, as they were more determined to win their contest, and six for the men, they needed to try harder.

As today was Saturday our old CO was returning to the mainland. The new CO should be in camp once we returned. Nobody knew anything about the new CO, only that he had been serving with the United States Marines for the past two years.

Once we had returned to camp all of us went into Operations. The Duty Officer said the three men arrested this morning had been transferred from the local RUC Barracks to the main one in Belfast. The older man was the main organiser along the border, he was known as a "Godfather of Death". The RUC had been after him for a long time. The two younger men were only bodyguards and drivers. All three were dressed in very expensive clothing, paid for by intimidated people. The money in the bags was for Republicans. A new scheme for collection had been devised, and the public house and fish and chip shop were now used as main collection points. The people living in the six streets had to take their money to either one of these collection points. The Unit's policy of high visibility patrolling each evening had forced the Republicans to change their methods of collection.

I heard that the "Godfather of Death" received nine years, and his two bodyguards two years each, detained at Her Majesty's pleasure.

The second patrol of the day, four till eight pm, was very quiet, thanks to the rain. Customers in the public houses stayed put. The fish and chip shop had very few customers, but remained open. No children or teenagers were in the streets or on the corners. We sheltered in house doorways and kept under eaves as much as possible. Good hard rain downpours do a lot to keep the area quiet and peaceful.

The final patrol of this duty was like walking streets of the dead. It was very cold, not even the cats were out. We returned back to camp, showered and slept in late.

The Sunday midday meal was something we all looked forward to, and our Chief Cook always did us proud. There was a choice of two roast meats, baked potatoes and plenty of vegetables to choose from. Also, it was good to gather and talk, to find out the latest news. The main gossip was about our new CO. The Corporal from the Orderly room sat at a table opposite, and he was asked, 'What sort of a person is the new Lieutenant Colonel? What's he like?'

The Orderly room Corporal said, 'I haven't got much time to stop and talk because I have to work this afternoon, but the new CO is rude, aggressive, arrogant and well overweight.' We all agreed that there would be problems to come. The second-in-command paid a visit to the main dining hall, he walked round all the tables and chatted to the Corporals and Marines. One of the marines had been hit in the face with a brick and his eye was closed and badly bruised. The 2 i/c chatted to him for about five minutes, and he was excused work and duties for a week. After the 2 i/c left the dining hall someone said, 'Why can't our new CO be like him?'

Someone else said, 'The new CO will not survive as this is his first time in Northern Ireland.' Sunday afternoon was dry and cold, we had a volley ball game for an hour. At six o'clock supper was served, then everybody not on duty went to the NAAFI.

The Orderly room Corporal came in but he was not his usual happy self. He said, 'The new CO shouted at all the staff in Headquarters Office, and he gave the Adjutant and Chief Clerk a hard time. He won't be up to the same standard as our previous CO, and he's not happy with the Unit, he thinks things are too easy; he's not happy with his new command. When the Unit returns to Plymouth everything is going to change.'

A corporal said, 'New brooms sweep clean, but he will also get rid of the good.'

The Orderly room Corporal replied, 'Tomorrow he is going out on his first mobile patrol.'

Someone muttered, 'Our new CO will go the same way as Majors Blunder and Incompetence.'

It was now Monday and my patrol had the second set of watches. Nobody liked them, they started late and finished at eight the following morning. I reported to the Operations Room for a briefing and any special instructions. The Duty Officer showed me a photograph of a young man who was to be arrested on sight. This youth was involved with Republicans as a delivery boy, of weapons, letters and verbal messages. I knew the young man by sight as we saw him frequently around the six streets. He was always quiet and well behaved. I was just about to leave the Operations room and gather up my patrol when the Duty Officer said, 'The new Commanding Officer will pay you a visit sometime this afternoon, so be careful.' I was not worried about a visit from our new CO, what did concern me was the last part, "be careful". It was a coded warning concerning this new CO, it is very unusual for an Officer to warn a non-commissioned officer about a senior officer.

We set off making our way to six streets, passing our opposite patrol returning back to camp. Their only question was, 'What's for lunch?' Going up and down the six streets was very cold. It was now the first week of December. One of the marines kept asking me the time, and I told him, 'There's a long time to go yet to the end of the watch.' The day was very cold, just below freezing, and the wind was strong. We did not want to move fast, just slowly killing time. The public house was full, the fish and chip shop had about 20 women in it. There was nobody on the streets, the children were at school and everything was very quiet.

At 1515 hours I received a coded message to rendezvous with our new CO at the junction of Fourth Street and Main Road at 1530 hours. The patrol arrived at the rendezvous point with plenty of time to spare. The children were now coming out of school We commenced waiting, the minutes passed slowly, and there was no sign of our new Commanding Officer. At 1550 hours four Land Rovers approached and pulled up at the rendezvous point. I went to the lead vehicle expecting to see and meet our new Commanding Officer, but in it was the Unit 2 i/c. I spoke to him and he told me that the new CO was in the second Land Rover. The marines in these vehicles disembarked and formed a cordon around all four vehicles. The 2 i/c stepped out of his vehicle, then went to the CO's Land Rover, telling him it was now safe for him to step out onto the Main Road.

The new CO disembarked, he looked round and checked that all marines were in place to protect him. He was very nervous and unsure of himself. I think it is called "lack of moral fibre". I approached him and introduced myself; he took no notice. He then went to the side wall of a house and pushed his back hard up against it. Then he called me over, looking up and down the road. There was only the odd car passing, he seemed very nervous. He asked me, 'What are you doing?' and 'Why is your patrol in this area?' I was just about to tell him when he stopped me, then asked, 'Why is there a group of young men on the opposite corner?'

I told him, 'They are teenagers out of school, just talking to each other before going their separate ways.'

He then said, 'Take your patrol and move them on.'

I replied, 'They are doing nothing, and all of them are harmless. There's no law prohibiting them from standing on street corners, and I'm not prepared to harass and push them around.'

The 2 i/c came to my defence telling our new CO, 'The marines are all subject to the law, and the young people are not interfering or bothering anybody.' I could immediately fell tension between the two senior officers. The CO then went to his Land Rover, got in and gave orders to move off and the marines maintaining the security cordon around the vehicles embarked. The 2 i/c/ thanked me and told me to carry on with my patrol. It was now 1620 hours, we were all cold, hungry, and looking forward to tea and a couple of rounds of toast.

Our old CO always went out with two Land Rovers, and he always sat in the lead vehicle. When the vehicles stopped he was always the first out, always leading from the front. He was not afraid of a few teenagers on a street corner. My first impression of our new Commanding Officer was a very poor one.

Once all the vehicles had left we returned back to camp. In the dining hall all the talk was about our new CO. He was like a large round ball, no neck, just a head on a large fat body. He was rude, arrogant, and very unsure of himself. We all agreed that he was a "Pratt" and we gave him the nickname of "The Blob". He was a disaster waiting to happen.

Our second patrol of the day was very quiet. Men leaving the local public house were in a hurry to return home. The fish and chip shop was empty; it closed at 2300 hours. The temperature was now nearly eight degrees below zero and the wind was increasing in strength. Time passed very slowly.

The third and final patrol commenced at 0400 hours, the duty Officer gave me two warrants to execute. Also, he told me that the suspect wanted by the RUC was arrested by a Corporal in charge of another patrol. They had to chase him up two streets before he was caught, but once apprehended he had given no trouble. Concealed on his person were two pistols, but no ammunition, he had been on his way to make a delivery.

We decided to execute the warrants first, as it was very quiet. Normal procedure was carried out, two marines went around to the back door. I knocked hard on the front door, which was opened straight away. A young man stood there, fully dressed, with his overcoat on. He just said, 'I'm ready to come with you; I'm glad it's all at an end.' We went into the house, opened the back door and let our two colleagues in. The suspect was searched, he was pronounced clean, then plastic cuffed.

His mother then came downstairs saying, 'I'm glad it's all over for him,' then she asked, 'what will happen to him?'

I said, 'a Land Rover will pick him up, he will be taken to an RUC Barracks, where they will take statements, care for him and follow the legal procedures.' I gave his mother a printed card with details of addresses and telephone numbers. This would enable her to keep track of her son. I radioed for a mobile, they came and picked up the young man. As we were leaving the house both of them thanked us, then the mother said goodbye to her son.

The Corporal-in-charge of the mobile vehicle patrol was a friend. He asked if we had met our new CO, to which we replied, 'Yes.'

The Corporal continued, 'Nobody likes him.'

It was now nearly 0530 hours, we went around to the second house to make our final arrest. As normal the two went round the back. I knocked hard on the front door and the upstairs window opened, a young man stuck his head out and said he would be down in a moment. Two minutes later we heard him running downstairs and opening his back door. Half a minute later the front door opened. The young man was plastic cuffed and the two marines said they had searched him, and he was clean. I showed him our warrant and he confirmed that he was the person mentioned.

Then his parents came downstairs and his mother laid into him with her fists. One of the marines had to get between them to protect the boy. The father then said to his son that it was his own fault, he should never have got involved with the Republicans. The son was now eager to leave, he was receiving a tongue lashing from his father and physical threats from his mother. Once we were out of the house he apologised for the behaviour of both parents. I arranged for a mobile to collect him. It was now 0630 hours and we still had time to kill. The next one and a half hours went very slowly, and it was very cold. Once we returned to camp we had breakfast and a shower, followed by bed.

*

Tuesday evening at supper there were rumours and stories going round regarding the new CO. Some said he had been arrested, and there were other stories that he had been returned to the mainland. Nobody had seen him around today and his Rover group had not left camp. Then somebody said the only way to find out the truth was to ask either Registry or the Orderly room Corporals. One of the cooks said, 'Both of them had early suppers and went back to work.'

They both always went into the NAAFI around 1930 hours and everybody not on duty proceeded there, and the rumours continued; we were all waiting for Registry and the Orderly room Corporals to arrive. It was nearly 2000 hours before both of them arrived, they bought their drinks and sat down. Everybody gathered around them and they were told to tell everything concerning our new CO and what had happened to him. The Registry Corporal said, 'I'll tell you, but on the condition that I'm not interrupted.'

This is what he said: 'Our new CO was invited to a Commanding Officers' dinner and reception, by the General

Officer Commanding Troops, Northern Ireland, at Army Headquarters. The dress requirement was mess dress, red jacket with miniature medals, white shirt, bow tie, black trousers and shoes. He wore a black coat over his mess dress and was driven in a civilian hire car, by his driver in plain clothing. Anyway, he had his dinner and drank a large amount of whiskey. When he left he threw his overcoat onto the back seat, displaying his nice red jacket to public view. His driver commenced the journey back to camp, and when he was going through a large Republican area, 15 miles from here, he was told to stop at a fish and chip shop. He told the CO that it was not a good idea as this area was dangerous. The CO replied that he was a Lieutenant Colonel and the driver was only a marine. So the driver pulled up outside the fish and chip shop; the CO got out of the vehicle and went in.

'As normal, there were young people and a large group of women in the shop. The CO stood out like a sore thumb, the teenagers called him names and the women ridiculed his mess dress. He then started to answer back and informed them of his position as a Commanding Officer of a Royal Marines Commando Unit. This rubbed salt into the wounds of all present. Women then started to push him around, the shop owner told him to get out because he would not serve him. The CO then went back to his vehicle and told the marine driver to follow him back into the fish and chip shop.

'The CO went in, his driver followed but tried to lead our CO out as he knew the situation was dangerous. The mood of the people was becoming very nasty. The CO then told his marine driver to arrest everybody on the premises. The driver tried to pull his CO out of the shop, but he was blocked. The driver forced his way out of the shop while the Lieutenant Colonel was still in there making a fool of himself and stirring everyone up. The driver was now in a panic, he was outside the fish and chip shop with no weapon or radio. Then he saw three Land Rovers coming along the road, so he flagged them down and all three vehicles stopped. He went to the lead vehicle and explained what was going on. The lead vehicle had a full Army Colonel in it, the head of the Royal Military Police, Northern Ireland. The other two Land Rovers were full of RMP's.

'The Colonel sent his men into the fish and chip shop to extricate our Royal Marine Lieutenant Colonel. His men managed to pull the CO out, but they had to fight off the women. Once outside the fish and chip shop the women followed, attacking the CO and the RMP's. The CO was pushed into the rear of a Land Rover. The RMP Colonel told the CO's driver to follow them, as he wanted to get as far away from the area as possible.

'They stopped two miles away in a lay-by. The Colonel sent for the CO's driver and asked for details as to what had happened. The CO's driver explained everything, and the RMP Colonel told him to return to his Unit. This was a gross breach of military discipline but the RMP's would take our CO back to their barracks and deal with him. He would spend the night in cells so that he could sleep off the effects of drink. The CO's driver returned to camp and informed the Duty Officer of what had occurred.

'Once the CO arrived at the RMP's barracks he was breathalysed, and a blood sample was taken; he was then stripped to his underwear and placed in a cell. In the morning GOC NI was informed, also MOD London and the Commandant General, Royal Marines. The GOC NI immediately asked for his removal as a Commanding Officer-in-charge of a Commando Unit. The MOD in London said he would face a Court Martial. The CO knew that his career was now finished, so he asked the Sergeant-in-charge of cells for a pen and paper. He wrote out his resignation letter. His letter was passed to the RMP Colonel, who informed the GOC NI, London and the Commandant General, Royal Marines. His resignation was accepted by everybody, with immediate effect. The Unit 2 i/c was informed, the CO's kit was packed and taken to the RMP's barracks, and he returned to the mainland today.'

One of the marines said, 'This is a total embarrassment to our Officers, this is the sort of behaviour you expect from young men.' The new CO had only been in command of his Commando Unit for four days; he was now a civilian. He lost his career, his standing and his good name, for a fish and chip supper. Everybody agreed that he had been a disaster, and a big cheer then went up from everybody present in the NAAFI. Somebody suggested that Lieutenant Colonel Blob, and Majors Blunder and Incompetence had all gone to the same public school for "Buffoons". It was also suggested that all of them should have done a petrol run for their first taste of Northern Ireland. None of them were ever seen again. Our Unit 2 i/c would be the Acting Commanding Officer until we returned to Plymouth, then a new Lieutenant Colonel would take over.

*

It was Sunday, and our last weekend of foot patrols, we all hoped. Two more days of duties, we all looked forward to Thursday, and it was the beginning of the second week of December. Our Unit had now been in Northern Ireland for five months. Our patrol had the first set of watches, which was good. We commenced our foot patrols, going up and down our six streets. Everything is very quiet first thing on a Sunday, life does not start till late morning.

It was still early, and as we were going up Fifth Street there was a young man walking towards us. I recognised him as he lived in this street. He was looking down at the pavement and had not noticed us approaching him. He looked up and noticed us, immediately doing a swift about turn. From the rear I could see that his coat pockets were bulging out, and this raised my suspicions that he was carrying something. I shouted at him to stop, and he then started to run. All of us ran after him, and one of the marines on the other side of the street sprinted across and blocked him off.

We all gathered around him; I made him spread with his arms up against a wall of a house. Two members of the patrol faced out and one covered him while I searched him. Both pockets contained live .38 bullets, a total of 70 rounds. All the bullets were placed in a plastic bag and he was plastic cuffed. I radioed for a mobile and informed them of the find. Control replied that a mobile was on its way and that a house search team would carry out a full inspection of his home. I knew his house, but I doubted that they would find anything; he was just an errand boy for the Republicans.

All the time we were waiting the curtains were twitching and people were watching us. The mobile arrived and the prisoner was placed in the back of one of the vehicles. I gave the bullets to the Sergeant-in-charge of the vehicle patrol, and he took a notebook out and asked me to explain briefly what had happened. This took a couple of minutes while he recorded the main details. We were all told that statements would be ready for signature once our patrol returned at the end of the watch. This was good news, normally we would have had to do statements in our rest period. The Acting CO was doing all he could to make life easier for the foot patrols. The house search team did not find anything in the errand boy's house, although it upset his parents. Close to midday we commenced our slow return back to camp, we reported to Operations, read our statements and signed them.

It was now time for our second patrol of the day, and we proceeded to the area of six streets. The weather was cold with rain showers, and there were very few people out. The public house was closed, as it was Sunday. The fish and chip shop had a few women in it; we were getting a wave of hands in a friendly gesture now. We all knew that most people wanted nothing to do with Republicans, but it all depended on the area they lived in. The rain increased in volume and pedestrians were few and far between. As we were walking along the Main Road a woman walked past us very slowly and said, 'There is a body at the old derelict building.'

We moved off towards the building and I informed Operations concerning what I had just been told, saying that we were going to investigate. Operations replied, 'Proceed with caution and keep us informed.' We arrived at the old derelict building, and nobody was around. On the other side of the Main Road, directly opposite the entrance was a lamppost, which gave out a limited amount of light. First we checked the outer fence, then went into the inside perimeter. We all had torches and we kept a gap of five yards between each one of us, as this would make it difficult for an ambush. Outside was clear. Then I went into the derelict building; I tripped over something as I went in and when I shone my torch down I saw that I had tripped over a human body!

I told one of my marines to stay at the door, then we checked inside the building very cautiously; there was nobody else within. We all shone our torches on the body, estimating that he was a man about 30. His face was a total mess, there was blood everywhere. His knees were also covered in blood. This was a knee-capping job. He was not breathing but blood was still trickling out of his wounds. The man had been murdered in the last fifteen minutes. We kneeled down, checked around him, and also under as body, as he might be booby-trapped. All of us rolled the body over with our feet. At the base of his skull was a neat hole. We then rolled the body back to its original position. We all knew that the body should not have been touched, but curiosity had got the better of us. He had been tortured, beaten, and then shot, obviously the work of Republicans. He had either informed against them or they had fallen out seriously. I radioed Operations, who said, 'Stay put, as a large number of marines will be sent to secure the area, and a police forensic team will join you.'

Ten minutes later the CO's Rover group arrived. The CO and RSM came into the building and viewed the body, both of them being disgusted at what they saw. Thirty marines arrived in two trucks, a Sergeant was in charge and he placed a cordon around the old derelict building. My patrol and I were glad that large numbers of personnel were now present, that the building was secure. The police arrived, their photographer took lots of photos, and once he had finished the body was put into a bag. Then a fingertip search was carried out; nothing was found. The Police Inspector-in-charge said, 'The dead man had been tortured, beaten and murdered elsewhere. His body has been dumped in this area, as a warning to other Republicans.'

The body bag was placed on a stretcher and taken to a black van. The Police Inspector asked, 'How did you know where to look?' I explained everything and he was satisfied. An autopsy would be carried out, which would tell them in detail what suffering he had been through before he died. After an hour everybody left and we returned back to our patrol area.

One day later we were told that this man was tortured, and an electric drill had been used on his knees before he was shot. The electric power drill had penetrated 14 times into his kneecaps; he was a Police informer. Fear is the main weapon used by the Republicans.

At midnight we set off for our third and final patrol, all of us longing for the finish at 0400 hours. It was very cold and frosty and the sky was clear. As we turned the corner of Fourth Street there was a large crowd of people assembled outside a house. Some of the men were throwing stones and bricks at the windows. There was a lot of shouting mixed with bad language. I radioed Operations and informed them of the presence of a large crowd causing a disturbance. Their reply was, 'Stay well back while reinforcements are sent.' We waited nearly 20 minutes, then two trucks and four Land Rovers arrived. The reinforcements moved slowly down the street and the crowd realised that they were outnumbered, and they dispersed. Our patrol moved down and joined the main body of marines, where a Sergeant was in charge.

We all stood outside the house. There was not a pane of glass left in any of the windows. The front door had furniture pushed against it on the inside. There were bricks and stones all over the front room floor. A mirror and two pictures were broken on the far wall, but the frames were still intact; well-aimed stones had done this damage. The Sergeant told me to go round to the rear of the property and see if anyone was in. My patrol went round to the rear, climbing over the outer wall; all the windows at the rear of the house were still in place. I tried the kitchen door, but it was locked. One of the marines shone his torch through the kitchen window, and we could see a small person huddled in a corner, a terrified old woman. She stood up slowly and approached the window; we shone our torches on each other to show who we were. She was crying and nervous.

She was told to open the back door and let us in and that it was now safe. After a little more reassurance she opened the door. We all went in and I turned the kitchen light on. The woman was old, frail and very small. Furniture was removed from inside the front door and the Sergeant came in. One of the marines made a cup of tea for the old lady.

Six marines were guarding the rear of the house and there were nearly 20 others in the street outside. Nobody else was in the area. After a few minutes the old lady calmed down and started to talk. She explained, 'I buried my husband yesterday, he died a week ago, age 72. I've lived in this house for 50 years, I have no family. My husband was a Roman Catholic but I am a Protestant, and everything was alright while he was alive, the neighbours were friendly and we were accepted by people in the community. But once his funeral was over the people just turned on me. They called me a traitor living amongst them.'

Of course, in Northern Ireland a mixed marriage is between a Protestant and a Roman Catholic.

The Sergeant went out to his vehicle and informed Operations of the situation. Ten minutes later he came back into the house telling the old lady, 'We will move you out tonight.' Half an hour passed, then two more trucks arrived. One had tea chests and the other six marines as a furniture removals party. The possessions she wanted were placed in the rear of one truck, but only four tea chests were required. Half the furniture was left as it was old and ready for the rubbish dump. After an hour the truck was ready to leave. An Army hire car arrived with three Royal Military Policewomen in it, they took over the care of the old lady and she was placed in a safe house for a few days. One week later she was allocated a small retirement bungalow, in a Protestant area, which was safe for her.

Once the old lady had left the unit carpenter arrived to board up the house. The additional marines and Sergeant departed, while my patrol remained behind with the boarding up party. It was nearly 0400 hours by the time the carpenter had finished, so we returned to camp with his party. We had expected a boring, tedious four hours, but it had been eventful and a total eye opener.

Tuesday was our penultimate day, we left camp at 1145 hours going at a slow pace to the six streets. There were a few people around, the public house was full and there were women in the fish and chip shop.

At 1445 hours I received a radio message to go to the local junior school, but no details were given. Ten minutes later we arrived and a schoolteacher was at the main entrance to meet us.

The woman teacher said, 'The Headmaster has requested help with a disturbance here.'

We all asked, 'So what is the problem?'

She replied, 'They were playing sport in the gymnasium when the two classes started fighting each other.'

'Is one class Protestant and the other Roman Catholic?' we asked, and she confirmed that they were. 'Is there a room where we can leave our rifles and equipment?' we continued. She led us to one of the school staff rooms and three of us removed our flak jackets and webbing, and placed our rifles on the table. I left one of the marines in the room to safeguard our equipment and rifles. The woman said there was no need to leave anybody behind to safeguard our equipment as the school buildings were safe, but we did so anyway, letting her know that if a rifle or any of our equipment went missing then a Court Martial would follow.

She led us to the gymnasium, and there was a lot of noise coming from within. The teacher responsible for sport was standing at the outer door. He was a tall man, all skin and bone. He told us, 'Both classes are fighting each other and nobody is taking any notice of what I say, I tried to stop them but they are out of control.' I said that we would go in but both teachers had to accompany us; they should stand behind us and witness events. They agreed to do this.

We opened the gymnasium door and found two groups of young boys fighting in the centre of this large open space, being cheered on by others standing around them. The average age was about nine years. I shouted as loudly as possible, 'STOP!' Complete silence followed, then I told them to stand with their backs to the wall around the side of the gymnasium. I think they were astounded at our arrival and they started to move as instructed. Once they were all around the sides of the gymnasium I told them all that they were a disgrace and should know better. I did hear the word "sorry" from someone amongst them. All three of us walked around the gymnasium, giving the young boys stern looks of disapproval.

The male teacher now came forward and instructed one class to go out and change, and the other one to remain behind. Once the first class had changed the remainder left too. The teacher explained that there was a problem with religion. Segregation was a normal pattern in the school, with one group Protestant and the other Roman Catholic.

The Head teacher then arrived and thanked us, and I pointed out that this was a very unusual event for us. He told us that he had rung the RUC, who in turn requested our Unit to deal with the situation. This had happened in the past. These children were brought up to hate each other, which was why they were in separate classes. We gathered up our equipment and left. All of us found this experience demeaning. The children were like little savages, full of hatred for each other. We finished the watch and returned to camp.

I told the RSM and Sergeant Major of our experience of the afternoon. They too were disgusted.

The next two patrol watches were quiet and uneventful.

On the last day of street patrols we were all looking forward to 0400 hours the following morning. We also considered ourselves lucky as we had the first set of watches. Operations told us that there was nothing out of the ordinary, things were normal. We commenced as usual going up and down our six streets. By now we were recognised by all local inhabitants. Later in the morning we passed the public house which was beginning to fill up. The fish and chip shop was not yet open, but a small group of women stood outside. As we passed they greeted us and we returned the compliments.

We turned into Second Street where we found three men beating up a boy in his early teens. All of us took out our batons and ran towards this small group. Two of them saw us approaching, and they turned and ran. One remained, kicking the youth on the ground. I hit this man as hard as I could across his knee, forcing him to stop his actions against the teenager. Two of the marines caught the other two men, and they, too, received a few blows to their knees, then they were dragged back. The third marine told me that a photographer had just taken some snaps of us, so I said to him, 'Get the photographer and bring him back to me.'

He chased the photographer for nearly 100 yards and caught him. Once the photographer was caught he became aggressive and abusive. When he was brought to me I said to the marine, 'Open his camera but don't damage it, and expose all the films that he has on him to the light.' The photographer had six films in his pocket which were all exposed and destroyed. I could imagine pictures appearing in a newspaper of a young man on the ground and of me with a truncheon in my hand, having just struck a man. I asked the photographer, 'Which newspaper do you work for?'

He said, 'I am freelance, the film I had exposed would have been sold to the "Troops Out Movement", and I would have got a high price.' I realised that if the pictures had got into a newspaper my career with the Royal Marines would have been over. We told the photographer to sling his hook and vanish, taking all his exposed negatives with him.

The youth, much to my surprise, sat up; his face was swollen and covered in blood. He then started to spit and cough up blood and it was obvious that he had internal injuries. The three attackers were searched and plastic cuffed and were made to sit cross-legged facing a wall. The day was cold and dry and the ground was like an ice block. One of them said, 'I'm in poor health and need to be in the warm.'

We all laughed and thanked him for his joke, pointed out the medical condition of the youth that they had all attacked. I radioed for a mobile and an ambulance. The mobile was the first to arrive and the Sergeant-in-charge said that he knew two of the attackers, they were low life types who carried out little jobs for the Republicans. All three were told to stand and move into the Land Rover. All three fell over whilst approaching the vehicles, none of them liked receiving bad treatment.

The Sergeant and I then asked the young boy where he lived and why he had been attacked. Slowly he told us his name, then with difficulty he gave us his address. I said, 'Your mother spoke to me a couple of weeks ago while we sheltered from the heavy rain under the eaves of your house.' The ambulance arrived and the young boy had to be stretchered in as he had lost consciousness. I gave the Sergeant details of my short conversation with his mother, and he said he would take his Rover group around to check out the family house. I was told to follow on foot and that he would inform Operations concerning the event. The three prisoners were complaining that they were cold, and our standard reply was, 'Tough!'

Ten minutes later our foot patrol joined the Rover group outside the injured boy's house. All the windows had been smashed and the mother, father and two boys were very pleased to see us. Normal procedure was being followed by Republicans, 'If you are not with us then you are against us, so you must leave.' Marines were sent to the rear of the house to safeguard the back entrance. The Sergeant radioed Operations and asked for a larger force to secure this street, as he knew that once we left this family's lives would be in danger. Half an hour later 25 marines arrived, together with a house removal team. Once the family was told they were going to be re-housed away from this area, they were overjoyed.

I pointed out to the Sergeant that my first watch was nearly finished, as it was coming up to midday. He told us to return, but that he would stay. The three prisoners complained again that they were cold and hungry, and I heard later that it was nearly mid afternoon by the time they were handed over to the RUC. The injured boy spent six weeks in hospital and made a full recovery. His family were re-housed somewhere in England.

One of the other areas our Unit was responsible for had suffered a lot of trouble this day. It all stemmed from six arrests that had been carried out early in the morning. Barricades were set up using vehicles, which were set on fire. The few remaining Protestants in the area had their houses burnt down. It had taken a full rifle company most of the morning to restore law and order.

I reported to Operations before going out on my second patrol, they told me to be very careful and to ensure that I radioed in my position every 15 minutes. We arrived at the six streets and commenced our normal duties of going up and down. Some of the people who had greeted us this morning either snubbed us or abused the patrol The whole atmosphere had changed, there was now an air of hostility in the area, that was very easy to feel. All of us were now more vigilant, we moved a little faster and avoided standing still in any one place.

At 1730 hours I received a coded message from our CO to meet him at the Fourth and Main Street junction. Our patrol arrived a few minutes early, then the CO's Rover group arrived. All of my patrol stood with our backs to a wall, and the CO got out of his Land Rover and came over and greeted us. He told us that the day had been very bad, and he reminded us to be on our guard. The RSM was in the second vehicle and he came over to us, accompanied by a young Second Lieutenant just out of Officer training, who had arrived the previous day. The CO said the Second Lieutenant would join the patrol for the remainder of the watch, to enable him to have a first hand taste of life on the street of Northern Ireland. We all introduced ourselves, and told him to stay between me and the marine bringing up the rear. The CO's Rover group departed and we commenced our patrolling again.

Going up and down the streets we received some abuse and hostility and the young Officer could not understand why we did not answer back. It was explained to him that this was normal behaviour today, and it was best to let the abuse ride over you. Remember, "sticks and stones can break your bones, but words can never hurt you".

At 1930 hours I radioed Operations and gave them my position, and we commenced our return to camp. At 1945 hours I radioed in again and gave my position as "old derelict building". Just as I finished my radio contact three of us outside the building were rushed by a large group of young men. They poured out of the old derelict building having waited for my patrol to pass by this spot, being on the main route from and to camp. The ambush had been planned well in advance as the men had been gathered and instructed to attack our small patrol. There must have been at least 20 of them, and they had learnt that weight of numbers will eventually overwhelm an enemy. Immediately the two marines on the other side of the road ran to join us. We all bunched together with our backs to the wire fence. It is better and safer to keep the enemy in front of you.

We did not have time to get our batons out, although I did press the transmitter switch and shout into the microphone, 'Help immediately.' Two men grabbed hold of my rifle but I kept hold of it, they held on tight but so did I. The only thing I could do was kick as hard as possible and one of the men let go as he received a hard kick to his shin. I was now receiving blows to my face, but I kept hold of my rifle. The man opposite, holding on to my rifle, was a little weaker than me and I managed to bring it up hard and hit him on his chin; he collapsed. Immediately another man took his place. I was now receiving a barrage of blows to my face and body. Then something hard hit me across my mouth, followed by blows to the nose and face. I could taste blood in my mouth and two solid small objects, I managed to spit, and they were two of my teeth. More blows were hitting me, I knew that time was against me; I was now unable to see since both my eyes had swollen and closed.

All of a sudden I could feel a sense of quiet around me. One of our mobiles had arrived and the attackers had fled, leaving us and six of their party behind. The next thing I could feel was gentle hands taking my rifle and reassuring voices. I could not see anything but I could feel warm blood flowing down my face and neck. I remember being put in the back of a Land Rover, and then I lost consciousness.

*

I awoke, sensing a little daylight, it was warm and something was in my arm. Both my eyes were still puffed up, my mouth was sore and my face was swollen. I was being spoken to by a female and I asked, 'Where am I?' 'How long have I been here?' 'Where are my mates?' and 'What happened to the young Officer?'

The reply was, 'You're in the Military hospital, you've been sedated for two days, you've lost two front teeth, you've had 70 stitches in your face, and you're on a drip. The rest of your patrol are all here and so is the young Officer. One of the marines had a broken jaw, but all of you are very lucky to be alive.'

I could only take liquid as my mouth was very sore, but after a further two days the swelling started to go down and I could see better and eat solid food. All the patrol were in the same ward, it was comfortable and friendly. When I could see a little I looked in the mirror. My face was still a little swollen and black with bruises, and the other members of my patrol, plus our young Officer, were in a similar state. The marine with the broken jaw had lost eight teeth and his lower jaw was wired up to his upper.

We all discussed events, and we agreed that the mobile patrol had saved our lives; if it had not arrived then we would be dead now. One of the marines said, 'It should not be forgotten that Sinn Fein IRA is a criminal organisation, they murder, torture, intimidate and rob respectable business such as banks, post offices, shops and off licences. Politics is only used as a front, to justify their criminality.

Our CO paid us all a visit. He told us that five of our attackers had been caught, and three were in hospital. The reason for the attack was to show that Republicans cannot be intimidated, and to emphasise to local inhabitants that Royal Marines can be beaten. The six streets were now being patrolled by mobile patrols in strength, and the area was now very quiet.

The RSM handed all of us a box of MILK TRAY chocolates and boxed sets of writing paper. We thanked him and said, 'We didn't think you cared!'

He laughed and told us, 'No more TV.'

After the CO and RSM left the boxes of MILK TRAY were opened and offered round to other patients in the hospital. Everyone in the hospital had suffered at the hands of the Republicans. On average one or two soldiers were brought in every other day, some with very severe wounds. The staff were excellent in their care and treatment, and they recognised my patrol from our days of doing security duties there a month previously. On the Wednesday afternoon our Sergeant Major arrived with clean clothes for all of us, telling the patrol that we were all going back to camp with him. We all dressed and thanked the nursing staff for their kindness, and we said goodbye to other patients.

Outside there were six Land Rovers, a vehicle for each of us accompanied by other Corporals and Marines as bodyguards. The Sergeant Major took the lead vehicle. Once back at camp we were all told that we were excused duties, and our equipment, rifles, and flak jackets were secure in the stores. That evening at supper we all sat together, and our friends and colleagues came over, shook our hands and told us how lucky we were. Later, we went over to the NAAFI and had a pint of beer. The marine with the broken jaw said it was the best pint of beer he'd had in his life.

On Thursday morning the camp guard came round to our accommodation at 0530 hours telling everybody that we were going home that day. On hearing this good news we got up and started packing our equipment. All bedding was returned and accommodation huts cleaned. Everybody was informed that there would be a parade at 1100 hours, either side of the camp road, as a very important man was coming to bid us farewell. Our patrol was issued with clean combat clothing, as this was the dress requirements for the parade.

The young Officer, the three marines and I had to stand together, just outside the Guardroom. At 1050 hours the main gates were opened and six Land Rovers drove into camp. The vehicles were manned by Royal Military Police. The third Land Rover had the General Officer Commanding Troops, Northern Ireland, as its occupant. The CO saluted and welcomed him, a Lieutenant General in the British Army; they chatted for a couple of minutes. The CO led the GOCNI over to the line of Corporals and Marines. My patrol group was the first to be inspected. All of us stood together, with yellow faces, caused by fading bruises and stitches. The young Officer was the first to be met and greeted, then it was my turn. The GOCNI thanked me for my endeavours, and for the hard work that was put in; and he said how sorry he was concerning my injuries. He emphasised that my patrol had been very lucky. Before he moved on he shook my hand. He was an Officer and a Gentleman. He spoke to every man and shook his hand. Before he left, he wished us all good luck and thanked us again for our hard work.

The Unit flew out from RAF ALDERGROVE courtesy of RAF Transport, back to RAF St Mawgan. We arrived in barracks late Thursday evening. On Friday morning leave passes and rail warrants were issued for two weeks Christmas leave.

Whilst on leave I reported to my local hospital, had the stitches removed from my mouth and face. This made me feel good. On completion of leave and returning back to barracks in Plymouth the scabs had gone from the wounds. As time passed the scars faded. All three marines and the Young Officer recovered fully.

During the third week of January a new Lieutenant Colonel arrived in the Unit, who had a good reputation. Our Unit was now back in very good hands.

Early in February I was promoted to Sergeant and posted to the Commando Training Centre, Royal Marines, Lympstone. I continued in the Royal Marines for a further eight years, serving in another two Commando Units. I was discharged into civilian life in the 1980s, leaving with the rank of Colour Sergeant.

Just a little about what happened to the Royal Marines that were part of my patrol. One left after he had served his nine years. Two others stayed on and completed their 22 years service. One left with the rank of Sergeant, and the other Sergeant Major, Warrant Officer Two. The young Officer who joined our patrol left the Royal Marines in 2003 as a Colonel. I meet the three members of my patrol once a year at Lympstone. The years are passing us by now.

The Royal Marines taught me self-reliance and gave me confidence in myself, and I took advantage of the Royal Navy education system. The services stood me in good stead for the remainder of my working life. I had left an organisation full of comradeship, which was structured and well disciplined. One thing everybody learns on joining up is that you never let the side down. I served with Pride an Joy. The Royal Marines are still Britain's sheet anchor, and are the best armed service in the world.

Chapter Eight
Civilian Employment

Now I was a civilian, aged 40, with 25 working years ahead of me. My service pension was small and although I knew that I would never starve, there were still standards to live up to. Also, you should always have something to occupy mind and body. I decided that it would be profitable to obtain a job with a small pension, as this would help me maintain a good standard of living on final retirement at age 65. I bought a National daily paper every morning and checked the situations vacant. If I saw anything available that I thought I was capable of doing I immediately wrote off. I always enclosed references and Curriculum Vitae. The response to my applications was very poor, there were few replies. Some of the letters received back were very rude, with insults to my former career, others were polite and to the point, stating my unsuitability to life in a civilian world. I did not give up and just kept pushing ahead. I also received the local evening paper every Thursday where there was a large selection of job vacancies advertised.

I had now been out of HM Forces for six weeks and there was one job in the local paper which interested me. The job was for an administration assistant at a heavy earthmoving machinery firm. I rang the telephone number listed and the man at the other end said that they did not send out application forms but only did face to face interviews. So I asked, 'When would it be convenient to come for an interview?'

They replied, 'Today at three o'clock.'

It was now Friday morning; I prepared myself, and arrived for the interview five minutes early. I reported to the front office and a young girl lead me into a small office which was that of the Depot Manager. There was a desk piled high with magazines, surrounded by empty, dirty cups. The waste bin was overflowing with rubbish. Three old chairs were in the room and there was a gentleman sitting in the most comfortable one. His dress was perfect, he wore a very expensive suit, a silk shirt, a club tie of some description, and hand made shoes. He was introduced to me as the Owner of the company; his manner was polite and exacting. The owner then introduced the Depot Manager, who was short, thin and filthy. He wore a good quality suit but down the left side were stains from tobacco ash. His shirt collar was worn and dirty and the shoes on his feet had not seen polish since they were purchased.

The owner started the interview with normal questions like, 'What have you done?' 'Where' and 'For how long?' I answered them all to his satisfaction. The Depot Manager asked if I was in receipt of a Military Pension, and I replied that I was. He said that I could only expect a very low wage, but I pointed out to both of them that I had earned my service pension, it was paid by HM government and was nothing to do with the wages paid by them. The owner then apologised for the abrupt manner of the Depot Manager and he offered me a reasonable wage. It was nothing near what I had received in HM Forces but I accepted his offer. Then I asked when I could start work. It now being Friday the Depot Manager said, 'Monday morning, eight am.'

I said, 'OK,' and this was accepted by the Owner and Depot Manager. I now had a job. I was grateful to be back in employment and earning some money. Beggars cannot be choosers, they have to accept what's on offer and take it.

On the Monday morning I arrived at the Depot just before 7.45 am. A welder unlocked and let me in, ready to start work at eight o'clock. The Depot Manager arrived at nine o'clock and the office girl at 9.30 am. He showed me around, telling me that the office girl knew everything. She would show me what to do. Being a Monday the Depot Manger had a clean shirt on, but the same dirty suit and shoes. At ten o'clock he departed, stating that he was doing his rounds of quarries and work sites. The office girl told me that the Depot Manager was only seen twice a week. Also, she said that we should go and meet the other two men working at the depot.

She led me into a workshop and introduced me to Stephen, the welder, who was a quiet polite man. His height was 6 foot 8 inches, and he was very powerful, no fat, just muscle. Stephen was friendly, polite and helpful. Then I was taken upstairs to meet the Depot Storeman, who was the complete opposite of Stephen, short, rude, nasty and aggressive. I told him "not to call me", and I wanted nothing to do with him. The office girl said he was always like that, he had no friends, and Monday was the worst day for him as he would have spent the weekend drinking. We went down to the front office and she explained what I was expected to do, which was not very much. She gave me the owner's telephone number and said, 'If there are any problems ring him because the Depot Manager is incapable of making a decision.' She also said, 'The owner only pays a visit to this Depot once a month as he has many other businesses.'

Stephen came into the office and made coffee, I asked if anyone took a cup up to the Depot Storeman, and the answer was no. The storeman never talks or drinks coffee with anybody. The duties were easy, I had to answer the telephone, update customer's accounts and take cheques to the bank each afternoon. The first two days were easy and uneventful, but on Wednesday the depot storeman did not come to work. At about 11 o'clock the owner rang me stating that the Storeman had left, and asking if I would I assist by helping with stores?

I said, 'I will help in any way possible.'

The office girl and the welder were glad to see the back of the Storeman. On the Thursday morning the office girl did not come in, and later the Depot Manager arrived, telling me that she had left the UK to go travelling with her boyfriend. Also, he was going to explain stores procedure to me. This took nearly an hour. Once he had finished explaining I was handed a set of keys for the depot and he departed. Friday was uneventful, I was glad that Stephen, the depot welder, was around, as it was very quiet. I received a few telephone calls for spares but this day passed by very slowly. My first week was an eye-opener. There was no proper system, everything happened by accident. I had now completed my first week's work in Civvy Street.

Two weeks later I was in my third week of normal routine. On the Monday the Depot Manager arrived with a clean shirt on, then left. During my second week the Depot Manager had paid a second visit on Friday in the afternoon. I knew that this was only to make sure that nobody left work early.

Wednesday started as normal, telephone enquiries, post and cheques to be sorted. Stephen, the depot welder, assisted me nearly all day as he had very little work to do. I gave Stephen the job of paying the cheques into the bank; one thing he hated was answering telephones. At around 11am a man walked into the depot office and introduced himself as "Ron, a mechanic". He said, 'I do permanent work at a quarry where the Owner has seven large machines out on hire and I have to be there permanently to maintain them.' Stephen came into the office and made three cups of coffee. Ron asked me, 'What did you do before you came here?' and I explained everything. He then said, 'I have worked for the owner on and off for the past 25 years. He is a big player in the earth moving business.' He then asked Stephen, 'Has Jim (the roving mechanic) been in lately?'

Stephen said 'No.'

I asked, 'What does Jim do for the Owner?' It was explained that Jim maintained all other earth-moving machines out on hire around County of Cornwall. Businesses that had machines out on hire rang Jim in the evening and informed him of any problems they were having, and he would visit the following day to rectify these. I then said, 'What does the Depot Manager do?'

Ron then started to laugh, he said, 'I'll tell you both about his history: The Owner's father was a man that liked young ladies, he was married to a very wealthy woman, richer than himself. They had two sons and they both went to Public School. The Owner's father travelled a lot on business, it was well known that he was a philanderer. The attitude of his wife was that what he did when away from home was none of her business, so long as she did not hear of it.

'They had a large house in the country, with numerous staff to run and maintain the property. One of the maids was young and very attractive, and the old man found her tempting. She lived in a nearby village. The girl was 17 and he had great difficulty keeping his hands off her. One day the old man's wife was away on business and he saw his golden opportunity. He asked if the young maid would like to go for a ride in one of his Rolls Royce cars. She immediately answered "yes". Off they went in the Rolls Royce, arriving at a very expensive hotel. A meal was provided, and the maid was now flattered that she was in great favour. After a couple of glasses of champagne she felt a little dizzy, and it was suggested that she should have a lie down. A hotel room was hired and the old man then had his wicked way, followed nine months later by the birth of a little girl.

'Now the cat was out of the bag. His wife played merry hell; the scandal had to be covered up. A story was put about that the young maid's boyfriend was in the Army, which had sent him to serve in Korea and he had been killed whilst on active service for his country. A small cottage was bought in a nearby village and the young maid was housed there. Money was provided in a way of a pension, and all the bills were paid by the old man's family. The old man was forbidden to go anywhere near the cottage and he was to have no contact with his illegitimate daughter. When the old man died he stipulated in his will that his eldest son would care for his illegitimate daughter. It was a shock for the Owner when he found out that he had a half sister, but he respected his father's wishes.

'The half sister later married a dump truck driver, who worked on building sites around the country. The owner brought a large detached house not far from the depot, installing his half sister in it. Her husband was then made manager of the depot, provided with a good salary and a company car.'

Stephen then said, 'The Depot Manager can neither read nor write,' and Ron added, 'That's why he stays away from the Depot. The house, furniture, car, and all company assets will never be owned by the Depot Manager, he is totally under control of the Owner. So if there are any problems just ring the Owner, who treats the Depot Manager like dirt.'

I said, 'A Public Schoolboy with a village idiot in tow.' Ron finished his story and left. Stephen and I carried on working. The Depot Manager did not pay a second visit that week.

I had been at the depot for nearly three months. Stephen and I had a routine going, and every Friday afternoon we gave the whole place a good clean. All rubbish in the Depot Manager's office was thrown out, the desk was wiped down with hot soapy water and dirty coffee cups were removed. When the Depot Manager paid his Monday morning visit he was amazed at the transformation, a tidy and clean office. One thing I did notice about the Depot Manager was that he was very frightened. He knew that his status and position was through his marriage. He was very insecure.

The Owner always paid a visit on the last Friday of each month, which meant that I had come into contact with him three times, once at the initial interview and twice since. During his last visit he invited Stephen and me into the Depot Manager's office and asked what both of us did for lunch. I told him, 'We normally have a cup of coffee in the main office, with a cake.' He then ordered the Depot Manager to go and purchase some cakes in the nearby small town. Stephen made four coffees. The Owner said that he was pleased how everything was running, and once the Depot Manager returned and passed the cakes round the Owner told everyone that he had ordered a teleprinter for the Depot.

I mentioned that nobody working here had any experience operating one of these. Then the Owner asked if I would be prepared to go on a one-day course to learn how to operate and work the teleprinter. The Depot Manager then piped in and said, 'The telephone always works for me, we don't need any of these new modern contraptions,' but the Owner told him to mind his own business, and that any decisions he made were not to be argued with. The Depot Manager realised that he had put his foot in it, then went very quiet. I think he realised that you do not object to ideas from the "hand that feeds you".

The teleprinter was delivered and installed. I did a one-day course with the telephone company. It proved to be very good, I could order spares and goods more quickly. It was far more convenient than Royal Mail, and it increased our efficiency. The Owner was happy how things had improved, and even the Depot Manager agreed that it had been a good idea.

One morning a self-employed man, a digger operator, called into the depot. He wanted some steel teeth for the edge of his buckets to enable greater progress for trench digging. The depot supplied him with the necessary bucket teeth, then he wanted to purchase a small ditch-digging bucket for pipe laying. He was told that we did not have any. Stephen said, 'I could make a bucket, but the Depot Manager won't allow me to. Plans and drawings are all in the office, and the steel plates and cutting equipment and welding gear are all in the depot lying idle. In the yard are steel plates from a quarter of an inch to one inch thickness, measuring nine feet by six, as well as a large expensive roller for shaping steel.'

I said, 'I will ring the Owner.' Once I had explained the situation to the Owner he was horrified at the waste of opportunity, so I told Stephen, 'Go ahead and make the bucket.' Stephen cut metal for three buckets, welded them and fitted steel teeth. I worked out a price which included the quantity of steel, the cost of welding gases and hours of labour. I then rang the customer who came to the depot, viewed the bucket and bought it straight away.

Word was now out, and during the next week the remaining two buckets were sold. Now we were receiving orders for trench digging buckets, also larger capacity ones. One Quarry Manager ordered three sets of steel plates to fit on the lower part of a bulldozer blade. These plates were two feet by eight and a half inch thick, plus he required the bottom six inches to be "hard faced". Hard facing is done to extend the life of steel plate, as sand wears steel away slowly when it constantly rubs against it. The steel plate was curved by rolling it; each piece was charged out at £700; the Quarry Manager was most pleased. Orders were coming in now at a steady rate. Stephen was earning the Owner an additional £2,000 per week.

One afternoon a customer wanted to purchase one of Stephen's small buckets when the Depot Manager was present. He turned to the customer and said, 'All these buckets are made from scrap steel.' The customer then turned on Stephen stating that he was not going to be sold shoddy goods. Stephen came into the office and told me what was going on, and I went out with Stephen to see the customer. We told the Depot Manager to go into his office, and also mentioned that the Owner would be informed about the mishap. The Depot Manager went white with fear once I mentioned the Company Owner, and he immediately proceeded to his office.

Stephen and I approached the customer who wished to purchase a bucket. We took him for a guided tour of the yard showing him the steel sheets and all equipment needed to make a trench bucket. I offered him a 15% discount on his proposed purchase, which he accepted and he bought the bucket.

Once the customer had departed Stephen and I went into the Depot Manager's office and confronted him. Stephen told him all sorts of unpleasant things regarding his incompetence. Once he had finished the Depot Manager apologised, then begged me not to contact the Owner. I then explained to him how successful everything was, and he apologised again. Then the Depot Manager said he would go out and return in about half an hour, and he left. Stephen said, 'What's he up to now?'

Twenty minutes later he returned with two bottles of whiskey, one for Stephen and the other for me. Then he started to apologise again; I told him to sit down. I reassured him that the Company Owner would never know about today's events and Stephen told him to go home. Once he had left, calm and peace settled back into our daily routine again.

A plant manager from a small firm came to the depot and ordered all necessary parts to recondition a machine engine. I gave him all the items he required then suggested it would be quicker to remove the whole engine and replace it with a factory re-build, which would have a year's guarantee. He agreed with this idea but stated, 'This service has never been offered in the past.' I rang the engine supplier who said that they had offered this service before but it had never been taken up by our depot. They agreed to send a price list. I rang the Company Owner and told him all the details, emphasising what a great benefit it would be to us and to plant operators in this county. Also, a delivery and collection charge could be added to the price of an engine.

Stephen said, 'I will collect the engines from plant operators, drive to the factory and deliver the reconditioned units back.' The Company Owner did a mail shot to all Plant Operators in the county. We received our first order, and the Plant Operator was impressed as his down time was short, being only two days instead of a week. Orders were now coming in, an average of four engines a week. One replacement power unit was for a massive V12, and this made the Owner a clear profit of £500. Now

Stephen was working flat out, making buckets, trips to engine manufacturers, and it was getting too much for him.

When the Company Owner paid his next visit I went through everything in detail to him, and I suggested that a delivery driver would be an additional asset, as he could take a good bit of unproductive work away from Stephen. A delivery driver would help to improve efficiency. The Owner confirmed that cashflow had improved during the previous two months and gave the go ahead to take on a delivery driver, and said he would purchase a five-ton truck. Once the Owner had departed I told Stephen that we could recruit and hire a delivery driver and that the truck would be provided. Stephen said, 'The Depot Manager can drive, why waste money recruiting anyone else.'

I replied, 'The Depot Manager only comes here twice a week, we need someone to work five days.' We recruited a driver and a five-ton truck was delivered. The new driver was ex-Army and he proved to be a good all round helper. The Depot Manager stayed away, sometimes we did not see him for two weeks. Jim, our roving mechanic, was most grateful for the service of reconditioned engines and said, This makes life a lot easier, so why hasn't this service been provided before?' Jim was a really nice bloke, he had a good sense of humour and was very helpful.

I had bow been working at the depot for six months, everything was running smoothly and efficiently and I decided it was time to ask the Company Owner for an increase in wages. He was to make a visit to the depot at the end of the month so I telephoned on the Thursday, securing an interview with him.

Friday arrived and at 11 o'clock I went into a clean depot manager's office to see the Company Owner. One thing I liked about the Owner was that he was always friendly and polite. I told him straight away that he would not like what I had to say. I was asked to sit down and the Depot Manager was told to bring in two cups of coffee, then to take a walk around the building. I explained how things were running, including the manufacture of buckets and replacement engines. Turnover had increased by nearly £10,000 a week, and our reputation had improved amongst plant operators in the county. I pointed out to him also that all invoices now went out at the end of each day, not once a week as was the previous practice. The owner pointed out to me that he'd had to take on an additional driver and he'd bought a five-ton truck. Then I mentioned that I was doing the work of a storeman, as well as the duties which were carried out by the office girl, so he was saving in wages by not replacing either of them. He agreed with everything I said and said that he would increase my wages by a further £500 per annum, and that he'd review my position once I had been there a year. I thanked him and left the office. As they say, "be grateful for small mercies".

On leaving the office the Depot Manager was standing outside with his dirty shirt, scruffy suit and badly scuffed shoes. He asked, 'What's been going on, and why wasn't I involved in this discussion?'

I replied that it was personal and private, 'If you need to know you will be informed.' The Depot Manager was worried, but I knew all would be revealed to him in due course.

After I had been there for nine months the Owner asked me if I would take a client out for a business dinner, and I agreed to this. The Owner told me the venue, a very exclusive restaurant out in the country. The restaurant had its own helicopter landing pad, and was well known in the South of England for excellent meals and service. I told the Owner it would not look very good arriving with a client in an old Ford car, and that I would need money up front to pay for the night out. I was provided with a top of the range Mercedes saloon car, apparently the Owner owned a Mercedes sales outlet. £500 was provided to cover the expenses of the meal and hospitality. The Owner told me that this client, who I was to entertain, was interested in purchasing a wheeled loader, cost £78,000. I knew the profit would be great, not to mention the follow up maintenance. The client's name and address was provided, together with the time of collection, 8pm.

I left work at 4.30 and took the long way home, as I told myself I had to familiarise myself with the handling and control of such a beautiful car, which was a work of art. I showered and put on a good suit and left home at 7pm to collect the client. His house was in the country, up a dirt track lane. I found the house, and the grounds around it were littered with old rusting vehicles of various types. His cottage was in need of repair, there were slipped tiles on the roof, and the wood on the windows was rotten. The machine the client wanted to buy was worth more than his property. I knocked on the front door and a tiny woman opened it. She had on an apron over a man's shirt, and a pair of jeans. Three young children were running amok in a large room downstairs. This room was the kitchen, dining room and living room combined.

I was invited in, where a large man was washing at the kitchen sink. I introduced myself and his wife invited me to sit down; the TV was on full volume and the children were shouting at each other. The client got dressed and he looked like something out of a Giles cartoon. He was a large man with a stomach hanging over his belt. He had on a bright yellow shirt and jeans, which he had worn to work that day. The sports coat he put on looked about two sizes too small for him. I told him that one of the preconditions of entry of the restaurant was a tie. His wife then went to a drawer and produced a bright green tie. We were just about to leave when I noticed that he still had his work boots on, and I suggested that he changed his footwear. He removed his work boots and put on a pair of "Dr Martins" boots, which were reasonably clean, but bright red. He reminded me of "Desperate Dan" in colour.

We eventually set off from his cottage. During the drive to the restaurant I tried to make conversation, but all I received back was a "grunt". Once we arrived at the restaurant, I parked the Mercedes well away from the other cars. The car park was full of very expensive vehicles and people going into the restaurant were immaculately dressed.

I lead the client to the main entrance. Once the Maitre D saw the man accompanying me I think he nearly had a heart attack. I gave my name, then I noticed my table allocation was changed. The waiter lead us both to a table in the far corner of the room, and heads were turning as we went by. I heard someone say, 'A Barbarian has arrived.' The client told the waiter that he wanted a pint of beer and a rum chaser before we had sat down to examine the menu. I ordered a fruit juice as I had to drive the client home later. The drinks arrived and before the waiter had time to put my fruit juice down the client had taken his pint off the tray and downed it in two large gulps. I ordered another pint of beer for him. People were looking at our table. I had thought this was going to be an interesting evening; but instead it looked as if it would be most embarrassing. There was no stimulating conversation concerning topics of the day.

I ordered from the menu; the client wanted two starters and a Porterhouse steak, rare. The beer was going down as fast as it was being served. The Porterhouse steak arrived on a large plate, I thought it was a serving plate, but it was the one which the client would eat from. A second waiter carried a large portion of fried potato chips, fried mushrooms, fried onion rings and a salad. The client shouted to the waiter, 'Take this salad away, I do not eat rabbit food.'

The portion of food placed in front of the client was enough for a family of six. Black looks were coming fast and furious towards our table. More beer was being consumed by the client, and once the steak was finished he wanted "pudding". The sweet trolley was brought over; the client chose three sweets, then covered them in a rich dairy cream. Now he was using his spoon like a shovel to convey food to his mouth as fast as possible. The client was either drinking or eating, occasionally he gave a grunt of appreciation followed by a loud "BURP". The alcohol was taking effect, his speech was slurred, also he was "F-ing and Blinding" at the people at the next table.

The Maitre D came over and asked him to refrain from using bad language, and I apologised. I felt like crawling under the carpet, then the client started F-ing and Blinding again. I then suggested to him that he go to the toilet, and I accompanied him. In the toilet I told him in no uncertain terms that he had to behave himself. He apologised. By now he had consumed nine pints of beer, six rums and a very large meal. All I wanted to do was get out, dump him, and go home. Then he asked for coffee and brandy. I ordered, had a coffee and asked for the bill. It was now 11pm and we were about to leave the restaurant, when the client announced that he could not stand, saying, 'My legs have gone.' I knew that the drink had had its effect.

I had to ask a waiter to assist me to get him into the car. As we were leaving loud comments were being made by other diners, "shocking", "disgraceful", "should be ashamed", and "where did he spring from?" I felt like telling all present that I agreed with their opinion. Once we arrived at the car he was pushed onto the back seat. Now my main concern was that he might vomit. I gave the waiter a £10 tip.

During the journey back to the cottage I had to stop twice so that he could relieve himself. Once at the cottage I knocked on the front door and told the client's wife that she would have to assist me in getting her husband into the house. The language she used on me and her husband is not worth printing. Once inside the cottage I pushed the big man onto a settee. Just as I was going out of the door he started to vomit. I ran to the car and drove away from the cottage as fast as possible.

The following morning a man from the Mercedes outlet collected the car. The Owner rang me at around 11am and asked how thing had gone. I relayed the events of the previous evening stating, 'It would have been better to take the client to a transport café and then a public house. The Owner had a good laugh at the other end of the telephone. He said that he would keep me informed of the client's intentions. Two days later the Owner rang me stating, 'The client has purchased a machine, and he enjoyed his meal out.'

I replied, 'More than I did!'

Two months later I was asked to take another client out for a meal. It was the same routine, a Mercedes and £500 cash. This client lived in an expensive area of town so I assumed that he was a decent, educated man. I arrived nice and early. The client's wife invited me in; she was polite and well dressed, and it was a beautiful house. We chatted in the front room while the husband made himself ready. The client came downstairs wearing a good business suit, a clean shirt, and good quality shoes, not "Dr Martins". Once we were in the car this client started to slag off his wife. I was feeling awkward as it would have been rude to agree or disagree. I kept my mouth shut.

Entering the restaurant the Maitre D recognised me from my previous visit, but this time I had a good table. The client asked for a bottle of Champagne and I had my normal fruit juice. All the time he continued to curse his wife, which was embarrassing. I changed the subject and asked him what he did. He told me that he was the Chief Technical Manager for an international construction company. His job took him all over the world, but he always returned to that awful woman, his wife. Again he started denigrating his wife. I ate my meal and ordered coffee and brandy for him. The bill was settled, and the client was a little unsteady on his feet going to the car.

Once we had set off he told me that he wanted a woman, and that he craved sex. He rabbited on and on about sex, so I told him that I did not know any prostitutes, but I knew the area of town where they hung around. I drove to the red light area of town where ladies of the street could be found. The client told me that he needed money to pay for services rendered. I stopped the car and gave him £50, and I warned him to be careful as the area was not safe. He got out of the car and a girl came out of a doorway. I watched both of them in the rear view mirror go up an alleyway, then I drove off.

The owner rang me the following morning. I described the events of the previous evening. He thanked me for this information. Two hours later the Owner rang again telling me that this client had bought three large earthmoving machines. The information concerning the ladies of the street had been put to good use, the client did not want his wife to know about the previous night's events and was pleased that we were discreet..

Customers were variable and colourful, the majority of them being small one-man operations. What I did notice about many small operators was that they could not read or write. When I used to make out invoices and hand them to customers they would often pass me their chequebook so that I could write out the amount. They normally checked the number against the amount on their invoice then signed. I never commented. The vast majority of small operators were excellent men, and I will describe a few of them.

*

One morning a man drove up in a beat-up, rusting old pick-up truck. He came into the office and ordered some spares. I gave him his spares and made out an invoice, which he signed. Just as he was about to leave Stephen came in, and they greeted each other. Stephen said he was going to make coffee, would Ron like a cup? Ron said, 'Yes, but I have my five border collies in the front cab of the truck.'

I told him, 'Bring them all in.' He went out to the pick-up truck and brought the five young dogs in, they were lovely.

Ron said, 'The mother bitch had died when the puppies were five weeks old, they are 18 months now,' and then he asked, 'Would it be possible for them to have a run around the back yard.'

I said, 'Yes,' and we all went out there. The dogs had a good run round, then we returned back to the office for coffee. When we sat down the three bitches climbed onto our laps and made themselves comfortable. Ron was a very pleasant man and I started to talk to him. I asked, 'How did you start up in the earth moving business?'

He answered as follows: 'After the war and demob from the Army there was very little work around. Any job that was going normally had 10 or more men after it. The local town had been heavily bombed and large areas were just rubble. I had a little money and I bought an old Army truck. Then I found out who owned which derelict bombsite in town, and approached the owner concerning clearing and levelling. After clearing my first site I was asked to clear two more. I took on two men who had served in the Army with me.

'By the end of the first year I had four men working for me and owned three trucks. Things were looking up. Then I met a girl who became my wife; she was bright, and she could read and write. She drew up contracts with customers for me to carry out work. Then I moved into road maintenance, ditch clearing and cable laying. By now I had 20 men working for me and my wife was the organiser of the business.

'In the 1960s we bought a quarry and since then we have never looked back. Sadly, my wife died two years ago and the business is smaller now, and I have to employ an accountant to do the books, which my wife did. I've sold most of the business off;

the only men working for me now are the original four I took on at the beginning.'

Ron finished his coffee and made his way out to his old pick-up, followed by his five beautiful dogs. I don't know how they all managed to fit in the front cab, but they looked snug and comfortable.

A few weeks later he rang up and ordered a battery. He was worried as it was late in the day and that we'd be closing in 15 minutes. I asked him where he lived, and as it was on my route home I said I'd drop his battery off in about half an hour.

I arrived at a large prestigious house, standing in five acres of land. I parked and went round to the side of the house, heading for the garage, carrying the battery. The kitchen door opened and five beautiful border collies ran up and greeted me. Ron came forward and took the battery from me. Then he asked, 'Are you in a hurry?'

'No, I'm not,' I answered.

'Would you like a conducted tour of the grounds?' and I said that I would. The gardens were well planned and immaculate.

I said to him, 'You must work hard to keep this large garden in such prestigious condition.'

He answered, 'I employ two full time gardeners, because the house and garden were my wife's passion. The kettle's on, would you like a cup of tea and a biscuit?'

We went into the large kitchen. In the centre was a large oak table, there was a comfortable soft chair in a corner, a wall-mounted TV and five dog beds around the edge of the room. He continued, 'I spend all day and evening in the kitchen keeping my dogs company. When my wife was alive they were only allowed in the kitchen, I've got no family and my dogs are as near as any relative.'

I said, 'It's such a large house.'

Ron replied, I will show you around.' The house had six bedrooms, a large living room, a study and a dining room. The furniture was beautiful, Ron said, 'Everything here was selected by my wife.' There were photographs of her in every room. 'I have a woman come in three times a week to clean,' he continued.

It was sad that Ron had lost his wife now that he was approaching retirement. He dressed respectably, but not in expensive clothing. He was a very wealthy man but with simple pleasures. He came into the depot at least twice a month, where he enjoyed a cup of coffee and a chat. He was a very decent man.

*

Part of the business was that the owner would apply for road construction projects and sub-contract them out. One afternoon he telephoned telling me that he required a progress report on a road-straightening scheme he had sub-contracted out. I asked, 'What does it involve?'

He answered, 'I've won the contract to build two miles of dual carriageway, straightening out a section of road.'

I said to him, 'I don't know anything about road construction.'

The Owner replied, 'I will send an artist's impression on how it should look now, as there are only two weeks to completion.'

The following morning a carrier arrived with an artist's impression and the address of this construction project. I left the depot at about 11am and travelled to the construction site. The first thing I noticed on arrival was that everything was quiet. I assumed it was a lunch break. I took out the artist's impression and compared it with the construction site; it was nowhere near where it should be. The site had been levelled, piles of gravel and earth were everywhere and the machines were lying idle. A pick-up truck pulled up by me and a man got out and approached me, telling me that I was trespassing. I explained my business and reason to be there, but he became abusive and hostile, so I decided it was time to leave.

On arrival back at the depot I telephoned the Owner, explained what I had seen and the general attitude of the contractor. The Owner told me there was a penalty clause in the contract. The sub-contractor would forfeit £1,000 a day for every day over the agreed completion date.

I told him, 'Somebody should have told the sub-contractor that.'

The Owner replied, 'I explained the terms and conditions of the contract to Mr Smith.'

I replied, 'He could not have been listening at the time.'

'I will send a photocopy of the contract and a letter down to him with you, and would you explain the terms of the contract to him again?' said the Owner.

The following afternoon I left to see Mr Smith, and took Stephen with me. On arrival I noticed one machine working, but then Mr Smith approached us telling us both that we were on a private site, and he ordered both of us off. I told Mr Smith, 'We have something for you, a letter from my boss and a copy of your contract. And you have just under two weeks to complete the project and for every day over schedule you will forfeit £1,000.'

He started to abuse me, then we left. I learnt later that he had taken on three sub-contractors for various jobs but they lacked the necessary skills, staff, and machinery to complete the project on time. Also, Mr Smith was behind in paying them. He was subsequently forced into liquidation one week before the completion date, which cost the Owner most of his profit as he had to hire another contractor at short notice.

Mr Smith owed money to banks and hire purchase firms for large expensive earth moving machines that he had bought. These machines were reported stolen. The police investigated and no trace was found. The insurance company paid out on completion of their investigation. Two months later a farmer was ploughing his field when he struck something hard and solid. He stopped to investigate, then took a shovel and removed some earth from around a solid object. The hard solid object was the cab of a large wheeled loader. The police were called. Further excavation was carried out and eight earth-moving machines were discovered wrapped in plastic sheeting for protection. The insurance company naturally wanted their money back and revenge. Mr Smith was charged with fraud and criminal deception, and he received seven years in jail.

When Mr Smith came out of jail he was stopped on the Queen's Highway, his vehicle was full of red diesel. Customs and Excise prosecuted him and he went back to jail for a further three months. A very nasty man.

*

Just after we opened one morning a very expensive Mercedes car drove up outside the front entrance, and a man got out and entered the depot. His dress was impeccable, blazer, white shirt, sober tie, black highly polished shoes and grey flannel trousers with a perfect crease in them. I greeted him and he returned the compliment. He said that a list had been prepared for his requirements, which he handed to me. The list of requirements had all the part numbers, descriptions and quantities. I checked that we had items in stock, ticking what was available. I told him, 'There are only three items out of stock, but it will only take a day to obtain them.'

He said, 'Go ahead and order them, and when the list is complete please ring me. One of my staff will collect the items.'

As the gentleman was leaving Stephen came into the office, he said, 'I see the richest man in the county has just left.'

I asked him, 'Tell me about him.'

He replied, 'That German gentleman came to the country as a prisoner of war, he was captured by the Eighth Army during their North African campaign. He was a Major in the Engineers, but once over here he did two correspondence courses, English and Business Studies, as he already had a degree in Construction Engineering. Towards the end of the war he was sent to this part of England to assist with repairs and construction of roads. During his time in the area he met an English girl and they eventually married.

'The girl's father owned two quarries that had lain idle for several years. Both quarries were used as collateral for a large loan. He bought some Army surplus earth moving equipment, and three former prisoners of war stayed on as his workers. For the next six years they struggled on, paying off loans and trying to keep their heads above water. Things started to improve in the late fifties, then in the sixties he experienced success after success.

'He now exports China Clay all over Europe, using his own small shipping fleet, and he now has eight quarries and the largest trucking firm in the area. There is a waiting list of people wanting to work for him, he never advertises any jobs. He has two sons who both went to good English public schools, then trained as lawyers. He is a County Councillor, and Chairman of several companies. But there is one person that he detests, and that's our Depot Manager.'

I completed his order and one of his drivers came and collected the items. The invoice was despatched and his cheque arrived the day after.

The German gentleman paid many visits, sometimes he would have a cup of coffee with Stephen and me. One day he asked me for some information concerning dump trucks. He said, 'My company requires five replacement 50 ton vehicles. They cost up to a quarter of a million pounds each. I gave him all the information that was available in the depot. After he had gone I rang the Owner and explained the situation.

The Owner said, 'I will send one of my technical salesmen out to see him.'

Everything was going well, the German gentleman wished to go ahead and purchase five vehicles. Finances were worked out and agreed, and there was to be a formal signing ceremony at a hotel in town, followed by a reception. I received a formal invitation and mentioned this to the Owner, who said, 'I will pick you up and we'll go together.'

The day of signing came and the Owner collected me from the depot in a chauffeur driven Bentley. The Depot Manager sat in the front seat. He had a clean suit on, a shirt with a collar badly frayed and black "Dr Martin" boots. We pulled up outside the hotel and proceeded in. The Depot Manager immediately went to the bar and ordered himself a pint of beer plus a large whiskey.

All the top managers from the German gentleman's firm were present. They were all well dressed; the German gentleman took me round and introduced me to his staff, and I was made most welcome. Everybody was relaxed, talking and enjoying themselves.

Then disaster struck; the Depot Manager had become drunk and he started to abuse people. The Owner told me to get him out of the building quickly as he was a total embarrassment. But before I could get to him the Depot Manager went up to the German gentleman and started to insult him. A deadly hush fell over everybody in the room, then our Depot Manager said to the German gentleman, 'What do you know about driving dump trucks?' I rushed forward, grabbed the Depot Manager by his arm and pulled him out of the reception room. The Depot Manager then started to use bad language on me and I told him, 'Shut up.'

But the damage was done, we were both standing outside the hotel when the Owner arrived. He said to the Depot Manager, 'I have just lost a large contract and a considerable amount of money.' The Owner's Bentley drove up, we got in and the Depot Manager was told, 'You can make your own way home.' As we left I saw him going into a public house.

A few days later I was speaking to the two mechanics, Ron and Jim, telling them what had happened. Jim said, 'The Owner should make the Depot Manager stay away from work, he loses more business than he gets as he has no idea what's required.'

Ron continued, 'Within a month the Owner will have forgiven and forgotten about the Depot Manager.'

I added, 'Life goes on.' Now I was determined to find another job, one with a pension.

*

It was a Friday afternoon, and Stephen and I had just finished cleaning the offices and the driver was out making his final drops for the week. The kettle was on the boil and in walked a well-dressed man, not a plant operator. He told me, 'I'm interested in buying a large earthmoving machine, what is the starting price?'

I said, 'They start at £78,000.'

Stephen added, 'Would you like a cup of coffee?'

'Yes please,' he said, and sat down with us.

I asked him, 'Where is your quarry?'

'I've just bought one on North Road, five miles out of town,' was his reply.

Stephen said, 'I know that quarry, it belonged to a couple and their son works with them. They are always in debt and spend more time repairing their machines than operating them. The machines are old and decrepit, ready for the scrap yard.'

The man said, 'I will tell you how the purchase of the quarry came about. I applied to supply stone cladding for the new Parkway being built through the town. My bid was the lowest so I was awarded the contract. I approached the owner of a quarry to supply the stone. He gave me a price, which I accepted. My profit margin would be 70%, but when I looked at his equipment I knew that he could not supply the stone to schedule, so I made him an offer to purchase his quarry, which would clear all his debts. His family could carry on working there, for me.

'They agreed to the sale. The quarry is good but all the equipment in it, is old and out of date, and his business methods left a lot to be desired - somebody tells him what they want, and he quotes a price, they both agree, spit on the palms of their hands and shake. Other quarry owners have been buying stone from him and then selling it on at a profit. The quarry only has three years life in it then I am going to apply for planning permission to use it as a household waste disposal site. I already have five sites, managed and operated by the German. The German management team collect all the fees for waste disposal, and manage and operate these sites. At the end of each month I receive a statement and a cheque.'

Stephen queried this, 'I didn't know that the German was into waste management.'

'The German has 12 sites of his own and manages another eight around Britain,' the gentleman replied.

Then I asked him, 'How did you become involved in quarries and waste disposal?'

He replied, 'I trained as an accountant, working for other people. I saw how people made money, some through hard work, and others by using their brains. One day I saw an old quarry up for sale, so I bought it with a large bank loan. The first five years were touch and go, and twice I just escaped going broke. I managed the project myself and employed three men, just drawing enough money to manage on, and then I purchased another quarry. With the two of them things were looking up. After two years I bought my third, and then things really took off.

The German manages all five sites, and I scout around looking for other opportunities.'

The accountant finished his coffee. Then Stephen ventured, 'Why don't you hire machines from us? How many do you require?'

The accountant replied, 'Three wheeled loaders. The German haulage firm is contracted to transport stone to the Parkway site.' He thanked us for coffee, went out and drove off in a very expensive Porsche car.

At the end of the month the Owner told me, 'I have just hired out another three machines to a quarry.' I knew where they were, but said nothing.

Now it was coming up to Christmas, business was steady and good. As the time came nearer to Christmas some contractors brought in bottles of spirits for Stephen, the delivery driver, and for me.

The Depot Manager came in two days before Christmas, and he saw a contractor give me a bottle. Once the contractor had left the Depot Manager came up to me and said, 'You must hand the bottle over to me, as well as any others in your possession, they are Company property.'

Before I could answer him Stephen walked in. There was an almighty row and the Depot Manager was the loser. Then the Depot Manager said, 'Alright, we'll divide the bottles four ways.'

'Why?' answered Stephen, 'You are never here, and you destroy work and drive customers away.'

I put in, 'We have been dividing the bottles up three ways, the driver, Stephen and myself.'

Stephen added, 'The off licence has plenty of bottles of spirits for sale, you can go there.'

The Depot Manager turned round, walked out of the door and drove off.

It was now Christmas Eve, and there was no visit from the Depot Manager. The driver had no deliveries to make so we gave the depot a good clean. At four o'clock the Owner rang and wished us all a Merry Christmas, and told us that we could lock up and go half an hour early. Half an hour given to us for our Christmas bonus, nothing else. We all returned back to work on

Friday the 28th December, but there were no visits from the Depot Manager or the Owner. They were very trusting.

Around Easter I had been at the depot for over a year, and the Depot Manager invited me into his office for a chat. He said, 'You have worked very well and helped to build up the business, but you are not a salesman or an engineer and you have very little experience of business, so the Owner cannot promote you to Assistant Manager of the depot. I thanked him for his plain speaking and honesty; although I knew that he was very much involved in the decision.

Now I doubled my efforts to seek a better position, and to look for a job with a pension. I carried on searching newspapers, and in early June a job was advertised with a firm on the South coast. I rang and asked for an application form, which duly arrived. I completed and returned it immediately. Two weeks later I was invited to attend an interview. I booked a day's holiday but kept the appointment details to myself. I was successful and accepted. I told my future employer that I had to give a month's notice to my present employer.

On returning to the depot I booked the last week of the current month and the first one of the following month, as holiday. Since I had worked at the depot everybody's wages were paid into their banks after the first seven days of the month were over. Wages were supposed to be paid in at the end of each month, but pay errors were always in favour of the Owner. The week before I took my holiday the German gentleman came in and told me that his welder had just retired, also three of his drivers. I told Stephen and our delivery driver to apply, but to keep this quiet from the Depot Manager and Owner. I gave them both my telephone number and told them to tell me if they were successful.

During the first week of my holiday they both telephoned me, they had been accepted for employment with the German gentleman's firm. Both of them were very pleased as they would be earning more, and there were perks to be had as well. I told them not to say a thing to the Depot Manager as it was now time for revenge.

I explained to both of them that their wages would be in their bank accounts at the end of the first week of this new month. All three of us would go in at the beginning of the second week, Stephen and I would return the Depot keys, and all of us would tell the Depot Manager that we were leaving with immediate effect.

I had my two weeks holiday, all three of us met up outside the depot building. The Depot Manager arrived and I unlocked the building. Stephen, the delivery driver and I followed the Depot Manager into his office. I put my keys on his desk and Stephen did the same. Then Stephen, the delivery driver and I said, 'We are all leaving, with immediate effect.'

The Depot Manager's response was, 'Your job contracts require a month's notice.'

All three of us said in unison, 'We have never had any job contracts or terms of employment.'

The Depot Manager was now worried, he said, 'What do I tell the Owner? There are a lot of invoices to be sent out.'

We all said, 'Goodbye,' and left the building. The Owner turned a blind eye most of the time to the Depot Manager's behaviour, but he forgot that bad management had a detrimental effect on staff and morale.

Stephen was made senior welder after working for the German gentleman for a month, because his work was always of top quality. The delivery driver went to night school and obtained some qualifications in management. After five years he was made Transport Manager.

The depot closed after we all left. The owner gave his half sister an allowance and she still lives in the house provided by him. The Depot Manager has gone back to driving a dump truck in a quarry. The accountant bought the depot, and he also employs the two mechanics.

My first experience of civilian employment was an eye opener, it's not what you know or capabilities that count, it's <u>who</u> you know, and relations count for a lot. I now work for a firm in the South of England.

THE END